"*This program will be a great help to lawyers and all others who make communication a profession.*"
    —John W. Kaufmann, attorney and partner, Eaton & Van Winkle

"*For as long as I can remember, I have dreaded public speaking to the point of almost declining an important promotion to avoid having to do it. I have taken several courses trying to eliminate my anxiety to no avail.* **TalkPower** *has done it, simply by teaching me self-control. It's about time!*"
    —Ralph A. Miro, educational coordinator, First Response

"*After thirty-four years and $25,000 spent on therapy, hypnosis, drug-therapy, and training programs, I walked away from the* **TalkPower** *weekend knowing I will never avoid speaking in public again.*"
    —Wayne Newcomb, president, Yankee Realty Inc.

"*I never thought I could put together a seven-minute speech, present it so coherently and feel so in control. I would have never been able to do it without the knowledge and calming support I received from* **TalkPower.**"
    —Pam Cressman, project coordinator, Thomas Jefferson Hospital

"*It's a great experience to sit and talk with a group of people who have the same, or similar, feelings as you about public speaking. I have taken my first step in overcoming my fear of public speaking.*"
—Claire Person, events marketing specialist, Philip Morris Companies

"**TalkPower** *is a powerful tool to overcome the phobia to speak out in public. Ms. Rogers is an expert in developing the building blocks to construct a speech and to stay calm while delivering. I am very grateful.*"
    —Salomon Cameo, associate systems analyst, United Nations

"*I thought no one could really understand the fear I had with public speaking. Your seminar proved me wrong.*"
    —Dr. Gail A. Lauro, Deutchman-Lauro Chiropractic Centre

"**TalkPower** *is an effective way to overcome the fear of public speaking. It allows you to experience the very doing of that which seems impossible. A powerful reminder that one must engage and participate in order to change a phobia.*"

    —Robert O'Conner, social worker

TALK POWER

TALK POWER

TALK POWER

THE MIND-BODY WAY
TO SPEAK WITHOUT FEAR

NATALIE H. ROGERS, MSW, CSW

Skyhorse Publishing

Skyhorse Publishing books may be purchased in bulk at special discounts for sales promotion, corporate gifts, fund-raising, or educational purposes. Special editions can also be created to specifications. For details, contact the Special Sales Department, Skyhorse Publishing, 307 West 36th Street, 11th Floor, New York, NY 10018 or info@skyhorsepublishing.com.

Skyhorse® and Skyhorse Publishing® are registered trademarks of Skyhorse Publishing, Inc.®, a Delaware corporation.

Visit our website at www.skyhorsepublishing.com.

10 9 8 7 6 5 4 3 2 1

Library of Congress Cataloging-in-Publication Data is available on file.

Cover design by 5mediadesign

Print ISBN: 978-1-5107-6009-7
Ebook ISBN: 978-1-5107-6010-3

Printed in the United States of America

In memory of
Harold Herbstman, my husband,
Beverly Rogers, my sister, and
Frances Kessler, my aunt . . .
my karmic cheerleaders.

If there's one thing I've learned in life, it's the power of using your voice.

—Michelle Obama

ACKNOWLEDGMENTS

When the Dalai Lama was asked, "What is your religion?" he said, "Kindness." I love this story and have quoted it many times. It sets a profound standard, bringing to mind the generosity of spirit surrounding the birth of this book.

I have been blessed with an abundance of helping hands and now is the time to say thank you.

Thank you Hector Carosso for your unwavering belief in the value of my book and for introducing me to Skyhorse Publishing.

Thank you Caroline Russomanno, my editor, for the loving attention you have given to every aspect of my book. When you wrote me that this was an awesome read, my joy knew no bounds.

A great big thank you to my assistant Manny Soloway, the young computer genius who appeared at my doorstep five years ago at the tender age of eleven and has worked for me after school ever since, demystifying my computer. When Manny first stepped into my office, little did I imagine how over time his ability to master the complexities of the computer, video camera, and the design of my website would prove to be so invaluable to me. In addition, thank you Manny for assisting me in the organization of my recent brain research and discoveries and the development of my stuttering program "Stop that Stutter" that I have incorporated into this new book.

This support has strengthened and informed my determination, setting the stage for an effort of teamwork and cooperation. I am so grateful for that.

A special thanks to the memory of my late husband, Harold Herbstman, for his excellent suggestions about the practices and procedures of lawyering. Also, his stamp of approval, which means so much to me.

To my daughter, Colette, I embrace you for your encouragement and editorial good taste in calling attention, in such a diplomatic way, of course, to the flights of fancy that I am occasionally subject to. Thank you to my son in law Alex Simon for your very insightful feedback. And to Leo my grandson for his piece about Stephen Curry. To my dear sister, Gail Meller, your enthusiasm for my work touches my heart.

Thank you Steve Bloom, not only for teaching me how to play chess, but for your invaluable feedback as far as the technicalities of my poems are concerned.

Thank you to the spirit of our Wednesday Women's Writing Group conducted in my apartment for the past twenty-two years. What a gift! Your very intelligent critiques week after week raised the bar higher and higher bringing out the best of me. Still going strong on Zoom with Tova Beck-Frieman now as the host. Thank you Tova for your generosity, organizing, and conducting our poetry meetings each week.

Thank you to the many thousands of TalkPower students I have had the privilege of working with over the past thirty-five years.

Without your courage and tenacity, your willingness to try the new and unusual drills and exercises in the TalkPower Workshops, this book would never have been possible. I learned so much from you as I witnessed the gradual loss of your terror and anxiety as you found your voice and finally delivered such interesting ten minute presentations after just two days of intense TalkPower training. I am especially grateful for your generous response when I requested sample speeches. I hope I have given your voices a proper representation.

To the patients in my practice, who expressed so much interest in this project, my warm gratitude. Thank you Karen Quinn and your staff at American Express, Financial Center, NYC: I so appreciate your support by including the TalkPower program in your training curriculum "Stress Seminar For Public Speaking" for nine years.

Let me not forget Leo and Goldilocks, my two omnipresent cats draped across the computer, sitting on the fax machine, good company from beginning to end.

This thank you list would not be complete without the expression of gratitude I feel to the Sivananda Yoga Organization, founded by Swami Vishnu Devananda. The guidance and inspiration that I have received over the years from my association with this remarkable organization has enhanced my intuitive understanding of the effects of mind-body training in changing behavior. The philosophy, the yoga, the meditation practice, and the exceptional teachers have prepared me for this task of demystifying the mind-body experience in regard to public-speaking phobia.

A special place of honor must be reserved for the memory of Constantin Stanislavski, the great Russian theater director. My debt of gratitude goes far beyond the writing of this book.

I first became acquainted with the work of Stanislavski in 1967 through the interest and dedication of my husband, Harold Herbstman. At that time we were the artistic directors of the anti war Dove Theatre Company in New York City. Since that time, my work as an actress, a therapist, a teacher, indeed every aspect of my life has been touched and illumined by the humanitarian ideals of Stanislavski and his Moscow Art Company.

Given this abundance of kindness and goodwill, the writing of this book has been an incredibly satisfying experience—an egg that hatched in a nest lined with joy.

TABLE OF CONTENTS

Part I. The Prelude

Part II. The Program

Part I

THE PRELUDE

INTRODUCTION

I am not afraid of dying. If you placed a gun to my head, I would not want to die. . . . I would be able to face it with dignity. Put me in front of a group, and I totally fall apart. I know a terror that is impossible to explain or understand.

—Charles, colonel, USAF

After twenty five years as founder and president of TalkPower, Inc., I can safely say that I have heard every horrific public speaking story imaginable. During this time thousands of students in my TalkPower workshops have recounted tale after hair-raising tale of sleepless nights, anxiety, public humiliation, excruciating stage fright, panic attacks, forgotten lines, and botched presentations, as well as disasterous job interviews, eulogies never given and wedding toasts never made

My job has been, and always will be, to repair the damage. Again and again, I have watched my students overcome their terror of public speaking by adhering to my simple, yet transformative, TalkPower program. I am convinced that the method I set forth in these pages can conquer even the most deeply entrenched fear. With proper training anyone can learn to speak before an audience with clarity, grace, and authority.

My Own Story

In 1978, I returned to college after many years as the Artistic Director of the Dove Theatre Company in New York City, a professional actress, director, and teacher, to prepare for my second career as a psychotherapist.

One day I was sitting in a class called "Oral Communication," waiting for the instructor to arrive. Snatches of conversation drifted across the room:

> *"I sound like a moron!"*
> *"My voice is so monotonous."*
> *"I hate this."*
> *"They don't like me. I know it; I can feel it."*
> *"Oh my God, the other day she was reading a menu during my entire speech."*

The students commiserated with one another until the instructor arrived and the class began. I watched the bobbing heads, waving hands, in continuous motion, nervous pacing, and listened to rapid speech and the many ums and ahs woven into every sentence of the repetitious presentations.

Each speaker looked extremely uncomfortable. Most of them had no experience speaking in front of a group. Tension in the room mounted as the students rambled on and on.

The instructor sat at the back of the class, taking notes and making suggestions. "Relax," she kept saying. "Relax."

Was I the only one aware of the discomfort and loss of concentration? Apparently, the instructor was not concerned. Apart from her command to relax, she ignored the students' profound distress and continued urging them to make eye contact and to speak more slowly. "Don't be so nervous," she'd add, trying to be helpful. "We support you." And when critiquing the presentation: "that was a good try but remember you have to have a beginning, a middle, and an end".

I was bewildered. This wasn't at all like the systematic training I had received in acting school, where we were given training for relaxation, attention, awareness, and authenticity. Here, the sole focus was on the preparation of the speech, with no serious attention paid to the painful anxiety and loss of confidence that many students were experiencing.

Filled with advice and lectures about how to know your audience, use body language, get to the point, try to relax, gimmicks, bits and pieces of superficial information and a hodgepodge of theory, this class was ineffective in helping the students calm down and take control of themselves. The most basic questions were never addressed. For example:

- Why do I feel so out of control in public when I am so confident in a one-on-one?
- Why does this feeling of dread come over me for days before a presentation?
- How do I deal with the adrenaline rush that I feel just before I have to get up and do my presentation?
- Why can't I catch my breath?
- How can I stop my heart from beating so fast?
- How do I keep from thought-blocking?
- How can I stop rambling?
- Why do I become unhinged when I have to talk at a meeting?
- Why do I feel that my talks are boring?
- Why do I lose my breath as my speech gets faster and faster?
- How do I stop my hands from shaking?
- What can I do about rushing to get it over with as soon as possible?
- How can I keep my voice from shaking?
- How can I prepare a talk that makes sense when I have so much to say and I don't know where to begin?

MY AHA MOMENT

Sitting in that classroom, I realized that there was no established procedure for training the mind and body for public speaking. Suddenly I had an "Aha!" moment. It occurred to me that a systematic approach like the new and original training program that I had been developing for actors when I was the Artistic Director at the Dove

Theater Company might help non-actors develop better concentration and self-control. In other words, a program for developing performance skills.

By performance skills I mean the ability to remain focused and clear-headed when people are looking at you as you perform some activity. For example gymnastics, golf, or public speaking. My reasoning went something like this. People who have intense anxiety about speaking in public believe that they are being negatively judged by the audience. This belief consciously or unconsciously triggers high anxiety, confusion, memory loss, rapid speech, and intellectual disintegration Thoughts like "I sound awful, they don't like me, I am too fat, I am too old, I am not smart enough, I am a fraud, I am too short, they can hear that my voice is shaking, etc." So in contrast to the traditional method of teaching public speaking that is based upon lectures, suggestions, tips, hints, and theory, and does not address this fearful reaction, my "Aha moment" dealt with a more practicle and effective approach. Instead of suggestions and lectures, I had an idea for a training program that would affect the brain and create the neurons that would equip one with the skills necessary for eliminating the threatening mind-set that speaking in front of an audience creates. Specifically training students with a set of original physical exercises, that could direct one's thoughts away from the speaker's fearful messages he was giving himself so he would have the ability to focus upon the talk he was giving. I called that training Program TalkPower. Little did I realize at that time how powerful that methodology would actually become.

Of course, a step-by-step program was the logical answer for eliminating the problem of public speaking distress. Envisioning an original mind-body training program based upon the concepts of neuroscience (dealing with the plasticity, the ability of the brain to change and transform itself), this new method would be effective for all performance situations. This includes delivering a presentation, speaking at a meeting, interviewing for a job, making a toast, asking a question in class, and even walking down the aisle.

Above all, my program would finally answer the most pressing question that people who are phobic or uncomfortable about public speaking ask: "How can I keep my concentration focused on what I am saying when everyone is looking at me?" I called the program TalkPower.®

And so I started teaching the TalkPower method thirty years ago in a class called "TalkPower: A Panic Clinic For Public Speaking" at Baruch College of Continuing Education.

The name was so promising that from the very beginning people who had registered in the traditional public speaking class canceled their registration and chose the TalkPower class instead. The demand for my class was impressive. Calls and inquiries poured in from people who shared a shameful secret: absolute terror about speaking. In front of people who were looking at them.

In the class, students shared their stories. Some confessed that as far back as they could remember they dreaded having to speak or read out loud.

We were a very big family . . . seven children. Whenever we went anywhere, we had to sit perfectly still. If you were thirsty or had to go to the bathroom, you couldn't go unless you got mother's permission. You had to sit there and be still. When I was in kindergarten, I did not utter a single word for the entire term. If I wanted something, I would point. Finally, they sent me to the nurse and there, alone with her, I had a conversation. My teacher was amazed that I could talk. . . . All of my life I felt as if I was not allowed to speak.

—Laurie, sales manager

Others reported a different story. For these students, speaking well had never been a problem until one day, in front of an audience, they became inexplicably speechless. This was so humiliating that they avoided all future opportunities to speak.

I was the valedictorian and I was giving my speech when I suddenly started to lose my breath. Before this time I was never afraid to speak in public. I would even volunteer to do so. That one incident seems to be the thing that set this off, because now I can't do it. . . . I get a wobbly voice, feelings of terror, feelings of embarrassment. I feel as though I'm completely losing control. I never speak in public.

—Phyllis, fashion coordinator

Testing my TalkPower method, I introduced the early students to a new kind of Body-Awareness Training designed to restore their shattered confidence. One of the unique features of the program is the attention paid to every detail of the presentation experience, from the moment one is waiting to be called upon to the moment one returns to one's seat. Step by step, the training begins with correct breathing techniques followed by original Inner Awareness techniques that train the students to maintain concentration when seated and are waiting to be called upon. Then students practice how to stand up so that they resist the impulse to rush to the podium, how to pause appropriately, and finally techniques for how to deal with keeping the focus upon the presentation under the gaze of the audience. (Speech phobic people know just what I am talking about.) Since great attention is paid to every detail, at first the student speaks only the first sentence of his presentation and then returns to his seat. Gradually the practice presentation includes more and more of the text. By the end of the second day of training, every student in the class is able to calmly deliver a ten minute presentation with appropriate pauses, the complete elimination of rushing speech and all signs of intense anxiety and panic.

THE TALKPOWER ACTION FORMULA

To help students organize their ideas, I created the "TalkPower Action Formula, "a writing procedure that guides the speaker with a structure for assembling facts and information into a logical flow. The goal is clarity. The TalkPower Action Formula helps the student to organize the text of the talk from a confusing tangle of information into a cohesive and logical script. And so following the structure of the Action formula, the student is able to stay on track. This plan produced a well-organized talk for every single student. Those early classes were a turning point. I was filled with enthusiasm as I watched each student find his or her voice.

TEMPLATES

I soon discovered that the TalkPower Action Formula was not a sufficiently complete instructional model to satisfy the challenges of a professional presentation. Even with the help of my Action Formula, most of my students had no idea about how to prepare a formal presentation for a listening audience (and judging from the talks that we hear every day, neither do most people). Participants in my classes, even though they were mature and successful professionals, had never been trained to write a tight script for a listening audience. Their schooling had only prepared them to create reports, letters, papers, and memos for a reading audience. As a result, their talks, although well–organized, were lifeless and repetitious huff and puff, filled with generalizations, numbers, and abstract concepts that wandered off topic and did not engage the audience. And so I set to work creating a series of fill-in templates for non-writers so that they could flesh out the facts of the talk into an engaging story-telling format. I composed these templates, with transitional phrases that framed the information and moved the presentation along. As a result well-edited, dynamic talks were created, much to the relief of the other students who enjoyed listening to these very interesting presentations. Included in this book is a selection of templates to help you flesh out your talk so that an engaging narrative emerges. With these tools one can create a polished speech in a minimum of time. The templates were a big success.

SELF ESTEEM AND LEADERSHIP

The final element of the TalkPower program revolves around self-esteem as it relates to leadership training, where the effects of false and negative personal messages are examined and discussed and preparation for leadership is introduced. This section completes the program so that all the aspects of the transformation are addressed. Now I really had something. The body awareness work, plus the

Action Formula, plus the templates, and my psychological expertise, made for a complete public speaking curriculum designed for transformation. My background as an actress-acting teacher, director, artistic director of the Dove Theatre Company, an anti-war theatre company in St. Peters Church in Chelsea, New York City, and psychotherapist, gave me a unique set of tools for solving this previously hopeless condition.

Today, TalkPower is a successful seminar business that has trained thousands of individuals. Some attend on their own initiative; others are enrolled through corporations that recognize the importance of public speaking. These organizations include American Express, Merrill Lynch, United Parcel Service, United Nations, National Westminster Bank, Texaco, J.C. Penney Company, AT&T, Dean Witter, Albert Einstein College of Medicine, IBM, The Wyatt Company, Women's Bar Association of the State of New York, MCI Telecommunications Company, Karpas Health Information Center, Chase Manhattan Bank, Organization of Black Airline Pilots, Hoechst Celanese Corporation, Otto Preminger Films, Toastmasters International, Howard J. Rubenstein Associates, Weil Gotshal & Manges, Ford Motor Company, The Skyros Center (Greece), and many more.

> *Your course is so helpful to people. It really changes them in a fundamental way after they attend. We are always able to fill your program when we offer it this is because the word-of-mouth around the company is so positive about the program. People really enjoy it and they feel it works. I would have to say that your seminar consistently gets among the best ratings of the many on-site classes we offer our employees.*
> —Karen Quinn, vice president for American Express

Fifteen years ago, with the publication of my first TalkPower book, I embarked on a journey of service and creativity, taking TalkPower training all over the world. The book was translated into twelve languages. Now, this new edition of *Talk Power* will bring you up to date on all the latest discoveries and techniques that I have developed since that first book was published in 1982.

What is TalkPower?

TalkPower is the only systematic technology for training the brain (re-patterning) for the skill of performance. This includes physical as well as hands on concentration exercises, drills, routines and correct breathing practice for developing and enhancing concentration skills. See chapter 4, Breath Is Life.

Clinically tested and perfected over a twenty-five year period, the TalkPower Mind-Body program has been compared to the systematic training that star athletes receive to prepare them for competitive events. This state of the art program with more than a 95 percent success rate has changed the lives of thousands of my clients and students.

SCIENTIFIC VERIFICATION

Based upon the enormous success I have had with the TalkPower program over the past thirty years, having worked with more than thirteen thousand students at large training seminars at American Express, in workshops, at conferences, one on one in my office, and now on Skype, I am proud to say that even the most phobic individuals in the TalkPower Workshops were able to eliminate their fear and avoidance of speaking in public.

I theorize that the extraordinary results achieved in the TalkPower Workshops are possible because of the unique exercises, repetition drills, and routines that are part of the TalkPower training program. These exercises which I believe cause the memory centers of the brain to develop the enzymes and genetic markers that initiate the production of new neurons (chains of cells) also reinforce plasticity: the brain's ability to remake itself. In other words, after participating for two days in continuous exposure to the TalkPower repetition drills and exercises, the brains of the participants were behaving like brains of people who do not in any way suffer from fear of speaking in public. As a result new and permanent performance skills are developed, enabling the speaker to face an audience with attention focused upon the presentation rather than on the judgement of the audience: Therefore speaking with no trace of the previous confusion and terror.

How Is TalkPower Different?

Unlike traditional public speaking courses that ignore the physical and emotional discomfort of students in their public speaking classes with bromides like "why are you so nervous; we support you," Talk-Power identifies *fear* as the central problem that must be *eliminated* before you can speak successfully in public. Contrast this approach with other methods that teach you to "manage your fear" or to "confront your fear" with lectures, theory, the importance of eye contact, body language, knowing your audience, positive thinking, and other superficial methods for teaching public speaking.

My experience tells me that for the person who is standing in front of an audience feeling out of control and totally embarrassed, the idea of managing or confronting your fear is meaningless.

Any serious study of public speaking phobia reveals that this is a complex condition arising from a history of some sort of abuse, public humiliation, harsh criticism, bullying etc. I have hypothesized that others who developed a fear of speaking in public later in life suffer from the effects of Post-Traumatic Stress. People with anxiety about speaking in public cannot overcome their problem with cavalier advice. The only reasonable solution is a method that will extinguish the fear and its devastating effects.

TalkPower accomplishes this with original exercises that synthesize neuroscience behavior modification, performance techniques, speech crafting, and self-esteem training. The result is transformation: a calmer state of body and mind, a clear speaking style, with appropriate pauses and a confident public persona.

How This Book Is Organized

Most of the chapters in this book are designed to duplicate the structure and content of an actual TalkPower Workshop. Beginning with Chapter 6, each chapter contains a new lesson or step, plus instructions for writing and practicing that step. As you complete the assignments outlined in each chapter, you will find that TalkPower training gradually re-patterns your brain for the skill of performance. As a result, step by step your fear response is eliminated. I have taken the liberty of repeating certain ideas in different places throughout the book. I feel that in these instances the material is so important it bears repeating.

The stories you'll find throughout the book come from just a few of the thousands of people TalkPower has transformed into proud and accomplished speakers. You are not alone. TalkPower will help you, too.

Dear Natalie:

It's been almost eleven months since I went to your weekend workshop last December. I've been waiting until I made my first "real" speech before I sent you this picture of me, in my gown, on the stage.

Two weeks ago I made my debut at a beauty conference where I was honored. I delivered a fifteen-minute speech, followed by an impromptu question and answer session. Natalie, I can't tell you how truly thrilled I was and am. I have been avoiding public speaking for years, and holding myself back.

I want to thank you for bringing me to this point today. . . . Going to your workshop, and the speech two weeks ago, were turning points in my life. I cannot adequately express to you how much it means to me. The speech went really well and I'll never be the same.

So, thank you, Natalie, for helping me change my life in such a major way.

I will never forget you or TalkPower.

—Betty, owner of a chain of beauty salons

Chapter 1

BORN TO SPEAK

They Are the Silent Many

In the beginning was the word
And then the spoken word.
All over the earth,
Every nation has a language.
Every tribe has a grammar
And a dialect with a meaning.
To speak is to be human.
To speak is to be seen.

—N. H. R.

Frances, a treasurer in a large corporation, has a group of male executives working for her. She goes into a state of shock when asked to give a weekly report. Her senior status does not lessen her anxiety. She fears her colleagues will criticize her for having the nerve to "stand up there and shoot her mouth off."

Frances describes her debilitating panic to a roomful of sympathetic nods from fellow TalkPower workshop participants. "I could see them sitting there, hating me." Her problem started when an older brother verbally taunted and bullied her. "He never let up." That hurtful, childhood voice haunts her everyday of her working life.

Frances is hardly alone. Another participant says:

When I first came in here and I saw all of you—so intelligent-looking, so successful—I wanted to turn around and leave. I said, "Oh no. This is not the right place for me . . . I am a nut . . . These people are probably a little nervous—not like me. I am going to stand out and be completely humiliated if I speak."

—Lisa, architect

Once this confession is made, others come forward:

"I had the same feeling."
"That's exactly how I felt."
"I almost left."
"I promised myself that I would not come back after lunch."

This scenario is not unusual. For the past twenty-five years I have had the rare privilege of working with and observing thousands of professionals who have attained the highest levels of achievement. These attractive, successful people, with every reason to feel confident and proud of themselves, all suffer from fear of speaking in public and feelings of low self-worth.

When people pass up opportunities for saying even a few words at small meetings, they lose the chance to become accustomed to speaking. Avoidance leads to further avoidance, and what began as a lack of confidence, or a feeling of inhibition, becomes an actual phobia.

A phobia is an irrational fear that leads to avoidance. *The Book of Lists* states that fear of public speaking is the number one phobia in the United States, affecting a majority of people.

Why Are You So Anxious?

Many of my clients and students are completely mystified as to why they become so anxious when they have to speak in front of a group. "After all," they say, "I am great in a one-on-one. My friends tell me

I'm very witty and persuasive. But put me in front of half a dozen people and I'm not just tongue-tied, I'm speechless."

"I spend days preparing for a speech, but when I face an audience, everything flies out of my head. I can't understand why!"

Where did this problem begin? Certainly, you were not born with it. Healthy babies come into the world kicking and screaming. They express themselves when they are wet, tired, hungry, or uncomfortable. No doubt about it, babies cry loud and clear.

When did your silence begin? Where did you learn to hold back? When was your impulse to express extinguished?

> *Even as a young child, I was often put down by my family and told that I should not talk because I didn't know enough about a subject. This made me very quiet and, I guess, shy. And now when I am sitting in a meeting and my boss asks me a question, I freeze up and I feel as if I am ten years old.*
>
> —Sheila, designer

In 70 percent of the questionnaires that are filled out in my classes, one theme resonates again and again: early experience with shaming, public humiliation, harsh criticism, and taunting.

> *During my preadolescence, when my voice was very high, often on the phone I would be identified as a female. . . . My two brothers and their friends would tease and humiliate me. I think it was then that I stopped talking. At least, I try as much as possible not to talk.*
>
> —Ted, editor

Self-Blame

I have found that many people who suffer from childhood humiliation and shame have no idea how damaging these experiences can be. Often, they are children from "good homes" whose families are models of familial devotion in the community. Hiding their pain, they blame themselves for their "problem," feeling guilty and ungrateful for having any negative thoughts about their parents, siblings, or teachers.

> *My father was a very respected orthodontist. All of my colleagues knew him and thought very highly of him. . . . He was a very accomplished man. I felt so inadequate next to him. . . . Of course he was very critical and tough on me. I really feel it when I am at a meeting with other professionals. I know people are looking at me and comparing me to my father, and I feel so demolished, I become speechless.*
>
> —Philip, orthodontist

Discipline or Abuse?

Verbal pounding is not considered child abuse nor does it fall into the category of criminal neglect. No social worker will show up to investigate a parent who calls his child "stupid" every day. Yet, this is psychological abuse. It destroys self-esteem and confidence, making any kind of public performance an ordeal, if not a devastating experience. As a matter of fact, studies tell us that psychological abuse can be more damaging than physical abuse.

> *I went to a very strict school. "Children should be seen and not heard" was the prevailing philosophy. We were discouraged from speaking up in class unless we were asked a direct question. In the beginning I was very outgoing, but I was punished so many times for speaking up that I became very quiet.*
>
> —Felicia, medical student

There is no escape. The incidents where one is required to make some sort of an appearance under the glare of public scrutiny are everywhere. While the necessity for performing has never been greater, the number of people who suffer from performance anxiety and fear of public speaking has grown to epidemic proportions.

Performance Anxiety Appears in Many Situations
- Presenting a formal speech in front of an audience
- Meetings
- In a circle where you have to introduce yourself
- Asking or answering a question in class
- Playing golf, tennis, or any spectator sport
- Making a toast
- Interviewing for a job
- Being photographed or videotaped
- Getting married, as in walking down the aisle or repeating the vows
- Speaking at a PTA or a board meeting
- Delivering a eulogy
- Appearing on the witness stand
- TV interviewing
- Giving a press conference
- Grand Rounds
- Speaking on a conference call
- Participating during a Zoom meeting
- Accepting an award
- Introducing a speaker
- PhD Orals
- A sales presentation
- Appearing in court, as an attorney
- As an actor performing at an audition
- As a musician, playing an instrument
- Having your name called, as in being paged, and having to stand up and walk across a room

There are many other times when you become self-conscious because you are the center of attention. In all of these scenarios, if you fear that you are going to be judged, you are no longer involved in the comfortable, safe, orderly exchange of dialogue that takes place in a conversation. Your mind jumps to negative thoughts about what the other person thinks about you and what you are saying.

My clients and students have the following thoughts at this moment of high visibility. Hard to believe, but at least one or more of these thoughts is actually what many, many people are thinking as they stand in front of an audience trying to talk

As shared in Talkpower workshops:

Nasty Self-Talk

"They don't like me."

"I didn't do enough research."

"I'm going to forget something."

"I sound so stupid."

"I am going to blow this."

"I'm taking too much time."

"I sound terrible."

"I'm going to get killed in the Q&A."

"I feel humiliated."

"My accent is awful."

"They see right through me and know that I am a fraud."

"They are disgusted with me."

"They look so bored."

"My voice is so monotonous."

"My suit is too tight."

"I look old."

"I am fat."

"I am skinny."

"My voice shakes."

"I am boring."

"My hair is a mess."

"They're smarter than me."

"I want to run out of here."

"I've got to get this over with."

"Who needs this?"

"If only there were a hurricane, then they'd cancel."

"I am embarrassed."

"I'm a mess."

"I wish I were dead."

"They can see how I'm shaking."
"I wish a bomb could go off somewhere so I could stop."
"I'm going to get sick."

People try to deal with their pain in therapy or, by hiding their low self-esteem so that it does not seem to intrude' or disrupt their lives, they manage to cope, even to become successful in their careers. However, when it comes to speaking in public, the effects of low self-esteem are devastating.

The following list describes the various conditioning factors that I have discovered result in fear of speaking in public. Do any of these apply to you? Check those that do.

- ❑ Authoritarian parents
- ❑ Abusive parents
- ❑ Overly critical parents
- ❑ Perfectionist parents
- ❑ Obsessive parental focus on child
- ❑ Alcoholic parents
- ❑ Depressed parents
- ❑ Parents with low self-esteem
- ❑ Jealous older brothers or sisters
- ❑ Victim of Bullying
- ❑ Abusive teachers
- ❑ Shaming relatives, neighbors, etc.
- ❑ Post-Traumatic Stress Disorder

Public speaking phobia can also be caused by negative attention that a child receives because of characteristics that are different.

- ❑ Large nose
- ❑ Overweight/underweight
- ❑ Skin condition
- ❑ Foreign accent
- ❑ Too short/too tall
- ❑ Unfashionable attire

- ❏ Large breasts
- ❏ Small or no breasts
- ❏ Racism
- ❏ Different sexual orientation

Social Silence

Always choosing to sit in the back row, invisible—silent—blaming themselves, phobic speakers hide among us. Millions of people are so afraid of public exposure that they invent the most bizarre excuses to avoid speaking in public. Accidents, dead relatives, illnesses, robberies, and playing hooky are the reasons used to avoid the fearful task. These people have a common despair yet do not know one another and have no idea that so many others suffer as they do.

Many other groups come out, talking openly about their problems. People in Twelve Steps programs, for example, find support and dignity by telling their stories. They have learned the healing power of sharing and do not avoid speaking out. However, people with public speaking phobia would be horrified by such an idea. They have a terrible need for secrecy. Memories of past denigration are so painful that they are paralyzed with shame. Avoiding the natural impulse to reach out, they do not ask for help. Embarrassed, they withdraw and remain silent.

Donald, a workshop participant, introduced himself as a nuclear engineer. He mentioned that he had an identical twin brother. Donald's fear of public speaking was so intense that he found himself literally hiding from his manager on the days of the month when summary presentations were made. Later, when I asked if his brother had the same problem, Donald said he did not know. So deep was his shame that he had never even shared his problem with his twin brother.

This story is typical. To avoid public speaking, speech-phobic clients turn down jobs, promotions, drop out of law school, refuse invitations to chair meetings, refuse opportunities to teach, pass on important job interviews, to make a toast, even to accept an award. One CEO of a major corporation told me sadly that he had been invited to speak all over the world, but could never accept.

Another man fainted when he was nominated for an Oscar, so terrible was his anxiety about standing up to receive his award in public.

> *I feel very damaged . . . like I have a major disadvantage when I stand in front of other people and have to speak. I am like a non-person.*
>
> —Arthur, architect

National Silence

Not only is there an individual silence about fear of speaking in public, there is also a national silence. The problem receives so little attention you would think it doesn't exist. For example, there are no public speaking phobia specialists attached to speech departments in colleges and universities. There is no National Public-Speaking Phobia Society; even the *Encyclopedia Britannica*, under the category of "speech," has no reference to this condition. In the speech category, although various esoteric conditions and maladies are cited, there is no listing of public-speaking phobia itself, although it has a name: *glossophobia*.

Why is it that in the United States—one of the few countries in the world where freedom of speech is guaranteed by a Constitution—fear of speaking in public is the number one phobia? This is a question I asked every time I appeared on radio or television during my first book tour. Nobody seemed to have an answer.

> *When I was studying to be a speech teacher, fear of public speaking and nervousness was never mentioned. The assumption was if you did it long enough, you would get over it.*
>
> —Helen Yalof, retired Chairman,
> Speech and Theater Dept., City University, New York City

The Symptoms

Speech-phobic people report three main categories of symptoms when speaking before groups: physical, mental, and emotional.

SYMPTOMS REPORTED TO ME BY STUDENTS
Physical

Physical symptoms of distress can begin weeks before making a presentation. High levels of stress trigger a nervous stomach, physical tension, and sleepless nights, which is called "anticipatory anxiety." Symptoms of physical distress that can occur just before and during the speech can include any or all of the following:

- Rapid heartbeat
- High anxiety
- Panic Attacks
- Trembling knees, making it difficult to get up and walk to the podium or stand at ease in front of a group
- Quivering voice, often accompanied by a tightness in the throat or an accumulation of phlegm
- A feeling of faintness
- Stomach nervousness, sometimes to the point of nausea
- Hyperventilation, involving an uncontrolled gasping for air
- Eye-tearing
- Trembling hands or limbs

Mental

Mental dysfunction that can occur during a speech includes:

- Thought-blocking—The speaker becomes speechless, having no idea what he intended to say next
- Repetition of words, phrases, or messages
- Loss of memory, including the inability to recall facts and figures accurately, and the omission of important points or complete speechlessness
- General disorganization

Emotional

Intense emotional distress brought on by having to speak in public, and all other types of performance, include symptoms such as:

- Feelings of confusion
- Feeling out of control

- Terror, which often arises before the beginning of the speech
- Feeling overwhelmed
- A sense of being outside of one's body (dissociation)
- Helplessness, a childlike feeling of powerlessness, being unable to cope
- Out of body feelings that you and your voice are coming from somewhere else
- Low self-esteem, a feeling of worthlessness, and failure
- Self-hatred, a feeling of disgust, and rage at one's self
- Embarrassment
- Panic (intense anxiety)
- Shame and humiliation following a presentation
- Fear of being discovered a fraud
- Tearfulness

These three categories of symptoms interact with one another. An initial feeling of terror as you wait to be introduced can cause your heart to race uncontrollably. Your pounding heart feels even more frightening as your throat begins to tighten. Physical symptoms disrupt your concentration, causing you to lose track of the organization of your speech. You stumble over your words, repeat phrases, or leave out ideas. You become embarrassed and feel out of control.

> *Whenever an opportunity comes up where I have to make a comment, address a group, or ask a question at a meeting, at that precise moment, all of my brain functions jam. And there I am, hopeless, shamed . . . I feel like a victim in front of a firing squad.*
>
> —Irwin, accountant

Phobias Acquired Later in Life
Some 70 percent of my students and clients recall that as far back as they can remember they were shy and didn't speak up. The other 30 percent who suffer from public speaking phobia have a different story. These people were once excellent speakers. Generally

outgoing, many were active in drama and debate clubs, were class valedictorians or presidents of school societies. They report this kind of experience:

> *I have about a hundred people working for me, and there I was, in front of my entire staff, nervous but doing all right, I guess. We had just been awarded a major contract and this was to be the announcement. Suddenly I looked at them and I couldn't say a word; or even think a word. They just looked at me and the room got very quiet, and I started to get very warm, and I could feel my face turning red. . . . And I was totally speechless. It was the most embarrassing thing that has ever happened to me. I can't talk in front of groups anymore.*
>
> —James, commercial real estate developer

Post Traumatic Stress Disorder (PTSD)

Behavioral psychology tells us that phobias happen after a traumatic event—usually an experience that shakes the individual to his core—like a psychological near-death experience. One's sense of personal control and safety is utterly shattered at the deepest levels of self, resulting in post-traumatic stress syndrome. The stress reaction takes many forms and can appear in the form of Public Speaking Phobia. It can appear immediately or up to two years after the traumatic event.

Precipitating Events

Another interesting fact about phobias is that they follow the rule, "Different strokes for different folks." For one person, the precipitating event could be tragic, like the death of a parent or child, a catastrophic illness, or a past sexual abuse, rape or incest. For another person, moving to a new community, going away to college, or losing a job can produce a similar post-traumatic stress reaction.

No matter what the cause, or the variety of precipitating events, the result can be a phobia, such as fear of flying, driving, fear of heights, or enclosed places. The phobia, triggered by a particular event, can then generalize to other areas, such as fear of escalators or trains, or a sudden panic attack in front of an audience.

The panic attack may cause an episode of thought-blocking and becomes another traumatic event that will not be forgotten. The next time an opportunity for speaking arises, you are psychologically transported to the past—and that moment when you were speechless. You simply cannot do it; you decline with some excuse. One avoidant experience leads to another, and in a very short time you have glossophobia: an irrational fear of speaking in public.

And so you join the silent many. Your voice is no longer heard, your reputation as a speaker, a thing of the past. You are silent, just like the person who cannot speak because of humiliation in childhood.

Understanding Why

These "late bloomers" are always relieved to discover why they suddenly lost their ability to speak in public and that TalkPower training can heal this mysterious malady. Time and time again I hear students say, "I lost my mother and we were very close. So that is why I became speechless at that meeting" or "It happened to me when I started college and I was so afraid I couldn't hack it."

One man who called me before he attended the workshop said he had no idea what could have caused a sudden panic attack he experienced at a Rotary Club meeting he was chairing. Later, when he attended the TalkPower seminar, he said, "I was thinking about what you told me, and then after several days I realized that we tragically lost our little girl to a terrible illness around that time." If you suddenly, for no apparent reason have had an episode of speechlessness, understanding why you lost your ability to speak in public will not cure the problem but it can help to motivate you to work with the training methods described in the following chapters.

Chapter 2

PRESENTATION, NOT CONVERSATION

The Big Chill

The difference between conversation and presentation is like the difference between ping pong and tennis.

People in my workshops learn that in addition to a history of public humiliation, there is another reason they are uncomfortable about speaking in front of a group. Much to their surprise, they discover that public speaking is not an extension of conversational speech. In other words, the skills used in conversation are not sufficient for a presentation because conversation and presentation are two very different endeavors.

The difference between conversation and public speaking can be compared to the difference between Ping-Pong and tennis. Suppose you invite a great Ping-Pong player to play tennis, assuring him that the two games are the same. In one game you have a ball, a net, and a racquet, just as you have in the other. How shocking for the Ping-Pong player to discover (especially if all his friends are watching) that he is overwhelmed by the size of the tennis court, the ball, the feel of the racquet, the height of the net, the rules of play—everything is different and strange.

*When I stand up to speak in public I feel as if I have been
catapulted to another planet or dimension . . . like walking into
outer space. It is really like an electric atmosphere, as if I am
an alien, or am among aliens. Even when I am with my own
family, at a family affair like a wedding or an anniversary, and
I have to make a toast . . . the air feels different, and the energy
around me feels strange. If I even think the words "hushed
expectancy," my stomach turns over and I stop breathing.*

—Richard, TV producer

That Silence

The passive attention of the audience is quite different from the
active give-and-take of a conversation. In a conversation you talk
and listen in an easy exchange. The only response you can expect
from an audience is restless movement, laughter, clapping, or silence.
That silence is certainly nerve-wracking. It carries with it an intense,
unfamiliar energy. All those faces stare at you and you feel as if you
are being judged. It's hardly the same as friendly conversation.

When the audience is attentive, actors say, "It is like being
bathed in a sea of warm love." The fearful speaker does not have
this poetic experience. To him, this special attention feels shamefully
intimidating.

*Sometimes I become numb and cold from head to foot. I can't
seem to think the simplest thought. My brain is frozen. Forget
it. It's a nightmare.*

—Diane, public relations executive

The Space Between You and the Audience

A speaker, who expects conversational signals, quickly loses his
confidence because of the absence of anything familiar. In a conversation, you are usually seated or standing close to the person with
whom you are speaking. You look into her eyes or face; you rarely
look at her entire body, or many bodies, as you do in front of a
group. The space between you and the audience can be disconcerting

if you are not used to it because you unconsciously miss the physical closeness of a conversation. Some of my students find this extremely threatening. They report a feeling of disassociation. "Standing at a distance from the audience feels like being out of my body and hearing my voice as though it doesn't belong to me."

Compounding the dilemma, since your heart is beating very fast, you have a tendency to speak more quickly. As a matter of fact, this is precisely what you should not do—the distance between you and the audience actually calls for a slower pace.

Me? A Leader?

Furthermore, since your presentation has a specific agenda, rather than the random path that most conversations take, your responsibility in leading the talk is totally different from your role in a verbal exchange. Unless there is a question-and-answer segment, as the leader of the group, you are engaged in a monologue with little, if any, feedback. The fearful speaker thinks, "Who am I to be standing up here, taking these people's time?" If you have any doubt about your right to be a leader, this uncertainty brings up other unsettling issues—low self-esteem and all of the feelings of shame and self-dislike that accompany this condition.

And about that question-and-answer segment—don't underestimate the strangeness of that situation, where you alone are fielding a lot of friendly or unfriendly questions from a body called "the audience." People are rarely prepared to stand alone, singled out, to respond and talk to an entire group. These subtle and not-so-subtle deviations from your habitual behavior and expectations, can wreak havoc with your sense of familiar reality.

> *I can remember one incident when I was in the middle of a very confrontational Q & A. Fortunately I was behind a lectern. By the end of the talk I was leaning on the lectern just to keep from falling over.*
>
> —Frank, entrepreneur

Inner Attention

Another important difference between a conversation and a presentation is one's mind-set. In social conversation your attention is outer-directed as you listen to what your partner in the conversation is saying. When you stand in front of a group, however, different rules apply. You must shift your customary social behavior to the unfamiliar state of inner-attention. The shift will allow you to think and concentrate properly on your presentation while the audience observes and evaluates you. *(We will discuss inner-attention in more detail in Chapter 6.)*

This ability to focus within empowers the speaker with the authority to withstand the scrutiny of the audience. The audience presses in; the speaker stands her ground. If you can stand up to this kind of pressure, you will own your role as the leader. As your talk progresses, your steadfast concentration draws the audience to you, and a magnetic field is created. Thus, the audience is engaged.

Leaders Know How to Perform

Once an audience is engaged, it is possible for the speaker to project a belief to each person that he will do any or all of the following: help, protect, cure, rescue, guide, teach, support, uplift, entertain, enrich, inspire, or transform them. This, of course, is an illusionary dynamic. Actually, the leader needs the support of the audience in order to maintain his leadership. And yet, because of his leadership skills and the ability to ground himself and stand firm, the audience responds with primal trust and attention.

This is exactly what happens when the powerful concentration of a good actor engages the audience with the persona of his character. As the actor Ed Asner once said, "I had those three hundred people in the palm of my hand. I could have asked them to jump off a cliff. That's the kind of power I felt."

The fearful speaker is afraid the audience will ask him to jump off a cliff. That's the kind of helplessness he feels. Lacking performance skills, he is unable to support himself in front of the scrutiny of the audience. Looking to see if he is winning the approval of the audience, he is totally distracted and cannot concentrate on his presentation.

When I was in elementary school, I was not a good speller. Once a week we had a Spelling Bee. We had to stand in front of the class and spell the words our teacher gave us. I was always wrong, and it was so humiliating to hear my teacher make clucking sounds with her tongue at every wrong letter. The other kids would get quiet and when they heard me going wrong, they'd snicker. I felt as if I was being roasted alive. That went on every week for a whole term, and I never spoke in class or anywhere after that. If someone asks me a question, I still get all hot and my mouth gets very dry and I feel as if I can't breathe.

—Becky, accountant

What About People Who Bask in the Limelight?

Not everyone has a fear of speaking in public. Even though many people feel uncomfortable and nervous when they first stand before the audience, they are able to overcome their initial discomfort and actually enjoy themselves. Their willingness to speak in public soon makes them comfortable with an audience. Without proper training, however, even if they are unafraid, they will probably never reach a level of professional elegance and authority.

The other day on television I saw a very famous businessman on a talk show. Even though this man is enormously popular and speaks with absolutely no difficulty, he came across as a fast-talking self-promoter with questionable credibility. His responses were defensive, he grimaced, and he expressed his nervousness by shrugging his shoulders after every few sentences. These mannerisms do not come across well on TV. With no technique for pausing, looking thoughtful on his feet, or projecting a mature image, the impression he left upon the audience was less than memorable.

Another celebrity I happened to catch really surprised me with his lack of physical control. Even though he seemed to be having an absolutely wonderful time, he fidgeted constantly and said *"umm"* after every other sentence.

Just as golfers and tennis players take professional instruction to improve their game—people who are in the limelight also need training for performance techniques that will polish their presentations.

Inconsistent Performance

> *Sometimes when I do a presentation, I feel as if I am flying by the seat of my pants.*
>
> —Susan, sales manager

Since most speakers have no fundamental technique to rely on, their presentations are inconsistent. One week, Bob J. did a sales talk that, as his manager commented, ". . . knocked the socks off all those guys."

The following week, in Minneapolis, with a bigger, more intimidating client, Bob felt so pressured that he omitted a very important part of the presentation and did not do well on the Q&A.

Lacking the basic skill of a trained speaker, Bob was unable to take control of his physical, emotional, and mental reactions. And so he could not concentrate properly during this highly competitive event. As a result, his anxiety grew until he lost his composure and his presentation fell apart.

The untrained speaker hopes to improve by speaking frequently. This is unlikely. Repeating the same mistakes over and over, like incorrect breathing, poor concentration, nonverbal fillers, and too-rapid speech, will keep her as unpolished as ever. Even if she were to give one hundred talks a year for one hundred years, her bad habits would be incorporated into every presentation. Usually people give up and say, "That's the way I am, and that's that."

> *I'm a complete wreck, and as the director of a corporate training program, I guess everybody would keel over if they*

knew that before I stand up to speak, I take a Valium or have a drink. . . . I've been doing this for the past twenty years. It has never gotten better. . . . I'm used to it; it's a fact of my life.
                                        —Harriet, director of training

Most People Who Speak in Public Don't Like To

At corporate conventions, we circulate a questionnaire that asks: "How much do you enjoy speaking in public?" Some 90 percent of our respondents indicate that they do not enjoy speaking in public.

The person in this category often speaks too quickly. He may not know how or when to pause for effect; he may pace, move around too much, or have poor organizational skills, which produce unclear and repetitive talks. He may use his hands too much, frequently say "ah" or "uh" (nonverbal filler), may have breathing difficulties (this he knows about), and sometimes clear his throat throughout the presentation. He usually has a sense of dissatisfaction and embarrassment about his presentations.

Not really phobic, he feels that his presentations do not go well. This feeling is shared by many people who speak all the time, yet have never been properly trained. This group includes managers, lawyers, teachers, trainers, salespeople, even movie actors and others whom you would never suspect suffer from discomfort related to public speaking. These people never avoid speaking in public; nevertheless, they are uncomfortable and need training just as much as those who have a serious fear of public speaking.

All my life I wanted to be a teacher, and now that I am, I find that I have begun suffering from the most horrible panic attacks. My job revolves around developing courses and presenting them, and I can't stand the pressure. I avoid as much as I possibly can. My self-esteem drops. I think about an upcoming presentation constantly . . . for days . . . I feel as if I am not myself. It's really hard to describe my misery to another person. No one would believe what I go through. The funny thing is, though, that at a training seminar my group had

*to attend, everyone in the group said that they were suffering
from terrible nervousness. I'm not sure it's not as bad as mine,
but I was really surprised to hear how all the others were so
uncomfortable. It made me feel a little bit better, but not much.
I still have this thing on my back that won't go away.*

　　　　　　　　　　　　　　　　—Dee, trainer, program developer

Can I Really Change?

Most of you have had performance anxiety for as far back as you can
remember. How can you change this? How can you train yourself
so that these performance situations become opportunities for you
to shine? How can you change a lifetime of discomfort and avoidance in one weekend? Time and again people ask me these questions
when they consider taking the TalkPower workshop.

I always reply by saying, "Do you think you could learn how to
ride a bicycle in one weekend? Or, if you were afraid of the water, do
you think that you could learn how to swim in fourteen hours?" Of
course you could learn how to swim in fourteen hours if you had the
proper training program. Learning how to be comfortable when you
speak in public calls for a similar systematic training approach. It's
not as if you have to learn a new language or how to think. You simply have to be trained to be in control, talk, and make sense while
people are looking at you. Twenty-five years of experience tells me
that the answer lies in the TalkPower synthesis. That synthesis will
train your brain for the skill of performance.

Performance, as we mentioned previously, is any situation where
you are doing some activity in front of people who are looking
at you. The person who suffers from intense anxiety at this time
feels that he is being negatively judged. The ability to detach your
thoughts from focusing on the audience by focusing upon your talk
is a skill that you will be able to develop once you commit yourself to
the TalkPower program as described in this book.

How Change Happens

Peter Russell, author of *The Brain Book* (Hawthorn Books,
New York) says:

The brain is unlike any organ in the body, in that its internal structure is always changing and developing as a result of experience. This gives it the unlimited capacity for learning.

The ability of the brain to change is called plasticity.

Although I have previously offered my explanation for the successful results accomplished in the TalkPower workshop, that were placed in the section on Scientific verification, I think that the information is so significant that is deserves to be repeated here.

I theorize that the extraordinary results achieved in the Talk-Power workshops are possible because of the unique exercises, repetition drills and routines that are part of the TalkPower training program. These exercises which I believe cause the memory centers of the brain to develop the enzymes and genetic markers that initiate the production of new neurons (chains of cells) also reinforce plasticity: the brain's ability to remake itself. In other words after participating for two days in continuous exposure to the TalkPower repetition drills and exercises, the brains of the participants were now behaving like brains of people who do not in any way suffer from fear of speaking in public. New and permanent performance skills were developed, enabling the speaker to face an audience with attention focused upon the presentation rather than on the judgement of the audience: As a result when speaking, there was no trace of the previous confusion and terror.

An article in the *New York Times* on March 24, 2000 discusses how London taxi drivers must be able to visualize an enormously complex map of their city in order to drive customers to their destinations as efficiently as possible. As a result, London taxi drivers appear to have brains that are notably different than other people's brains.

In a study conducted by the University College London, the brain anatomy of London taxi drivers was compared to the brain anatomy of control subjects. The drivers in this study had spent two years in a required taxi driver training program, followed by an average of fourteen years on the job. Researchers used scanning equipment to examine the brains of both groups. A direct correlation was discovered between the size of the driver's posterior hippocampus and the number of years he had spent on the job. The posterior hippocampus is the area of our brain that is believed to store a spatial representation of our environment.

The study concluded that "it seems there is a capacity for local change in the structure of the healthy adult human brain in response to environmental demands."

If You're Still Not Convinced . . .

Looking at the field of neurobiology, Dr. Eric R. Kandel, Professor at Columbia University in the Center for Neurobiology and Behavior, has experimented with the gill-withdrawal reflex of sea slugs and has shown that "new neural connections" can be made to grow in response to experience. This provides an objective model of what happens during the TalkPower training process. Building on Dr. Kandel's theory, the systematic repetition of the TalkPower training exercises probably alters the functional connections between neurons and then repatterns these functional changes in the actual structure of the cerebral cortex. This explains how such a dramatic transformation can occur in one weekend for more than 95 percent of our participants who have suffered with public speaking phobia for most of their lives.

The TalkPower Training Process

The TalkPower method is a behavioral program designed to help you overcome your fear of public speaking. Drawn from three different areas, the program includes performance training, speech crafting, and self-esteem training.

I. Performance Training: Mind-Body Control

The exercises in the first part of the program will allow you to feel calm and in control. In a surprisingly short time, you will know how to make the shift from social behavior to performance behavior. You will be able to stand in front of an audience without panic, projecting excitement and confidence. At the same time, you will be able to think and talk clearly. Eventually (hard as this is to believe), you will actually enjoy giving a talk.

II. Speech Crafting

Speech writing is a craft that is easy to learn. Several chapters of this book are devoted to speech construction using the unique Talk-Power Action Formula plus the speech templates to guide you in the development of a presentation. This formula enables you to write an interesting speech quickly and easily. Eventually you will internalize this formula, using it to speak well extemporaneously.

III. Self-Esteem Training

By dealing with the psychological aspects of public-speaking phobia, the self-esteem exercises in chapter 15 will help you to examine where your fear may have come from and reframe the negative core beliefs that trigger anxiety when you have to speak in public.

While psychological insight alone cannot change your phobic response, once the basic performance techniques are in place, psychological insight will enhance and reinforce your transformative experience.

Rather than waste time with traditional approaches, people should investigate TalkPower—a quick and effective method that has withstood rigorous scrutiny.

—Nick Catalano, PhD
professor of literature and communications, Pace University

Chapter 3

DEMYSTIFYING THE "PROBLEM"

I've Tried Everything

I have spent thousands of dollars and years of my life trying psychotherapy, hypnosis, dropping out of major training programs, to overcome a problem that TalkPower eliminated in one weekend.

—Christine, human resources director

To understand fully what happens to you when you perform—speaking before an audience, on the tennis court, or on the stage—let's take a look at the physiological composition of the brain. Looking inside this amazing organ is like opening Pandora's Box containing all kinds of fascinating instruments and gadgets. Made up of three separate brains, each of which developed independently at different stages of our evolutionary history, the average human brain is about the size of a grapefruit and weighs about three pounds. It is composed of an estimated hundred billion neurons, more neurons than there are stars in the galaxy. Each neuron is as complex as a small computer.

The Reptilian Brain

The most primitive part, which is located at the base of the skull, is called the reptilian brain, or autonomic nervous system. This brain controls behaviors that deal with survival, escape from danger, speed, strength, and activation of the "fight or flight response." The reptilian brain regulates our breathing and heartbeat and maintains equilibrium and muscle tone. It is the seat of our autonomic nervous system, which has two parts. One part is responsible for automatic arousal; the other is responsible for automatic relaxation. The role of the autonomic nervous system is important for understanding the breathing exercises in the next chapter.

The Mammalian Brain

Our second brain, called the mammalian brain, or limbic system, surrounds the original reptilian brain and developed in the earliest mammals about 150 million years ago. This brain is the center of our emotions, sexual drives, maternal instincts, and bonding impulses.

The Cerebral Cortex (The Enchanted Loom)

In the wrinkled top layers of the human brain (about an eighth-of-an-inch thick) lies the neocortex, the new mammalian brain, commonly referred to as the cerebral cortex. The cerebral cortex is more intricate in structure and more complex in function than anything else known to us. It is with the cerebral cortex that we think, speak, learn, reason, solve problems, and perform the many human functions that separate us from all other creatures. The cerebral cortex has a right side and a left side.

Left Brain/Right Brain

The left side of the cerebral cortex controls things that act in an orderly and conscious progression like speech, language, grammar, logic, reason, analysis, counting, writing, reading and organizing. The right side helps us to arrange seemingly disparate elements into a whole as in visual images, recognition of faces, depth perception, problem solving, creativity, musicality, synthesis, rhythm, empathy, feelings, and love.

In regard to public speaking, a well-balanced presentation includes organizational and analytical components handled by the left side of the brain, as well as the emotional, inspirational, and active components that are evoked with the right side of the brain. To speak effectively, both sides of the brain must be functioning harmoniously, freely, and smoothly. The following story illustrates exactly what happens when brain activity is disturbed by intense fear.

> *My parents always made me recite and sing songs for the family. I hated it. They put so much pressure on me that I became very shy. And eventually I couldn't speak in class, certainly not to an adult. . . . We had a big family, and every Easter we had a big Easter egg hunt in my aunt's backyard. One year the prize was a bike. I was six years old and I dreamed about the bike. My uncle had shown it to me in his garage. On the day of the Easter egg hunt, we must have had thirty kids running around screaming and squealing and looking for that special painted Easter egg. . . . And there it was: I found it tucked away in a bed of high grass near a big tree. I was so excited when I saw it, my heart almost jumped out of my chest. But then I couldn't say anything. I became paralyzed. I just could not take the egg and bring it to my uncle and say, "Look, I found it!" Hard as it is to believe, I left it there. I left it there, and my cousin Bobby found it and got the bicycle. I am fifty-six years old and I've had a lot of therapy, but I still feel like crying when I think of that story. . . . And I still can't stand being the center of attention.*

> —Michael, psychotherapist

Fight or Flight . . . In the Boardroom?

When you are called on to speak and you feel threatened, the reptilian brain (the autonomic nervous system) is activated, sending adrenaline and sugar into your bloodstream, revving up your body to meet the supposed danger, urging you to escape. As a result your heart beats faster, your muscles feel tense, your throat becomes dry, your stomach tightens, and you breathe using your chest muscles.

This reaction to threat is known as the "fight or flight response." This is exactly how you would react if you heard strange sounds outside your window in the middle of the night.

Since you are usually sitting or standing still as you wait to speak, and you cannot fight or run, you begin to feel trapped. This feeling of being trapped triggers such high levels of anxiety that your cerebral cortex (the thinking brain) shuts down and reasoning, logic, and speech are affected.

"I can't seem to think straight," you say. "I block, I become incoherent. I can't make the most obvious connections."

The interference with your thinking process is similar to what happens when you are worried, eat dinner, and then have a case of indigestion. The indigestion occurs because, in a state of worry or stress, your brain does not send signals for the production of digestive juices. In other words, your digestive system, like your ability to think clearly, shuts down when your fight or flight response is activated.

SAN DIEGO, FEB. 18 (AP) - *A judge who resigned after developing what he called stage fright has won a lifetime disability pension at the age of 44.* . . . *Despite efforts to hide the problem, he said it worsened to the point that he panicked in any public setting where he was expected to speak. The problem, complicated by depression with anxiety, interfered with his ability to perform routine judicial tasks and forced him to take "inordinate amounts of tranquilizers to get through the job," he said.*
—*New York Times,* February 19, 1990

Does Therapy Help?
Even though fear of speaking in public usually originates in childhood, or a post-traumatic stress reaction, the fact remains that speaking well in public is a complex skill. This skill requires systematic training to develop and manage the vast array of necessary neurological underpinnings, like thinking, organizing, remembering, and performance skills, as well as physical control. Compounding this is the element of high visibility, which is part and parcel of the public-speaking situation. This is why trying to learn to be comfortable

when speaking in public, in a therapist's office (as many of my clients have), is like trying to learn how to swim by talking about it.

As I have said, when people experiencing intense anxiety speak in public, their fearful thoughts trigger a fight or flight response that is an automatic reaction, similar to a knee-jerk. This condition does not respond to reason, insight, positive thinking, understanding, or other cognitive processes.

It is true that other phobias, like fear of flying, fear of tunnels, or fear of heights, respond positively to various therapeutic desensitization techniques, like systematic desensitization, relaxation training, flooding, Eye Movement Desensitization Reprocessing (EMDR), and visualization techniques. But the one-dimensional aspect of these nonperformance phobias, where only you and your therapist are privy to your fears, is very different from the element of high visibility that accompanies public speaking. Consequently, these approaches do not diminish public-speaking anxiety.

If you have spent time in therapy, hoping to reverse your fear of speaking in public, and have had little or no results, don't lose hope. As a matter of fact, in the past twenty years, hundreds of therapists, psychologists, analysts, lay counselors, psychiatrists, and priests have attended the TalkPower seminars and have overcome their own public-speaking discomfort.

Additionally, a much prescribed remedy has been treatment with drugs like Inderal—marginally effective, but with alarming side effects.[1]

Demystifying the "Problem"

I always take a combination of Inderal and Ativan before important presentations and meetings. This makes me tired,

---

[1] INDERAL: generic name propranolol hydrochloride. Possible side effects: May decrease heart rate; may aggravate or worsen a condition of congestive heart failure; may produce lowered blood pressure, tingling in the extremities, light-headedness, mental depression including inability to sleep, weakness, or tiredness. [Harold Silverman, PhD, and Gilbert I. Simon, DSc, *The Pill Book*, (Bantam, 1980).]

*gives me headaches, and I worry that the effects of the drugs
will make me forget. Or else they might not even work.*
                              —Anita, marketing sales manager

What about Visualization Techniques?

A popular idea suggests that if you visualize yourself speaking successfully, you will be able to overcome your anxiety. I have worked
with thousands of speech phobic people, and I cannot recall a single
case where visualization significantly reversed this fear. The reason
for this is that in order to visualize successfully, a high degree of
concentration is necessary. This kind of concentration is not possible
given the anxiety that arises in a public-speaking situation. However,
once you have completed the TalkPower training and you have the
proper skills for concentration, visualization techniques can enhance
your presentation.

Gaining Control

To be an effective speaker, your reptilian brain must be brought
under control. But, you can't shut off its signals altogether. You
are giving a performance, and you need the proper bounce you get
from the adrenaline. On the other hand, you don't want the reptilian brain (the fight or flight response) to take over completely, to
paralyze the cerebral cortex. How can you keep the necessary and
valuable impulses from the reptilian brain flowing and, at the same
time, control them so the cerebral cortex can function?

TalkPower Techniques

In addition to the ground breaking exercises, the success of the
TalkPower program lies in the program's attention to detail. This
SLOW and careful step-by-step approach demystifies the problem and offers a new methodology for the elimination of the fear
response. In addition, TalkPower's correct breathing techniques
(next chapter) train you to deliberately diminish that fight or flight
response, bringing it under control, so that you are able to think
clearly and speak clearly. Finally, the concentration techniques

in chapter 6 will help you grow the neural networks (wiring) to develop new concentration skills so that you are able to focus on what you have to say while the audience is looking at you.

In chapter 6 you will learn how to direct your attention from an outer attention state to an inner-awareness state. In other words, we can say that your social attention is outer directed for good social skills and your performance attention must be inner-directed so that you are able to concentrate on your presentation.

Usually people develop a sense of inner-awareness through Yoga, meditation, or martial arts practice. These paths of self-realization, though significant, are not effective for helping you to face an audience because all of these disciplines are done in silence with no apparent observers. Once you add the element of speaking in front of an audience you need additional elements for dealing with the challenge of the high visibility and performance. Chapter 6 describes the very special TalkPower Inner Awareness techniques that are specifically designed for training people to speak in in public. These techniques derive their effectiveness from the principle of hemisphere synchronization.

> *The electrical activity of the brain's two hemispheres becomes coherent, in phase, effectively fostering a state of whole-brain consciousness, in which both brain hemispheres work together integrating two different modes of thinking (verbal and visual-spatial; analytical and synthesizing) and producing gains in certain types of mental functioning.*
> —Michael Hutchison, *Mega Brain* (Ballantine Books)

Chapter 4

BREATH IS LIFE

Why Deep Breathing Doesn't Work

I have conquered my fear, which I did not think was possible.
I did the breathing exercises, prepared my presentation with
your guidelines . . . and each subsequent presentation got
better and better.

—Philip, social worker

Whenever I meet a new group of students in a TalkPower workshop, I am astonished to learn that 98 percent of these people do not know how to breathe correctly. Even after all these years it still amazes me that so many are misinformed about the most basic of life's activities—breathing. I have even taught physicians and stress-reduction trainers with severe public-speaking anxiety, who didn't know how to breathe correctly.

When you do not breathe properly, this is what happens; you are sitting, waiting for your turn to speak and you are very nervous. Your stomach muscles are locked, so that your chest pumps the air in and out of your lungs. Chest breathing is called hyperventilation. When you hyperventilate you activate a body chemistry process called the "fight or flight response." This automatically raises your tension. Becoming more anxious by the minute, you think that you are so nervous because you are worried about having to get up and talk in public. That is only partly true. Actually, your anxiety is growing by leaps and bounds because you are using your chest muscles to do the pumping instead of your abdominal muscles. Chest breathing causes you to exhale too much carbon dioxide. This brings on a carbon dioxide depletion in your bloodstream.

Why Does Your Heart Race?

You probably don't know this, but carbon dioxide is a very important manager of Ph (acid-alkaline balance). When this carbon dioxide depletion occurs, the fight or flight response is automatically triggered. Looking at what happens to your body in a fight or flight mode, we notice that sugar and large quantities of adrenaline are pouring into your bloodstream so that your body is prepared for vigorous physical activity. It's true that adrenaline is very necessary when exercising, but large amounts of adrenaline production that is not accompanied by actual vigorous physical activity will certainly trigger anxiety. Everyone knows what happens when you are waiting for your turn to speak and you begin producing lots of adrenaline and sugar; your heart begins to beat wildly and you tense up, ready to fly out of the room. But you can't fly out of the room—you are about to be called upon to speak.

Dread

As the rapid chest breathing continues and your heart beats even faster, a vicious cycle emerges. Hyperventilation increases anxiety and the resulting anxiety produces more hyperventilation. What happens then—well, you begin to feel trapped and helpless. It is this perception that you are trapped and helpless that brings on that surge of dread before a presentation. The equation is as follows: Trapped + Helpless = Dread.

As your brain function seems to slowly dissolve, your ability to think clearly disappears. There you are, sitting in your seat waiting to present your talk. This is the worst possible time for such a thing to happen. What a nightmare!

I was waiting for my time to speak, sitting there with my stomach all knotted up in a ball. My heart was beating as if it was going to jump out of my chest. I felt utterly trapped and helpless. A feeling of dread descended on me, like a dark cloak, totally enveloping me. I no longer felt like a normal, competent, sane self. My personality just left . . . my sense of humor, my confidence. Instead, I was left with a horrible feeling of isolation, and a shameful feeling of terror. When I say this I feel as if I am becoming so melodramatic, even morbid. But this is just what happened to me last week.

—David, portfolio manager

In *Hyperventilation Syndrome: A Handbook for Bad Breathers* (Celestial Arts, 1992) Dinah Bradley gives us a clinical translation of David's story:

In a terrible *Catch-22* cycle, natural anxiety about symptoms increases the tendency to over-breathe (hyperventilate), further increasing respiratory problems which leads to more unpleasant or frightening symptoms. Not only nerve cells are affected, smooth muscle cells are galvanized into action by lowered carbon dioxide levels, which leads to tightening or constriction of the blood vessels. . . .

The heart and pulses start pounding, and the one hyperventilating may feel panic stricken, with palpitations and chest pain. The brain may have its oxygen supply cut by as much as 50 percent, making it difficult to think, concentrate or even feel part of this planet. Ultimately, all systems in the body are affected, leading to a puzzling constellation of symptoms.

Brown Paper Bag Technology
If you have ever wondered why doctors recommend breathing into a brown paper bag when having a panic attack, it is because you can then breathe back the carbon dioxide you lost when you were hyperventilating by breathing with the chest.

Some people who suffer from anticipatory anxiety due to hyper-ventilation tell me that at times the symptoms of distress are so severe, they feel as if they are losing their minds. If you have ever wondered whether there was something wrong with you for feeling this way, let me assure you that the loss of thinking ability is a common occurrence for many people who normally hyperventilate when they breathe. As a result, when they have to speak in public they become extremely anxious. This even happens occasionally to people who speak all the time.

Confusion about Breathing

So you see, the way you breathe can contribute to a state of high anxiety. Most people do not know this, nor do they understand how the chest works. It's all so confusing, my students say. The top chest, the middle chest, the bottom chest? Should it move or not? Where should it move? How should it move?

And then there is this word, *diaphragm*. What is the diaphragm? How does that work? A diaphragm is a sheet of muscle under your rib cage which pushes your breath up and out of your lungs. (More about the diaphragm later.) Should I breathe through the mouth or the nose? Also, "Is deep breathing good? It makes me feel so spacey. I never know if I am doing it correctly. It's so hard, and I know I do not breathe right, because I get out of breath but I am not sure what to do."

As a trainer who works with people who suffer from high anxiety when they have to speak in public, I have spent years trying to find a simple way to teach my students to breathe correctly.

Breathing Correctly

It was obvious that breathing with the chest was causing the panic my students were feeling. They needed to learn how to calm themselves with slow diaphragmatic breath. I tried many different methods and finally, I devised a way that worked. I asked my over-anxious students to keep their chests still and breathe by moving their bellies in and out. This is called "belly breathing," or diaphragmatic breathing.

The first time I tried this system, it took only ten minutes to get the entire class doing it correctly. The results were miraculous! I had 100 percent belly breathing and every participant felt calmer and more relaxed. Of course, there were the usual comments: "This is like breathing backward. I never breathe like this. I am not getting enough air," proving that most people breath incorrectly all the time.

Nevertheless, soon everyone was breathing correctly, and not one person was confused about what to do. With a few students, I had to actually push my fist into their stomachs, asking them to push back so that they could feel how their abdominal muscles move. (Some had not moved their abdominal muscles for years!) At last they were clear about how to breathe correctly. Most importantly, they would never again go through the torture of severe anticipatory anxiety while waiting their turn to speak.

Deep Breathing vs Shallow Breathing

A common misconception is that deep breathing is good and shallow breathing is bad. Students always ask: "You mean when they tell you to take a deep breath, it's all wrong?" The fact is you can breathe incorrectly when you do deep breathing, when you do shallow breathing, when you take in big gasps of air, or when you are barely breathing. The only criterion for correct breathing is whether or not your chest is still as your belly moves in and out.

However, there is a time when chest breathing is correct. And that is when you are doing any kind of cardiovascular activity, such as jogging or dancing. For our purposes, learning a simple procedure (like belly breathing) can mean the difference between a panic attack and remaining in control, before and during your talk.

How to Move Your Belly

The purpose of the following warm-up is to help you feel how your abdominal muscles move in preparation for correct belly breathing.

1. Sit in a chair in a quiet room. Place both feet on the floor.
2. Put one hand on your belly and the other on your chest.

3. To the count of five, slowly and gently pull your belly in. (Do not pull in tightly.) As you do this, your chest should be as still as possible.
4. Hold this for three counts. (Think: "1-2-3.")
5. Slowly release the belly to the count of five (do not move your chest).
6. Do this three times. Place your hand on your stomach, and feel the abdominal muscles (belly muscles) tighten and relax.

Note: *Since you probably breathe incorrectly, using your chest to do the pumping instead of your belly, the only way that you will be able to learn how to do slow belly breathing properly is to try to keep your chest as still as possible.* **Don't worry if your chest cannot become still immediately.**

Some people must continue to practice very carefully for several weeks before they feel comfortable using the belly to do the pumping.

Adding the Breath

Now that you know how your belly should move, you are probably asking (as many of my students do): "When do I breathe?"

The following exercise will review the correct procedures for inhaling and exhaling through the nose. (Following the Yoga tradition, use the nose for breathing and the mouth for eating.)

1. Put your hand in front of your nose and exhale a gust of air onto your hand. Relax your stomach muscles. Do this three times.
2. Do you feel that gust of air? That is the breath of nostril breathing.

Note: *You will notice that when you relax your stomach muscles, the air flows easily into your nostrils. This is an automatic reflex called a "passive posture."*

Correct Breathing Technique (Abdominal Breathing)
Combining Nostril Breathing with Belly Contractions

1. Concentrate, and pull your belly in slowly as you exhale with the nose. Keep your hand in front of your nose for the first five breaths only.
2. Hold this for three counts. (Think: "1-2-3.")
3. Relax your belly muscles and take a small breath. Do not fill up your lungs or breathe so hard that your chest moves. (This is one complete diaphragmatic exhalation-inhalation set.)
4. Continue breathing in this way, counting "1-2-3" in and "1-2-3" out each time for ten breaths.
5. Now that you have completed ten breaths, take a moment to see how you feel.

Note: *Please remember that abdominal breathing has nothing to do with deep breathing vs shallow breathing. The only determinant of abdominal breathing is that the stomach muscles do the pumping, not the chest muscles.*

Note: *Always begin your breathing exercise with an exhalation, never an inhalation. Take in small gusts of air. Be careful not to breathe too deeply. If you become short of breath at first, stop and take one large breath. Then resume the slow belly breathing.*

The Diaphragm
In this last exercise as you exhaled, you felt your belly contract. This contraction is caused by the diaphragm, which pushes your breath up and out of your lungs. Curved in an arch at the base of the rib cage, the diaphragm rests under your lungs. Correct breathing occurs when we use our stomach muscles as a bellows to cause the diaphragm to move up and down and thus empty or fill our lungs with air. When you take your small inhalation, the intake of air causes a slight expansion of the belly as the diaphragm pushes down to make room for the inhaled air. This is called diaphragmatic

breathing (or abdominal breathing); we will refer to it as slow belly breathing. The technique is invaluable for overcoming the effects of hyperventilation (chest breathing). When you hyperventilate, you do not feel the expansion and contraction of your belly. Instead, your chest will be moving up and down as you inhale and exhale.

After this belly breathing exercise, most people feel very calm. If you do not, however, read the next section carefully.

Complaint Department

1. If at first you feel you are not getting enough air, don't let this worry you. This is happening because you are not gasping in great breaths of air using your chest the way you did in the past. As you keep practicing correct breathing, you will get rid of your old hyperventilating habit and your brain will learn to be comfortable with smaller breaths of air. Eventually you will feel comfortable taking in as much air as you need with small breaths.

   If this way of breathing feels totally strange to you, you probably breathe incorrectly most of the time. So that even when you are sleeping you are hyperventilating and activating the fight or flight response. This is what causes your state of low level anxiety that you feel most of the time. I suggest you read Dinah Bradley's *Hyperventilation Syndrome: A Handbook for Bad Breathers*. I recommend this very readable gem to all my students and clients.

2. Often several students in a class report that belly breathing makes them feel very tired and sleepy. My theory about this is that these people have come to the class extremely fatigued and could use some rest. When they breathed with their chest, adrenaline was released into their bloodstream (activating the fight or flight response), causing them to feel active and alert. With correct belly breathing and a decrease in adrenaline production, their true fatigue appeared.

3. If the slow belly breathing exercise makes you feel spacey and light-headed, you are probably not doing it correctly. Check your chest. Is it moving too much when you do this exercise?

To correct this, relax and pull your belly in less deeply and gently release, so you have more control and your chest does not move as much. Do ten gentle belly breaths. A very helpful way of practicing Belly Breathing is to lie down on your bed or couch, put a small book on your stomach, keep your chest as still as possible, and watch the book on your belly go up and down as you breathe.

Rules to Breathe By

Whenever you do a rehearsal or a practice session, always begin with a series of ten belly breaths, and remember to start with the exhalation. Eventually your brain will learn to be comfortable with this healthy way of breathing.

After a slow belly breathing practice, you'll feel profoundly calm. When you are sitting in the conference room waiting for your name to be called, keep your eyes open, and give 50 percent of your attention to the person who is speaking. Subtly do your breathing practice as you keep the other 50 percent of your attention on your counting. Count fifty breaths, and then from one to fifty again, until your name is called.

As you count you will be perfectly aware of what is being said because when you breathe correctly and you are in a calmer state you will be able to count your breaths and still be able to concentrate on what the other speakers are saying. As time goes by, the longer you practice this, the easier and more natural it will become.

Follow-up studies of TalkPower students show that one of the most transformative elements of the workshop is the correct breathing technique. Participants are delighted with the level of calm and control they maintain during highly volatile situations.

When to Do Belly Breathing

"Should I breathe this way all the time?" students ask when they experience the calming effects of belly breathing. It is impossible to breathe this way if you are rushed or busy or tense, or jogging or exercising, or in any situation where your stomach is automatically locked. When you sit down and relax, watching TV, during a break at work, before you have the first bite of your dinner, or when you are at the movies, or in a plane or even before you fall asleep—those are very good times to do belly breathing.

Certainly before you go to sleep, do from ten to fifty SLOW belly breaths for a calmer, less adrenaline-laden sleep. And, of course, as you sit in your chair waiting for your turn to speak, belly breathing is what you should be doing.

Additional Perks

If you seriously make slow belly breathing a regular practice in your life, you will probably live many more healthy years than is likely at the present time. I make this extraordinary prediction based on the fact that adrenaline is a known immune system inhibitor. Unnecessary amounts of adrenaline production (as in incorrect breathing) will, over time, compromise your immune system. Your ability to regulate and diminish your adrenaline flow (with correct belly breathing) will result in a healthier immune system, capable of protecting you against the onslaught of disease, infection, and assorted germs. In addition, people who suffer from chronic low-grade anxiety and insomnia will find these breathing techniques hugely beneficial and sometimes miraculous.

> *My experience with a major presentation started with high anxiety. However, I took my abdominal breaths, centered myself, and relieved my anxiety. No one even noticed. I then had the ability to answer any question from the audience, and most importantly to think clearly and verbalize my thoughts.*
> —Rosemarie, sales manager

Breath and the Autonomic Nervous System

Now that you are learning to breathe correctly, you may be interested in knowing how your breathing process is tied into the fight or flight response.

Your breathing processes are controlled by the autonomic nervous system. Located at the base of your skull and governed by your reptilian brain, the autonomic nervous system is composed of two separate systems—the sympathetic nervous system and the parasympathetic nervous system. The sympathetic nervous system regulates bodily arousal including the rapid heartbeat and quick chest breathing experienced under stress (fight or flight response).

The parasympathetic nervous system regulates inhibitory functions, slowing down the rate of arousal, causing your heart to beat more slowly (the relaxation response).

In the *Human Nervous System* (Appleton Century Crofts, New York), David Jensen states:

A generalized activation of the sympathetic system prepares the individual for intense muscular activity, such as is required in defense or offense [the so-called fight or flight reaction]. Parasympathetic activity, on the other hand, is concerned primarily with mechanisms responsible for maintaining resting bodily functions such as reducing the heart rate, and promotion of digestive activities.

Here's how Karen, a psychologist, described her experience.

I had to introduce the main speaker at a professional conference. I totally blanked out on the stage. My eyes were tearing, and I couldn't even read my notes. After what seemed like an eternity, someone began prompting me from the side, so I stumbled through somehow. It was terrifying. I felt as if I had totally lost control. I avoid all situations where I have to talk in front of a group.

The sympathetic and the parasympathetic systems are complementary. Either one or the other is dominant at any given time in the body. When you have to get up to give a presentation and you become anxious, it is your sympathetic nervous system, responding to fearful thoughts, that has been activated.

Stopping the Fear Response
If you can activate your parasympathetic nervous system, you will inhibit, or stop, your fear response and become calmer. How can

you do this if these two systems react automatically? Remember that we said they are a part of the autonomic nervous system? Well, the fact is that these systems are not completely automatic. Jensen says:

> It is now clear that a number of supposedly involuntary processes are indeed subject to modification by application of conscious mental effort on the part of the subject.

Belly Breath: The Invisible Tranquilizer

When you deliberately control the way you breathe, as you did in the belly breathing exercise, you activate the parasympathetic system (relaxation response). As a result, you feel calmer. Can you see what a wonderful tool this belly breathing technique becomes?

Breathing this way anywhere, at any time, will help you calm yourself, and it is virtually undetectable to an observer. Just sit quietly on the speaker's platform, or in your meeting room, with your hands in your lap, breathing slowly out and in, out and in. Don't forget to start with the exhalation and to count each set until you reach fifty, then start again, so that you don't begin daydreaming.

It's Not Over Yet

Correct breathing will certainly help you to feel calmer when you sit in your seat waiting for your turn to speak. However, when you stand up you will probably lose all of the benefits you have just received. To learn how to walk up to the podium calmly, please see chapter 6.

Chapter 5

PANIC CLINIC FOR PUBLIC SPEAKING

How-to for the Hopeless

Having to give a presentation is enough to bring on a nervous stomach that lasts for days. It doesn't matter whether there are ten people or fifty people present, when I stand up in front of a group, I have palpitations, my voice eventually fades to barely a whisper, and my knees give way....
I even went to therapy for this problem. It didn't help.
—Marla, bank vice-president

Many people who are so phobic that before they can begin the TalkPower Program, which begins with chapter 6, they really need to work with the following exercises to prepare them for the program. These exercises include:

- Alternate Nostril Breathing
- Inner-Awareness Exercise
- Slowing down your speech
- Thinking in public.

Symptoms

If you suffer from any of the symptoms listed below, the Panic Clinic section in this book is a powerful resource for you.

- Rapid heartbeat that is intolerable
- Fear of actual fainting when speaking before a group
- Hyperventilation (uncontrolled gasping or breathing)
- Feelings of suffocation in front of a group
- Feelings of deep humiliation and shame in front of a group
- Acute disorientation
- Blocking of thought and speech and loss of memory
- Soft or cracking voice
- Dizziness in front of a group
- Rapid, uncontrolled speaking
- Avoidance of all public-speaking situations
- Shaking in body

The Panic Clinic for Public Speaking

Actually it has come to the point where I avoid speaking in public because I just can't handle it. For example, several years ago I had to give a small talk on a project I had designed. It was for a local group of politicians. I became so self-conscious that from the very first sentence my voice started to tremble. I was really petrified and I forgot what I was going to say. It was so embarrassing. Well, I stumbled through the thing somehow, but I don't think they had the foggiest notion of what I was talking about. The worst part was the awful shame I felt afterwards. I slunk to the back of the room and sat down. Just sat down, burning with humiliation. It was the worst experience of my life.

—George, civil engineer

If you feel that your case is hopeless, that you will never be able to speak in public successfully, *The Panic Clinic* in this chapter has been specifically created to help you prepare your mind and body for the TalkPower program that begins in chapter 6. If you feel you need such basic help, do the Panic Clinic exercises right now. But remember these are just helpful exercises and you can skip them and go on to chapter 6 at any time.

Note: *These special programs should take you about two to three weeks to complete. If you work on the exercises for ten to twenty minutes a day, you will then be ready to begin the regular TalkPower regimen that begins with chapter 6.*

ATTENTION TO DETAIL

One of the distinguishing factors of the TalkPower program is the attention paid to details found in each part of the training program. I believe that this meticulous approach is responsible for the successful results experienced by the thousands of TalkPower students when they leave the workshops with their new skills for speaking in public. These skills will be part of their skill set for the rest of their lives.

Alternate Nostril Breathing (Analoma Viloma)

If you suffer from panic attacks, an extremely helpful exercise for self-calming taken from the Yoga tradition is the alternate nostril breathing technique. This ancient practice is immediately effective in calming the mind and bringing down your level of anxiety. Alternate nostril breathing is done by slowly inhaling through one nostril while you cover the other nostril. In this way you alternate from the right nostril to the left. (*Detailed instructions follow.*) Use a count of four for inhaling and eight for exhaling. If the exhalation is too long for you, make the count shorter and just do the best you can. The benefits of this exercise are a heightened sense of calm and well-being.

Note: *Alternate nostril breathing is not appropriate for public situations. Do this in your rehearsal when you are alone or else in the privacy of the washroom before a public presentation. In order for this exercise to be effective, it must be done on a daily basis. Do not expect it to work if you only use it when you have a panic attack.*

Exercise: Alternate Nostril Breathing

You may do the alternate nostril breathing before or after the other
Panic Clinic exercises. Sit in a chair and follow the steps below.

Sit down in a relaxed posture, close your eyes and send your
attention within. Be aware that the right side of your body is perfectly balanced with the left side.

1. Vigorously exhale through your nose, pulling in your belly as
   you do. Now you can open your eyes if you wish.
2. Place your right thumb against your right nostril. Hold the
   right nostril closed with the right thumb, inhaling with the
   left nostril, counting 1-2-3-4.
3. Close both nostrils with the thumb and forefinger. Count
   1-2-3-4.
4. Release the right nostril and exhale 1-2-3-4-5-6-7-8. Then
   inhale through the right nostril, counting 1-2-3-4.
5. Close both nostrils with the thumb and forefinger. Count
   1-2-3-4. Release the left nostril and exhale 1-2-3-4-5-6-7-8.
   Then inhale with the left nostril. Close both nostrils and
   count 1-2-3-4. Open the right nostril and exhale.

As you can see, this simple pattern of exhaling and inhaling repeats itself. Continue this exercise for five rounds at first.
Then increase to ten rounds. A round is a complete left and right
inhalation-exhalation.

After you have completed ten rounds, sit for a moment and see
how you feel. The point of this exercise is to force your breath into
one nostril and then the other, thus balancing and quieting your agitated mind and body. Do this practice before you begin any of the
other exercises.

Inner-Awareness Exercise

The TalkPower Inner Awareness practice is a procedure where one
sends one's attention within while sensing the weight of the hands.
This practice of sending your attention from an outer awareness
mode to an inner awareness mode while sensing the weight of the

hands is fundamental to the TalkPower series of original exercises and drills. The purpose of this exercise is to develop the brain wiring for the skill of performance.

Based upon my experience with thousands of previously speech phobic TalkPower students, I theorize that when one sends one's attention within, while sensing the weight of the hands a connection is made with the memory centers of the brain, where enzymes and genetic markers initiate the production of neurons that are responsible for actuating plasticity. (Plasticity is the brain's ability to change and transform). As a result transformation occurs as the brain of the previously phobic speaker resembles the brain of a person who has no problem thinking and speaking well in front of an audience. And so practicing these inner awareness exercises regularly will develop your ability to think clearly by focusing your attention upon what you are sensing, rather than upon your fearful verbal thoughts. As a result, your concentration will be much stronger and you will feel that you are in control when you face an audience.

After practicing these inner awareness techniques, in a short period of time all highly phobic students were able to significantly enhance their concentration, pause appropriately, think clearly, and lower their level of anxiety when facing an audience.

INITIATING AN INNER-ATTENTON CONNECTION

Day One (*Five-Ten Minutes*; two times a day, once in the morning and once in the evening)

Begin with a quiet room—no distractions, no phone calls. Your utmost attention and concentration are necessary. Use a kitchen timer and plan to stop after ten minutes.

You will need an object (a book, a paperweight, a plant) weighing about one pound. A can of soda or a can of tuna fish is just right.

1. Place the object on a table. Now sit down and pick up the object. Hold the object in your hand and feel its weight as if your hand were a human scale. Do not tighten your hand around the object; hold it loosely. Do not lean your hand on the table. Do not jiggle; just keep your hand still and keep feeling the weight of the object.

2. Move the object SLOWLY from your right hand to your left hand (count to five). When you move the object from one hand to the other, keep concentrating on the weight in your hand. Do not clutch or tightly hold it as you move it from one hand to the other hand SLOWLY. Move it back and forth from the right hand to the left hand and back five times. Put the object back on the table SLOWLY. Feel the weight until you release it.

3. Sit down and rest. Close your eyes and very slowly count to ten. Try to let go of all the tension. Then repeat the Inner Awareness exercise until ten minutes have passed. After this, go about your normal routine. Do not look for results. If ten minutes is too long for you, start with five minutes and increase the time as you go along. Use your own judgment.

When you concentrate on the weight of the object you are creating the brain wiring necessary for the skill of performance. It's the same principal for transformation (change) as when you lift weights to develop the cells that form a muscle.

Day Two (Ten Minutes)

1. Once again in a quiet room, with a kitchen timer set to ten minutes, use the same object as the day before.

2. Go through the Inner Awareness exercise once as you did the day before. Then rest.

3. After resting for a slow count of ten, pick up the object and walk very SLOWLY with it in your hand to the opposite side of the room. Look straight ahead. Concentrate on sensing the weight of the object at all times. Walk SLOWLY. Put the object down. Sit down and rest, close your eyes, and SLOWLY count to ten.

4. Pick up the object again. Concentrate on its weight. Walk SLOWLY back to your original place, put the object down, and rest, counting to ten with your eyes closed. Repeat until kitchen timer rings. Do not look for results yet—this is only

the second day! By the end of the week you should be feeling the first signs of an inner-awareness sensation.

Day Three

1. Set up as on Days One and Two. You will need the original object plus two or more objects that are of different weights than the original object. (For example, a one-pound paperweight and a two-pound book.) It is not necessary to weigh the objects as long as they have body and feel as if they are of different weights.

2. Standing, pick up each object SLOWLY, one at a time, being aware of its weight. Then put it back down. Be aware of the difference in weight of the three objects. Try to keep your body as relaxed as possible while you do this. Be aware of any tensing-up you experience. When you put one object down, try to relax as much as possible before picking up the next one.

3. After you have picked up each object in turn, sit down, close your eyes, and SLOWLY count to ten. Then stand up and repeat the exercise from the beginning. Continue until the timer goes off.

Day Four

1. Begin with the exercise for Day Three. Go through the procedure once, as you did on the previous day. Sit and rest.

2. After resting for a slow count of ten, pick up any one of the objects and SLOWLY walk across the room with it. Be aware of the weight of the object at all times. Come back and rest, and then pick up the next object and SLOWLY walk across the room. Be sure to rest after every trip. Continue for ten minutes.

Day Five

Now that you've had almost a week with the inner-awareness exercise, you are ready to include a longer round of breathing into this exercise. Turn back to chapter 4, correct belly breathing, sit down and do one round of ten breaths. Start your practice with ten belly breaths, pulling your belly in and blowing out through your nose, then relaxing your belly as you take in a small breath.

1. Choose one object weighing two to three pounds. Focus on a nursery rhyme that you know by heart. (If you do not feel comfortable with a nursery rhyme, use a song or any poem that you know well.)
2. Stand up and pick up the object, concentrating on the weight as you did on Day One. As you do this, begin reciting your chosen lines in a soft whisper. Remember not to hold the object tightly, just firmly enough so that you do not drop it. Hold the object in your hand and stand in place until you have completed your chosen song or poem. Look straight ahead and be aware of the weight of the object at all times as you recite or sing. If your mind begins to wander (this is a break in your concentration), as soon as you become aware of this, bring your attention back to the weight in your hand.
3. Sit down and rest. Close your eyes and count to ten. Then repeat the exercise until ten minutes have passed.

Day Six
Do ten belly breaths, pulling your belly in and blowing out through your nose, and then relaxing your belly as you take in a small breath.

1. Follow the instructions for Day Five, except this time walk across the room holding the object and reciting or singing.
2. When you have crossed the room, put the object down and count to ten. Then pick up the object again and walk back while reciting or singing. Do not rush. Be aware at all times of the weight of the object as you recite/sing and walk. It is very important that you walk as SLOWLY as possible.

Day Seven

Do ten belly breaths, pulling your belly in and blowing out through your nose, and then relaxing your belly as you take in a small breath.

1. Stand up. Working with three objects of different weights, pick up each object one at a time, being aware of its weight as you recite or sing. Put each object down before you pick up the next object. Repeat for ten minutes.
2. Walk SLOWLY across the room with each of your three objects one at a time. Be aware of the change in weight with each one. After you cross the room each time, rest. Repeat for ten minutes.

This inner awareness exercise has now prepared you to do the "standing up and walking to the podium" exercise in chapter 6.

LEARNING TO SLOW DOWN YOUR SPEECH

Many people speak too quickly when they have to face an audience. For the untrained speaker the shock of having to talk when one is being observed causes intense anxiety, rapid heartbeat, and a complete body-acceleration. As a result, speech becomes extremely rapid. This is an automatic response, so telling yourself to speak more slowly if you can will not work. Here is an exercise that I have developed for training your brain to break your rapid speech reaction to speaking in public.

Give five minutes a day to this practice and eventually you will end your tendency to rush your words when you speak in front of people who are looking at you; for example, at a meeting.

1. Place two chairs facing one another about two feet apart.
2. Place a wastepaper basket on one of the chairs.
3. On top of the wastepaper basket, place a large ball (basketball or soccer ball), a Styrofoam wig holder or a large empty box. **Note:** *If you wish to further simulate a face, draw eyes, a nose, and a mouth on the ball or box with a marker.*

4. Sit facing the chair with the wastepaper basket.
5. Use the sentence, *"Today I am going to talk about
_____."* (fill in the blank) Say this sentence out
loud as you tap your fingers after each word.
5a. Now the idea is to break up the sentence: "Today I am going
to talk about _____" by tapping SLOWLY on a
table or on your leg in between each word.
     It should sound like this:
     "Today (fingers) *I* (tap) *am* (tap) *going* (tap) *to* (tap) *talk*
(tap) *about* (tap) _____."
6. As you tap, look at the top of the ball (not behind the ball)
at the place where the forehead of a person might be if the
ball were a head. Do not look at the place where the eyes
might be.
7. Repeat the sentence twice, tapping between each word.
8. For a third time, as you look at the top of the ball, try to
see each word as if it were written on a blackboard. You
probably will not be able to see the word, but making the
effort will build your concentration skills.
9. Repeat the exercise in its entirety.
10. Do this entire exercise five times consecutively, twice a day
until your rapid speech is under control.

Thinking in Public

*I find that I have organized my entire career around strategies
to avoid speaking in public. Each day brings a new possible
threat. . . . It is like jungle warfare: sometimes the dread and the
fear of discovery is too much for me. . . . I barely get through
the day.*

—Paul, insurance actuary

The hardest thing for a speech-phobic person to do is to think
his own thoughts while other people (the audience) are looking at
him. The reason for this is probably that, as children, they were

interrupted by powerful others with loud voices who barged in upon them and humiliated, challenged, or criticized them. Again and again, students report that they were punished for speaking up and voicing their opinions. Little attention was paid to their feelings or boundaries as mothers, fathers, sisters, brothers, and teachers dismissed their expressions as if they were worthless. As a result the child develops an inability to think clearly, a sort of mental paralysis when confronted by authority figures.

Another way that thought-blocking is developed is when parents or teachers pressure a child with "What is the answer? Quick, quick, answer! Hurry, hurry! Tell us the answer! Talk, talk," as if to say "What is the matter with you? Are you stupid or something?"

Such a forceful intrusion into the mind of a young person is terrifying and causes a freezing-up or again a temporary mental paralysis. As a result, the ability to think or talk clearly when others in authority are present is lost. This condition persists into adulthood and occurs in all performance situations. Although people may have no problem speaking and thinking in a one-on-one, where a friendly or even a professional conversation is the usual style of talking, whenever the speech-phobic individual is in a performance mode, where she feels that she is being observed or judged by others, intense anxiety occurs and the result is thought-blocking, and an inability to perform.

THINKING IN PUBLIC EXERCISE

The following exercise is especially helpful for growing the neural patterning (chains of cells) in the brain to develop the concentration skills necessary for pausing and thinking in front of an audience. (It is similar to the talking and tapping exercise for slowing down rapid speech.) The production of neurons (chains of cells) will result in the plasticity of the brain (the brain's ability to transform itself) to restore your sense of personal boundaries and help you to separate emotionally from your audience (performance skills). As a result you will be able to think freely when you face the audience like during the Q and A.

The exercise combines talking and feeling as a left brain/right brain activity. It should be done twice. The purpose is to get you to talk and be aware of what you are feeling simultaneously, as well as to heighten your concentration.

1. Place two chairs facing one another about two feet apart.
2. Place a wastepaper basket on one of the chairs.
3. On top of the wastepaper basket, place a large ball (basketball or soccer ball), a Styrofoam wig holder, or large box. **Note:** *If you wish to further simulate a face, draw eyes, a nose and a mouth on the ball or box with a marker.*
4. Sit facing the chair with the wastepaper basket.
5. Start with both hands sitting on your lap, palms up.
6. Bring your hands barely off your lap, as you feel the weight of your hands and say, out loud *"Today (Pause) I (pause) am (pause) going (pause) to (pause) talk (pause) about (pause) _____ (Fill this in).*

After each word in the pause space bring your hands down to your lap and then after the next word lift your hands up off your lap.

Bring your hands slowly down to your lap and say *today (hands down) I . . .*

7. Lift your hand, barely, and say *"am." (Feel the weight of your hands throughout this entire exercise.)*
8. Continue in this way so that it sounds like: *"Today (lift) I (lower) am (lift) going (lower) to (lift) talk (lower) about (lift) _____ (lower)."*
9. As you do this, look at the top of the ball where the forehead of a face would be and try to feel the weight of your hands when you aren't speaking.
10. Repeat the exercise in its entirety.

If you feel ready to go beyond this set of preparatory exercises and begin the TalkPower system in chapter 6, you will experience:

- A general feeling of calm
- A slowing down of your heartbeat

- A slight awareness of body weight or heaviness when you walk
- An inhibition of your impulse to rush and move quickly

If you do not feel sufficiently grounded yet, by all means repeat the Panic Clinic exercises again. If necessary, say the steps out loud and narrate your actions, e.g., "I feel my hands," "I feel the book." Only rarely does anyone not respond to these exercises within three weeks.

Panic Clinic Schedule
Self Rating: Calm—Nervous

Day	Attitude	Time Start/Finish	Comments
Example 1	*Skeptical*	*7:30 - 7:50*	*Very Difficult*
1			
2			
3			
4			
5			
6			
7			
8			
9			
10			

Part II

THE PROGRAM

Chapter 6

THE ROAD TO TRANSFORMATION

Who knows what happened to me? I may have a cold. I may have a hangover. Maybe I couldn't sleep last night because my wife left me. I have to be good for a sharp audience that demands only the best. My voice, my body, my everything has to work for me. That is what technique is.

—José Ferrer, *Actors Talk About Acting*

Many ideas from my theatre background have inspired me to create the TalkPower program. They are my interpretative takes, of the teachings of Stanislavski, the great Russian theater director, in my attempt to create new exercises that would be useful for training a phobic non-actor.

Stanislavski founded the Moscow Art Company more than one hundred years ago. His vision inspired the Method School of Acting in the United States.

At the core of Stanislavski's concern was his interest in how to train the actor.

Stanislavski's approach involved the importance of awareness from within and relaxation training. His purpose was to condition and transform the instrument (mind and body) of the actor so that he was able to express the inner truth of the role he was playing. By inner truth I mean the physical, emotional, psychological, and spiritual nuances of a character. In addition, Stanislavski was greatly concerned with the problem the actor had in maintaining his concentration and not becoming distracted by the audience or by his personal problems.

> *How can I find a basis for doing on the stage what I do not do off of it? How can I address my very self? To determine that, we must choose a subject and an object . . . unless I can find those two inwardly connected centers, I am powerless to direct my roving attention, always ready to be drawn toward the audience.*
>
> —Constantin Stanislavski, *An Actor Prepares*

My Great "Aha!"

In 1978, I took a course in Public Speaking. I was surprised to see how nervous the other students were. Suddenly I had an idea: I thought about Stanislavski's method for changing the behavior of an actor and I felt that if a clumsy self-conscious actor could be transformed into an elegant gentleman, it might be possible to change the behavior of a non-actor who was afraid to speak in public. I was so intrigued by this idea that I started working on a Public Speaking program that could do just that.

Trying various approaches I tried to extract the essence of the Stanislavski training (Inner awareness) into a new and original method for training a person who was not an actor to be calm and in control when facing an audience. Soon I realized that the Stanislavski training actors receive for portraying a character would not give me an understanding of how to train the person who has a fear of public speaking. By this I mean that as I compared the professional actor on the stage to the nervous speaker making a presentation, it became very clear that learning how to create a role had nothing to do with fear of public speaking. For example, when we see an actress acting on the stage we observe that her acting skills enable her to behave in character by taking on the emotional and physical qualities of her role. This is how a role is created. On the other hand, I asked myself what is it that enables the actress to concentrate, move freely, and speak fluently with confidence as she presents her characterization to the audience. I realized that if I wanted to change the behavior of my speech phobic students I would have to create a new kind of training that dealt with performance skills. Even though I had worked for years as an actress, the idea of performance as a skill separate from acting was totally new to me.

What Is a Skill Anyway?

In order to acquire a skill like swimming, riding a bicycle, or speaking in public, your brain must re-pattern itself by growing the neural pathways (wiring) for that particular skill. This happens when you deliberately perform certain movements over and over again in a specific order, like practicing scales on the piano. From these repetitive movements, your brain grows the neural patterns (chains of cells via axons and dendrites) that produce chemicals, electrical signals, and, finally, impulses that allow you to execute that particular skill automatically. So, if performance is a skill, I had to ask myself, *"What are the repetitive movements for training a speaker so he can develop the skills for control and concentration when facing an audience?* Having studied the scientific principles of how different activities affect the brain, I decided to try the original techniques that I had been developing when I was the artistic director of the Dove Theatre Company. I thought that perhaps this systematic step by step program of unique exercises might help non actors develop the concentration and self-control that I was looking for. In other words, a program for training people to have performance skills."

Exploring This Theory

Back at my TalkPower workshop, the first problem I had to tackle was the transition the speaker makes from sitting in her chair as a member of the audience to that moment when she stands up and walks to the front of the room. Now she becomes the leader of the group and has to speak. This has always been a big problem, not only for those who are phobic, but for everyone. Even the most experienced speakers have a nervous reaction before and during the first two or three minutes of their speech.

I envisioned a step-by-step training for the speaker. I broke down the "problematic transition" of sitting, standing up, and walking to the podium into separate steps. Now that things were slowed down, I could look at the details of each event separately. By doing this, I could try to deal with the enormous anxiety the speaker feels when her fear of not performing well turns to terror and dread. I had to find a way to eliminate her fearful thoughts while she sits in her seat waiting for her turn to speak. How could I keep her attention focused on what she had to say, and not on the audience? I decided to do this by first teaching her a correct breathing routine for when she sits in her seat waiting to speak, then training her to go into a state of inner awareness that she would maintain as she stood up and walked to the podium. This would create a continuum of concentration until she finally faced the audience.

Here was my plan: After my students calmed themselves with the belly breathing technique, I asked them to focus on their body balance as they sat in their chairs. This would establish a core of inner stillness. So far, so good. The students became calm.

Not So Fast
Now a new problem arose. When their names were called, the students jumped out of their seats and walked very quickly to face the audience. This completely did away with the calm they had just been feeling. Body balance no longer worked when you were moving. A new place to concentrate on had to be found. I asked the students to lift their hands up off their laps slightly and to feel the sensation of the weight of their hands. In this way they could remain focused within and stay calm. Of course, as they shifted their attention from their body balance to the effect of gravity pulling on their hands, their inner focus became stronger and thoughts about the audience disappeared.

Standing Up and Walking
The next step was to ask the students to stand up slowly while continuing to concentrate on the weight of their hands, to walk up to the podium, and finally, to face the audience. Doing this, the students were able to hold on to their concentration until they faced the

audience and had to speak. Thought-blocking totally disappeared and much to their amazement, the students felt calm and in control. For some, this was the first time in their lives they were able to stand in front of a group, talk, make sense, and answer questions intelligently.

Later, I put small weights in their hands to reinforce the feeling. I had once designed a similar walking/hands exercise for the actors in my company when I was the artistic director at the Dove Theater and was trying to get them to slow down. For my TalkPower students, this technique was again a success. They could immediately slow down their rapid heartbeat when they concentrated on their hands.

Inventing different methods to get all of my students to work on focusing within (even the Type-As), I created a uniform and systematic procedure for the sitting, standing, and walking exercises. I patterned it into a self-talk routine and every student in the class spoke the instructions out loud together. It was terrific; it really worked. I called this exercise the Transitional Mantra.

Walking Up to the Podium
- Sitting
- Standing
- Walking
- Facing the Audience

The following set of exercises are training exercises. They will condition your mind and body so that you remain calm as you sit in your seat waiting to speak, stand up, walk to the podium, and finally face the audience. The last exercise is the Transitional Mantra. This is the pre-speech routine you will use every time you have to speak in public.

Sitting
Inner attention is the foundation of performance technique and should be practiced with careful step-by-step dedication. The purpose of the following exercise is to train you to shift from your outer social mode to an inner performance mode so that you can concentrate under intense public scrutiny.

Exercise: Sitting in a State of Inner Awareness

You will need two paperweights, each about the size of a small fist. (You can also use two small cans of tuna.) Two rolls of quarters will also do. They will help you remain inwardly focused.

1. Sit in a chair in a quiet room. (Keep this book in your lap.) Place one paperweight or roll of quarters in each hand. (Always keep your hands still.) Do five slow belly breaths, pulling your belly in and blowing out through your nose, and relaxing your belly as you take a small breath in. Count each exhalation and inhalation.

2. With the paperweights resting in your hands, lift your hands and hold them still, about two inches off your lap. Keep your hands as relaxed as possible. Your palms should be facing up. Feel the weight of the paperweights as you count slowly to three, "1-2-3." Feel your attention on your hands when you do this.

3. Bring the paperweights back to your lap. Rest your hands on your lap, palms up, and do three belly breaths. Again, lift the paperweights about two inches off your lap. Hold this position and do five belly breaths. Feel the paperweights as you breathe. Bring the paperweights back to your lap.

4. With your hands resting on your lap, focus on your buttocks and feel how your right and left sides are perfectly balanced as you sit. (You may close your eyes here, and then open them slowly. When you open your eyes, you will find that they are out of focus. This happens because when you focus on an inner sensation like your balance, you activate the right side of your brain and this causes your eyes to go out of focus. You will have to refocus each time you read the new instructions. Do your best and don't worry about being perfect. We call this awareness of your balance "centering yourself.")

5. With your eyes closed, focus attention on your head. Feel it centered between your right and left shoulders. Gently exhale, and open your eyes.

6. Focus your attention on your back against the chair . . . Gently exhale and release . . . Focus your attention on your feet, in your shoes, on the floor . . . Exhale once and release . . . Compare how you feel now with how you felt at the beginning of the exercise . . . Feel how your attention has dropped down into your body . . .

7. Do five more belly breaths in a state of inner awareness and count your breaths.

From this sitting position, you are ready to learn how to stand up.

Bolting Out of Your Chair

When your name is called and you quickly leap out of your chair, you lose the benefit of the slow breathing and inner-awareness practice that you have been doing.

Despite your good intentions, it is useless to promise yourself, "Next time I won't rush," because hearing your name called activates the fight or flight response. Then a tremendous rush of adrenaline makes your heart beat much faster and urges you to move very quickly.

Even though your heart is beating as if it will jump out of your chest, practicing the following *standing up, walking,* and *slow walking* exercises will stop you from bolting out of your chair and rushing up to the podium. I know that this is hard to believe, but in the past thirty years I have trained thousands of people to get up and face the audience with poise and control. I have broken down this part into tiny steps to help you develop the necessary "brain brakes" for resisting the impulse to rush.

This exercise will teach you to stand up slowly and get ready to walk to the podium slowly. As I mentioned before, these exercises activate the right side of the brain, and slow down the activity of the left side of the brain. (The left brain produces the negative fearful thoughts that make you lose control.) In this way, you can eliminate your fearful negative thoughts. Do this exercise out loud for maximum benefit and keep this book open on a chair next to you.

Exercise: Standing Up
(Set a kitchen timer to five minutes.)

1. Sit in a chair and hold one paperweight in each hand. Let your hands relax palms up, in your lap.
2. Do five slow belly breaths. (Pull your belly in, exhale through your nose, hold it to the count of three, and relax your stomach muscles. Do not move your chest.) Count each inhalation and exhalation set as one count, and repeat each for a total of five belly breaths.
3. Say out loud, "*I am sitting in my chair . . . I feel my body perfectly balanced.*" (Feel your balance.)
4. Lift your hands no more than one inch off your lap so that no one else would notice. Say, "*I feel my hands.*"
5. As you bring your hands to your sides, say "*I drop my hands to my sides slowly.*" (Let them hang.) Say, "*I stand up slowly,*" as you stand up.

Exercise: Walking
1. You are now standing in front of your chair. Slowly take a step with one foot; take a step with the other foot, and then take another step so that both feet are parallel, about twelve inches apart. Stop. Feel the weights in your hands.
2. Repeat Step 6 over and over—taking three steps and stopping— walking around the room until the timer rings.

Exercise: Slow Walking Practice
Now you are ready to practice walking without stopping. This is a very important exercise. It will train you to maintain your concentration as you walk to the podium with the audience looking at you.

1. Take a step. Think of the weights in your hands. Take another step. Think of the weights in your hands. Keep walking around the room, and with each step, send your attention to your hands. Walk about fifty steps.
2. Sit down and do ten belly breaths.

Can I Really Eliminate My Negative Thoughts?

The following information is so crucial to your understanding of the TalkPower mind-body training, I would like to repeat what I said before about left brain/right brain function. The slow-motion walking practice is important because it helps you to learn how to walk without having verbal thoughts. In this way you empty your mind of negative, self-demeaning, fearful thoughts like, "I am so boring" or "I'm not going to get through this." These negative thoughts trigger the fight or flight response.

Many years of observing my students tells me that when you focus inwardly, concentrating on your hands (or any other part of your body), you activate your right brain, the nonverbal side. Since verbal thoughts come from left brain activation, when you activate the right side of the brain, you shut off the negative verbal thoughts that trigger your rapid heartbeat. My students are always amazed at the immediate calm that comes over them when they practice this exercise. Eventually, this technique will become a part of you so that you can walk normally, losing the robotic look you have in this exercise. In rehearsal, however, continue the slow walking exercise until you feel as though you can click into a calm state at will.

The Pre-Talk Routine: "The Transitional Mantra"

This exercise will give you the instructions for sitting in your chair before you speak, for getting up, and for walking to the podium. I call it the Transitional Mantra because it guides you through all the steps you take from sitting in the audience to standing in front of the audience. During this early training period, everything you do will be slow and robotic.

Set up several chairs, with a sheet of paper on the floor where you will be standing to practice.

1. Sit in a chair and hold one paperweight in each hand. Your palms should be face up, your hands lying relaxed in your lap.
2. Do five belly breaths. (Pull your belly in and exhale through your nose. Hold it to the count of three. Relax your stomach

muscles. Do not move your chest. Repeat five times. Each inhalation and exhalation set is one count.)

3. Say out loud, "*I am sitting in my chair . . . I feel my body perfectly balanced.*" (Feel your balance.)
4. Lift your hands off your lap no more than one inch—so that no one else would notice. Say, "*I feel my hands.*"
5. Say, "*I drop my hands to my sides slowly.*"
6. Say, "*I get up slowly . . . I take a small step and stop . . . I wait until I feel my hands.*" Get up and take a tiny step (no more than three inches) in front of your chair. Stop. **This is a key movement. You must wait in place until you feel your hands grow slightly heavy, as gravity pulls them down.** Then, walk slowly to the podium, keeping your attention on your heavy hands.
7. Say, "*I walk slowly to the podium . . . I feel my hands.*" Take as many steps as you need to get to the designated podium. Feel your hands at all times. Say, "*I turn around slowly . . . I face the audience . . . I stop.*" Say, "*I look straight ahead at the faces or heads of the audience . . . I stand with my feet comfortably apart . . . I feel my hands.*"

Note: *This is a training exercise. However, before a real presentation, say these words silently to yourself.*

Facing the Audience . . . In Control

When you first face the audience, you will feel a slight shock. It is in this moment that you shift from being private to relating to the audience. A few seconds of silence before you speak will help you to make this connection. The silence allows an introductory process to begin so that you and your audience can tune into one another.

On the other hand, if you start speaking immediately, you will be skipping a very important step. Imagine meeting a new person and launching right into a conversation, instead of introducing yourself and shaking hands. This behavior is just as awkward as facing your audience and starting your talk without an initial pause.

A good way to do this is to stand still and SLOWLY squeeze your toes three times before you say the first words of your speech. This gives the audience time to focus their complete attention on you.

Now that you know how to pause, before you begin your speech we will work on how to return to your seat.

Returning to Your Seat . . . Still In Control
Note: *You have just spoken the last words of your speech and thanked the audience with a simple expression: "Thank you."*

Returning to your seat is just as important as making your entrance, especially if you want to eliminate the wave of shame or self-consciousness that hits you at the end of your presentation. You must practice your exit slowly to avoid that shock.

Exercise: Returning to Your Seat
1. Say out loud, "*I walk slowly back to my seat. I feel my hands.*"
2. Sit down.
3. Do five belly breaths when seated and see how you feel.

Now that you have completed several of the inner-awareness exercises you should be feeling the "inner click."

The Inner Click
The inner click is the immediate sensation you feel whenever you bring your attention to:

1. Your body balance
2. The weight of your hands
3. Belly breathing

This inner click accompanies the shift in your brain that happens when you go from outer attention to inner attention—the inner click tells you that:

a) You are anchored or grounded within your own body *(centered).*
b) The activity in your right brain *(non-verbal)* has been initiated and the activity in your left brain *(verbal)* diminished.
c) Your eyes are somewhat out of focus.
d) You are not leaning on the audience for support.
e) Now the attention of the audience is being pulled in your direction.

As you continue practicing the body balancing, the belly breathing, and the Transitional Mantra, your awareness of the inner click will grow stronger and stronger.

Eye Contact
Should you make eye contact with the audience before you begin speaking? The answer, you may be surprised to learn, is no. When you first stand in front of an audience, and you are in a state of inner awareness, your eyes will be out of focus. If you try to focus on specific people, you will strain your eyes.

Where to Look
Look straight ahead at the faces in your audience, perhaps at their foreheads or even their hair. Look neither too high above their heads, nor so low that you appear to be looking at the floor. Making eye contact is not necessary because if the audience looks into your eyes and you are looking at their faces, they will feel as if you are making eye contact. The necessity for eye contact is a myth. For example, when you go to the movies and become involved with the actors on the screen, you laugh, you cry, you become terrified, yet none of the actors on the screen makes eye contact with you. In the same sense, when you are speaking, it is not necessary for you to look into the

eyes of your audience for them to feel involved with you. Just don't look above or below their faces.

Making eye contact (which means having a nonverbal eye-to-eye conversation) distracts you at a time when you need your concentration to focus on your first words, your adjustment to the high visibility, the strangeness of the distance between yourself and the audience, your rapid heartbeat, and the general shock of the performance situation. You need time, about thirty seconds to two minutes or even more, to get used to all of this.

Adjusting to the Audience
The next phase involves your awareness of the audience, so that you can slip into an easy and comfortable relationship with them. This will happen automatically if you stand still when you first face your audience. You don't have to do a thing except squeeze your toes three times slowly before you speak your first words. This phase is enormously important. If you do it correctly, you will feel very much in control.

After two or three minutes have passed, if you feel that you have established yourself in front of your audience and your presentation is flowing, you may choose to make eye contact as long as it does not disturb your concentration. Do what feels comfortable to you.

While keeping your gaze at the face level of the audience, do not fix anyone with a prolonged stare. Actively staring into the eyes of your audience implies that you are pursuing them, asking "Do you like me? Is this good?" Don't look for approval. The audience looks to you for leadership. Lead!

Scanning the Room
When you first stand in front of your audience, please—do not mechanically scan the room, moving your head from right to left as if your eyes were great floodlights emanating from a control tower. This is extremely awkward and looks unnatural. Instead, as I have just said, when you first stand in front of an audience, before you begin to speak, be as still as possible and look straight ahead in the

general direction of their faces. Smiling is nice, but it isn't essential. If you can smile a small smile, smile. If you want the complete attention of the audience, your physical stillness, rather than your physical activity, will make this happen.

As your speech progresses and you become more comfortable, from time to time you can move your head slowly, looking at your audience to the left or right. Once again, naturalness and comfort should decide when and if you look at various people in the room. If at first this pose seems stiff and robotic, do not change back to your old nervous behavior. Eventually you will relax into physical stillness so that you feel comfortable and empowered.

The Likability Factor

I frequently ask a TalkPower group, "In terms of the impression you create, what is your personal objective in giving a presentation?" The answer usually is: to communicate a message, to sell a product, to unite people, to convince them to do something, and other variations on that theme. The answers are always about the speech, never about the speaker. From my point of view, the most important personal objective is *to be likeable*. By this I mean the general impression of confidence, ease, and warmth you project so that people feel comfortable with you.

Likability happens when you are in control of yourself. Then you are able to be clear, not talk too fast, so that your words flow with ease. A likeable speaker has a much better chance of getting an idea across, selling a product, convincing people to vote for him, and certainly winning an election. Our recent history abounds with stories of politicians who seemingly came out of nowhere to capture the vote, simply because people "like them." I could go on and on, but you get the idea.

Now, the reason I make such a fuss about this likability notion is because so many people secretly believe that before they have the right to ask others to listen to them, they have to be brilliant, innovative, super-intelligent, clever, witty, dynamic, or else they do not deserve to stand in front of an audience and talk. As a result, either your talk is top-heavy with facts, statistics, attempts at inspiring generalizations, huff-and-puff, or you avoid speaking altogether. How unnecessary! Just use the TalkPower Formula, tell stories, look away from your script at the audience, look calm, look thoughtful, handle yourself in a leader-like manner . . . in other words be likeable, and you will be a huge success. Remember, leaders are rarely geniuses. Leaders have the good sense to hire geniuses to work for them and we never hear or see the names of this invisible army in *People Magazine*. We call them think tanks. A presentation is very different from a think tank. So, the next time you prepare your remarks for a talk or a toast or a sales meeting, the question you must ask yourself is, "Am I taking the time to rehearse properly, to do the TalkPower exercises, and to slow down my racing motor, so that I appear likeable to the audience?"

Me, Likeable?
Many of my students who feel very nervous and uncomfortable at first cannot believe that their discomfort is not visible to the audience. Yet, as long as they practice the TalkPower techniques they appear very likeable and are easy to listen to. Time and again, after a wonderfully entertaining talk, a student in my class reports "Oh, I thought I was speaking so slowly . . . you mean you really liked my talk?"

"Yes, yes!" the class responds "You were not slow at all. You looked so confident up there. It was really a pleasure to listen to you."

Likability is a Skill
You realize, of course, that appearing likeable is a learned skill. You can have that skill. You really can, if you apply yourself to the training program that follows. If you have any doubts about this, take a look at the quote from José Ferrer, at the beginning of this chapter.

Looking Thoughtful
People know when you are thinking. They can feel it as you draw within for a mini-second to think about something—to answer a question, to find just the right word—and people like thoughtful

leaders. They like to know that someone is responsible enough
to care about how he will handle their destiny or deal with their
fears and concerns. Thoughtfulness is a very attractive quality for
a speaker, a leader, or a salesperson. In contrast, stand-up comics don't have to be too thoughtful, because stand-up comics are
only entertaining you and not attempting to impact your life. However, leaders, speakers, and salespeople should look thoughtful
because when they don't, people don't trust them. How does one
look thoughtful? Don't talk too fast, pause before you answer, and
practice the TalkPower program so that you can look thoughtful in
a relaxed and natural manner.

Chapter 7

THE TALKPOWER ACTION FORMULA

Making Order Out of Chaos

What physics looks for: the simplest possible system of thought which will bind together the observed facts.

—Albert Einstein

Visitors to my workshops often mention how enjoyable it is to listen to the speeches. There is a sense of fluency and excitement, not only in the delivery but in the content as well. This sense of vibrancy is due to the TalkPower Action Formula, which helps the students to organize and develop their ideas.

The Formula divides a speech into eight sections, each one with a specific function. How you handle each section will, of course, be determined by the amount of time allotted to your presentation. Whether you are preparing a five-minute presentation, a two-day seminar, or writing a book, you can use the TalkPower structure as a model. As a matter of fact, students will find the formula tremendously helpful for writing term papers.

This method is much more effective than a laundry list type of outline because a general outline will not infuse your talk with life. An outline simply lists items, one after the other, with no structure or internal dynamic (the placement of elements that brings a speech to life).

As language theoretician Eric Lennenberg noted, a sentence is analogous to a mosaic: "Put together stone after stone, yet the picture as a whole must have come into being in the artist's mind before he began to lay down the pieces." In this sense, a talk is put together section by section, yet the basic premise must be in the speaker's mind before he begins to lay down the pieces.

To help him identify this organizing principle, the TalkPower Action Formula gives the speechwriter a place for stating this basic idea (the Message Sentence) and a method for sorting out the overwhelming amount of information that confronts him (the Point Section). In addition, the Formula gives a detailed plan showing exactly what belongs in the "beginning, middle, and end" of a successful talk.

In the following chapters, I will take you through the TalkPower Action Formula, step by step. Each section of the model will be reviewed, with examples and an assignment for that section. A complete rehearsal is included to help you practice all you have learned.

Why Use a Formula?

For the inexperienced speaker, every new presentation becomes a risky foray into uncharted waters. That's the beauty of the TalkPower Action Formula. With this system you will be able to approach each new presentation with a familiar procedure. Although the content of each talk will be different, if you follow the guidelines as they are presented here, you will have a familiar method for organizing your talk.

Many of my students do not do formal presentations. They only speak at meetings or want to make a toast or perform in some other public speaking situation. And so it would seem that this program has not been designed for them. Actually, in order to be trained to overcome the fear of public speaking, you must go through the formal presentation model of exercises, drills, and routines as given. Then you will have the performance skills necessary for any type of meeting, talk, toast, or any other kind of public presentation.

The TalkPower Action Formula

Speech Section	Contents	Words & Time
1. Introduction	The first thing you say—a joke, anecdote, or other. *(25 word minimum, 300 maximum)*	The beginning section has approximately 300 words or two minutes of speech, including pauses.
2. Topic Sentence	Subject of your speech— "Today I am going to talk about _____." *(12 word maximum)*	
3. Message Sentence	The central and most important idea. Begin with the words "I think," "I feel," or "I believe _____." *(12 word maximum)*	
4. Background	This story shows the connection between the speaker, the company, or the organization, and the topic. *(150 words)*	150 1 minute
5. Menu	This list of points divides the topic into manageable segments. "I will discuss the following items. . ."	13-43 15-30 seconds
6. Points	Here you fully develop each point in your menu.	450 3 minutes
7. The Climax	The last point, the high point of your talk.	150 1 minute
8. Conclusion	You summarize the points.	150 1 minute
Note: *In each minute of speaking time you say approximately 150 words, including pauses.*		Total 7 minutes

Sample Speech

Although the following example, using the TalkPower Action Formula, was written for an eight-minute speech, the formula can be used for a speech of any length.

Note: *Certain phrases in this sample speech are underlined. These are the transitional phrases found in the templates that were used to write this speech. The templates, which are story guides, will be introduced and discussed in later chapters.*

Introduction

Some people love to putter in their gardens.

Others look forward to sailing on the weekends.

I can think of nothing more enjoyable than working on my house. (*PAUSE*)

Topic Sentence

<u>Today I am going to talk about</u> tackling a remodeling project. (*PAUSE*)

Message Sentence

<u>I believe</u> that one can get a great deal of satisfaction from seeing a project through to completion. (*PAUSE*)

Background

<u>I became interested in</u> home construction about twenty-five years ago. <u>At that time I was</u> working in an office as the administrator for a company. My good friend Mark had graduated from Colgate with a degree in philosophy but chose to go into the family home-building business. <u>I became aware of the fact</u> that there is an entirely different language and set of skills associated with building. <u>For example</u>, in the evening we would get together to play cards and Mark would talk about plumb lines, surveying, headers, and copper versus aluminum wiring. <u>And so I</u> became intrigued with this process of ideas, ingenuity, and hard work that produces a tangible, useful, and necessary result. <u>I also</u> was somewhat jealous of Mark's abilities. <u>As a result,</u> I attempted to educate myself in matters mechanical and

practical. <u>Today I</u> can say that although I still work in an office set-ting, I have learned a few things along the way. I don't know if I have saved any money by doing these things myself, but it proves to be a nice distraction from the pressures of office work. (*PAUSE*)

Menu

The five aspects of remodeling that I shall now discuss include:

- Envisioning the finished product
- Planning the space and materials
- Knowing the local codes
- Anticipating snags
- Finally, learning new skills

Note: *In this sample we are going to develop just one point, to give you an idea of what a speech looks like, using the TalkPower Action Formula.*

Point #1
Planning the Space and Materials

    <u>Trying to</u> plan for space utilization and materials <u>can be</u> an extremely frustrating and time-consuming experience unless you have a clear view of your priorities and a good planning tool. <u>I realized this</u> early on when my wife and I spent a lot of time and many legal pads attempting to agree on a design. When we first decided to finish our basement, it never occurred to us that there were so many decisions to make.

    <u>For example</u>, how important were storage space, a full bath, a workout area, and an entertainment center in relation to each other? Also, how far did we want to stretch the budget in favor of enhanced resale value?

    <u>And so</u> we had to articulate our objectives. <u>Also</u>, it took a lot of time to keep drawing walls and doors. It occurred to me that there had to be a smarter way to get through this step. <u>Finally</u>, I found a software program called "Floor Plans Plus" that facilitates computer-aided design and creates a list of materials. <u>This resulted</u>

in our quickly coming to an agreement on a utilization scheme and then proceeding to the next step.

<u>Today</u>, I am happy to say that I have gotten a lot of satisfaction from planning the work and working the plan. (*PAUSE*)

Q&A

Before I conclude, does anyone have a question? (*PAUSE*)

Conclusion

<u>In conclusion, I would like to suggest that</u> you consider taking on a small project. <u>You may be surprised</u> to find how much you enjoy the process of creating a new area of usage and/or beauty in your home. <u>I feel confident in saying</u> that you will be gratified as you learn to do something new.

<u>In my discussion of remodeling</u> my basement I have tried to familiarize you with:

- Envisioning the finished product
- Planning the space and materials
- Knowing the local codes
- Anticipating snags
- Finally, learning new skills

<u>But above all</u>, imagine how delighted you will be when the last nail is in place and you look around at the new, clean, beautifully designed addition to your home. (*PAUSE*) Thank you.

(Once again, we have only developed one point—even though five points are indicated.)

So you see what a very basic, no-frills speech, using the Talk-Power Action Formula plus template looks like. In the real world, where more time and information are available, the writer would be able to add quotations, jokes, interesting anecdotes, and research that would have fleshed out and enhanced his talk.

So Many Words, So Little Time

Students tell me that their inability to edit material is a major problem. Often they accumulate enough research material to talk for hours even though they only have ten minutes to do their presentation. Cutting this down for your allotted time is a Herculean task, leaving you feeling totally overwhelmed.

> *It's like a dream I sometimes have. In this dream I go into my office and all of my filing cabinets have been turned upside down and emptied out on the floor. I need certain documents quickly, to prepare a summation for a jury, and I don't know where anything is. I feel rushed and helpless; I don't know where to begin. That's what it's like when I have to prepare a summation or a speech, or any kind of presentation.*
>
> —Jason, attorney

The TalkPower Word Budget

This section will give you a structure so that you can easily select and organize your information to fit your material into your time allotment without overloading yourself with more information than you can possibly use.

Beginning (Introductory Section)	1) Introductory Paragraph 2) Topic Sentence 3) Message Sentence
Middle	4) Background 5) Menu 6) Point Section *Point A* *Point B* *Point C* *Point D* 7) Climax
End	8) Conclusion

Almost every presentation has a time limit. Since there are approximately 150 words to one minute of speaking time, once you know how much time you have for your talk, you can keep track of the amount of material you need by using a word count to limit yourself. This is how you do it:

If you are given ten minutes to make a presentation, you will have to prepare fewer than 1,500 words, including time for pauses. The combination of a time limit and word count gives you a word budget to work with. (There are about 250 words per double-spaced typewritten page, given one-inch margins and a twelve-point font.)

If this idea seems radically different from your normal procedure, don't panic. Writing a talk will become as familiar as driving to work, when you understand the rules. Once students learn how to edit themselves in terms of minutes and word counts, they are amazed at the beauty and clarity of their talks. In addition, the timesaving factor when using this formula is considerable.

Planning Your Talk

No experienced host or hostess ever plans a dinner without first deciding exactly how many guests will be invited, what the menu will be, and how much of each ingredient will be needed for each dish. Your presentations need the same kind of attention. When preparing a talk, you need a timetable. Here is a sample for a ten-minute presentation.

		No. of Words	Time (in minutes)
Beginning	1) Introductory Paragraph 2) Topic Sentence 3) Message Sentence (pauses)	225 (plus pause time)	1 ½
Middle	4) Background 5) Menu 6) Three to five subheadings 7) Climax	975	1 ½ 5 1
End	8) Conclusion	150	1
Total		1,350	10

The Beginning

No matter how long the speech is, the first three sections—introduction, topic sentence, and message sentence—should take no longer than two minutes, depending upon your introductory story (plus time for your pauses). This is enough time for you to get into your speech.

The Middle

The middle is composed of the background, menu, and point section—the body of a speech—you may add as much material as you wish, as long as it fits into your time budget. The point section is the most flexible part of a speech. Some points take less than a minute to cover; others may take much longer. The climax is your last point and should be more dramatic than the other points. In chapter 11 we will look at the point section in greater detail.

The End

The conclusion summarizes the main points of your speech. No matter how long you have been talking, the conclusion should never exceed one minute in length. Many inexperienced speakers conclude by simply coming to a halt without properly summing up. Like a motorist about to overrun his exit, they simply jam on the brakes or veer wildly across lanes, trying desperately to get where they're supposed to be, with no thought of the consequences.

A summary is a very brief recapitulation. Book and film critics often summarize a three hundred-page novel or a two-hour movie in a single paragraph. You should not take more than one minute to summarize a speech.

Verbal Graphics

The TalkPower Action Formula provides a perfect vehicle for stylizing the look and sound of your talk. Verbal graphics is the TalkPower method of breaking a speech down into sections and then shaping the speech with strategically placed pauses. These pauses give your presentation the same design you would find in a poem or an essay. Just as the written page is designed with headlines, margins, bold print, bullets, and spaces, spoken words need the contrast of silence and sound for style, beautiful design, and dramatic effect.

Verbal graphics create the space (silence) for the audience to take in and reflect upon what you are saying. These pauses create a rhythm that brings the presentation to life. The rhythm causes the speaker and the audience to move back and forth, figuratively, in unison. This movement is the catalyst for the intensity that occurs between speaker and audience when so-called dynamic speakers perform. For example:

Speaker: When I was doing my research for this talk I got the strangest telephone call. (*PAUSE*)

Audience: (Leans in, listening more intently)

Contrast this with the following:

Speaker: When I was doing my research for this talk I got the strangest telephone call. It was a young man who claimed he had been abducted by aliens!

Dramatic Tension and Timing

As you can see, a pause brings dramatic tension to a speech, providing the speaker with a mysterious quality called presence or charisma. I can think of many well-known speakers (I will not name them because I do not wish to embarrass them) who speak well, but are not thought of as dynamic presenters. They speak in endless loops of sentences with no pauses at all. In that case, the entire speech becomes one long ribbon unraveling with no values, colors, shade, or changes.

> *If speech without the logical pause is unintelligible,*
> *without the psychological pause it is lifeless.*
> —Constantin Stanislavski

Even if the speaker has an interesting voice, filled with a variety of intonations, he will not project a dynamic personality if he or she does not pause properly. What begins as an exciting lift-off for the audience when the speaker appears, fades as the speech progresses and the attention of the audience subtly begins to diminish. I have seen this happen on numerous occasions, and I thought, if only there were ten or fifteen well placed pauses in this speech, the speaker would surely receive a standing ovation instead of polite applause.

Prevailing wisdom tells us that only very special people possess the ability to be dynamic presenters. I beg to differ. People can learn to be dynamic when they speak in public and you can, too.

Dynamic Presenters

Commitment can be communicated in many different ways. For example:

- A laid-back style: the way Tom Hanks projects his personality—controlled, relaxed, wry.
- High energy: personified by Jim Carrey—a bombastic character of great enthusiasm and extreme gesture.

Here we see two entirely opposite styles of personality, yet both are effective in projecting an image that is dynamic and charismatic. These stars' unerring sense of timing in using pauses creates a brilliant performance that is universally recognized. Just as actors rely upon timing and pauses, so too should people speaking in public.

This chapter will introduce you to exercises that will develop the muscle memory necessary for skillful pausing. As time goes on and you continue to practice the verbal graphic skills, you will develop an intuitive sense of when to pause.

Learning to Speak

Now it's time to get up on your feet, face your audience, and begin talking. This is not as simple as it seems. The shift from silence to speaking can be shocking, and must be handled skillfully.

Even though you have learned to slow down internally with the breathing exercises and the inner-awareness walking exercise, be prepared to feel a more rapid heartbeat as soon as you hear your name called and it is time for you to face your audience. This is to be expected. Making the transition from being an anonymous member of the audience to the speaker causes your level of excitement to jump up a notch or more. As a result, the intense inner acceleration urges you to rush your opening words in a burst of rapid speech.

From Silence to Speaking

Now you must learn new habits of control for speaking, just as you learned new habits for walking to the podium.

The best way to learn how to make the transition from silence to speaking is to work with two short sentences: the Topic Sentence and the Message Sentence—the second and third parts of the TalkPower Action Formula.

The Topic Sentence

(*PAUSE*)　　"Today　I　am　going　to　talk　about _____."

(fill in the blank)

The Message Sentence

(*PAUSE*) "I think that _____." (*PAUSE*)

(fill in the blank)

Example:

(*PAUSE*) "Today I am going to talk about stress management."
(*PAUSE*) "I think that everyone can benefit from learning about stress management." (*PAUSE*)

Assignment: Complete your own two sentences (Today I am going to talk about . . . I think that. . . .) on a 5 x 8 card, using my example as a model. We will use them in our rehearsal.

How to Pause

Because we do not pause in conversations the way we do in presentations, our pausing ability is underdeveloped. Besides, if you pause in conversation the way I am suggesting, you will appear artificial and overbearing. Add the excitement of a rapid heartbeat and you can understand why you lose control and speak too quickly when you address a group. Once the talk has started, expecting to pause before you introduce an important idea will not work because your brain is patterned for conversational speech. Yet, in a presentation, knowing how to pause is a sure sign of a polished speaker. It can make the difference between a rambling diatribe and a talk that is a pleasure to listen to.

> **Question:** If telling yourself to pause will not work, then what does?
>
> **Answer:** At the end of the sentence stop talking and **SQUEEZE YOUR TOES THREE TIMES.** This provides an action that counts off your time. Here is how this looks and sounds . . .

(Squeeze, squeeze, squeeze . . .)
Today I am going to talk about Global Warming
(Squeeze, squeeze, squeeze . . .)
I think that Global Warming is a serious threat to this planet
(Squeeze, squeeze, squeeze . . .)

Try this out loud. But don't say, "Squeeze . . . squeeze . . . squeeze . . . ." Just let your toes do the squeezing. I know this sounds ridiculous, but it works!

Some time ago, my staff and I were doing a two-day seminar for a major corporation. One of the participants balked. "Look, Ms. Rogers, this pausing business will never work for me. I am a fast guy. I talk fast. I walk fast. I eat fast. I think fast. I even sleep fast . . . Fast, fast, fast, that's me!"

I thought for a moment and then said quickly, "Think of how we would remember Martin Luther King if he had said, 'Ihaveadream.'"

Martin Luther King said, "I . . . have . . . a . . . dream . . ." Sensing those pauses, we feel his miraculous power as a speaker.

The fast fellow then said his lines, squeezed his toes, and his speaking was appropriately slower.

The class applauded. And he looked impressive.

Today . . . I . . . Am . . .

Not only am I going to ask you to squeeze between each sentence, but I am also going to ask you to put pauses in between the first three words that you say so that you can ease into the spoken word. Your first sentence would be as follows:

> Today *(PAUSE)* I *(PAUSE)* am *(PAUSE)* going to talk about Global Warming. *(Squeeze . . . squeeze . . . squeeze . . . those toes.)*
>
> I think that Global Warming is a serious threat to this planet. *(Squeeze . . . squeeze . . . squeeze . . . those toes.)*

"Why the pauses? Doesn't it sound weird like that? It's so unnatural."

At first, most of my students and clients are quite resistant to my suggestion that they pause, even though their colleagues assure them that they sound so much better. The fact is that pausing is essential for holding back that rapid-fire explosion of words just waiting to burst out of you when you first face the group.

Say I!

You need to get used to saying "I . . . am . . ." and not "I'm . . ." Let's say it again:

> Today *(PAUSE)* I *(PAUSE)* am *(PAUSE)* going to talk about wearing a mask *(Squeeze . . . squeeze . . . squeeze . . .)*
>
> I think that wearing a mask is essential for remaining healthy. *(Squeeze . . . squeeze . . . squeeze . . .)*

Stop hiding and whisper the following positive statements about yourself. Be sure to say the "I" separately. Say this every day, looking in the mirror after you brush your teeth and before you go to bed at night. Say it even if you can't believe it.

"I am a very important person."
"I would like you all to listen to me."
"I have something very meaningful and interesting to tell you."
"I feel good about myself."
"I am proud of myself."

If these statements make you curl up with embarrassment, then you really need to say them over and over again until you are comfortable with saying nice things about yourself. Your discomfort indicates that you need to separate your "I" from the "am" and say, "I *(PAUSE)* am." There is no such entity as "I'm." Who is "I'm"? "I'm" is you hiding. Sometimes it's even you saying "I'mgoingtotalkabout." I suggest that every morning when you look in the mirror, and repeat these words of self-support out loud, this will eventually help you to develop your "self-esteem." Don't get discouraged if you don't see immediate results.

Getting back to the pause lessons, even though you feel strange at first saying, "Today *(PAUSE)* I *(PAUSE)* am going to talk about . . ." eventually it will feel quite comfortable.

If you begin your talk with a joke, and the first three words are "My cousin, Fred . . ." you would say, "My *(PAUSE)* cousin *(PAUSE)* Fred." This pausing technique will give you tremendous control, helping you to pace yourself as you find your "talking stride." I promise you that not one person in the audience will remember that you said the first three words slowly.

Finding Your Talking Stride

Beginning a talk slowly, easing into the spoken word and resisting your impulse to rush ahead, will put you in a perfect position to find your proper talking stride. This means finding a speed and rhythm that is most natural for you and comfortable for the audience. A talking stride is exactly like a running stride. It is a speed and rhythm that is determined by the flow of the activity, rather than by fear and the compulsion to rush to the finish line. Once you learn what your talking stride feels like, you will be able to enjoy speaking in public.

Speaking Names Clearly

Many people mumble and stumble through names and abbreviations of names, making it impossible to understand what they are saying. I am calling special attention to this because time and time again I have to remind the participants in my workshops to speak the names of people, places, and things slowly and clearly. This is true even for many experienced speakers. When you have a written text, names and letters and abbreviations are always printed in bold type or italics or some form of capital letter. The same kind of special attention should be paid to names when they are spoken. Actually, more attention is necessary because the spoken word is so fleeting. Even if your associates tell you that your talk went very well, ask if they were really able to understand all of the names you mentioned.

Rehearsal

Set up several chairs, and a designated podium with a sheet of paper on the floor.

This is where you will be standing to practice.

1. Sit in a chair and hold one paperweight in each hand, your palms face up and your hands lying in your lap.
2. Do five belly breaths. (Pull your belly in. Exhale through your nose. Hold it to the count of three. Then relax your stomach muscles and take a SMALL breath. Do not move your chest. Repeat five times.) Each inhalation and exhalation set is one count.
3. Say out loud, *"I am sitting in my chair . . . I feel my body perfectly balanced."* (Feel your balance.)
4. Lift your hands off your lap no more than one inch so that no one else notices. Say to yourself, *"I feel my hands."* Feel the inner click.

5. Say, "*I drop my hands to my sides. (Let them hang.)*
6. Say, "*I get up slowly . . . I take a small step in place and stop . . . I feel my hands.*"

   Get up and take a tiny step in place (no more than three inches) in front of your chair. Stop. Say, "*I wait until I feel my hands.*" Do you feel the inner click?
7. Say, "*I walk slowly to the podium.*" Say, "*I feel my hands.*" Take as many steps as you need to get to the designated podium. Feel your hands at all times. Say, "*I turn around slowly . . . I face the audience . . . I stop.*" Say, "*I look toward the audience . . .*" Say, "*I feel my hands.*"
8. Squeeze . . . squeeze . . . squeeze . . . those toes!
9. TOPIC SENTENCE: "Today . . . I . . . am . . . going to talk about _____." (*fill in the blank*)
10. Squeeze . . . squeeze . . .squeeze . . .
11. MESSAGE SENTENCE: "I think that _____." (*fill in the blank*)
12. Squeeze . . .squeeze . . . squeeze . . . feel those toes!
13. Say, "*I slowly walk back to my seat . . . I feel my hands.*"
14. Sit down and do five belly breaths.
15. Repeat this entire exercise one more time, without the paperweights, feeling the weight of your hands. Try to memorize the Transitional Mantra for future use.

Can I Read My Speech?

Many of my students come to the workshop with the notion that reading a speech is unprofessional; they fear that reading will make them lose their spontaneity.

This is the silliest thing I ever heard and completely impractical. An all-or-nothing approach will only serve to discourage you from ever taking the risk of speaking in public.

Isn't it better to feel confident, using a written script? Why avoid an opportunity to speak because you are afraid you will forget what you wanted to say? If you do accept an opportunity to speak and you choose not to use a script, isn't it foolish to run the risk of rambling on and on, feeling insecure and embarrassed? Is it any wonder that there are so many terrible speakers out there when people are taught that using a script is a big no-no? *Of course* you can read. Common sense will tell you that confidence comes from feeling secure and this can happen only if your speech is right there in front of you.

A Listening Audience, Not a Reading Audience

The fact is people lose their spontaneity when they read from a paper because they prepare a talk as if it were a term paper. "Fill up as many pages as possible and you'll get a better grade." If the professor had to skim over repetitions and irrelevancies, that was his problem. A listening audience cannot skim. Go off the beaten track for half a millisecond and you lose your crowd. The audience tunes out, planning dinner, lunch, the weekend, counting the tiles on the ceiling . . .

The TalkPower guidelines will help you write such an entertaining script that your audience will be hovering over every word. Learning how to write for a listening audience, not a reading audience, makes all the difference. After you have been using a written script for some time, and have internalized what a real beginning, middle, and end are all about, you will be able to speak without a script. For the time being, if you follow the TalkPower Action Formula, plus the rehearsal techniques, and the pausing, your scripted presentations will be as well received—or even better received—than a talk done off the cuff. (This, of course, does not apply to speaking at meetings. We will deal with that later.)

Looking Up

An old wive's tale maintains that if you read from a script you will sound stilted. Actually, you sound stilted when you constantly read with your nose in the text. The secret of appearing spontaneous lies in rehearsing the script so that you look up at the audience, then back at your script. Practice your talk looking at the text, then looking out at your imaginary audience, then finding your place and looking at your text again. Not only will you feel secure, but you will also appear charming, knowledgeable, and in control.

Each year I subscribe to a series of play readings in New York City produced by a very talented theater company called TACT (the

Actors Company Theater). There is no scenery, and every actor reads from his script. These readings rank among the best theater that I have ever experienced. Much work and rehearsal goes into each production, yet not one actor memorizes or improvises his part. Every word is read from a script, and the results are always delightful.

Politicians read their speeches, of course they use a tele-prompter but everyone knows that they are reading and they usually go off without a hitch—and I have seen many professional speakers read their speeches with complete charm.

Perhaps last month you saw a professional speaker giving a long, magnificent, hilarious presentation without reading from a single note. And perhaps you felt envious and inadequate. Let me assure you that this professional speaker has probably given this same talk one hundred times in the last five years!

> *I was scheduled to talk at two colleges on two successive days.*
> *On the first day my talk on ecology went over so well I decided*
> *to get more mileage out of it by giving it the second day. My*
> *teenage son was with me and during dinner, prior to the second*
> *talk, I suddenly became aware that my son was regaling the*
> *head table with an exact account of the speech I had given the*
> *night before—and was about to give again!*
>
> —Isaac Asimov

Losing Your Place

Often, anxious speakers are afraid of losing their place if they look up when they are reading. On the contrary, losing your place is good because in the few seconds that you take to find your place, you create an uneven rhythm. This is quite attractive to an audience, since an even rhythm is monotonous and hypnotic and causes people to fall asleep.

Try to practice your introduction, topic, and Message Sentences without reading from the script. Since the Topic Sentence and the Message Sentence are short and are always preceded by the same words, it should not be too difficult to look away from your script, with your face open to the audience. If this causes you too much anxiety, then by all means read the entire speech.

With each new rehearsal, you will look away from your cards more frequently as you become accustomed to your script. Gradually you will feel more confident in public. The point is to get you up on your feet. You are learning; you don't have to be perfect the very first time—or even the tenth time. At the end of each TalkPower seminar, I see people who have never spoken before, sounding better, and looking more in control than many experienced speakers.

What Is a Good Speaker?

In *Anna Karenina*, Leo Tolstoy wrote, "All happy families resemble one another; every unhappy family is unhappy in its own fashion." Much the same could be said about good and bad speakers. There are many ways that a speaker can fail. But good speakers have certain characteristics in common.

A good speaker holds our attention. His thinking and speaking are clear and logical. The information included in his speech backs up his main point, telling us what we need to know without overloading our capacity.

A good speaker keeps us entertained with stories and examples that illustrate the points being made. In this way the speaker engages us, drawing our attention and making us think about what he is saying. Finally, a good speaker leaves us with a feeling of admiration. And that can happen even when we disagree with what he has said. He or she projects an aura of authenticity that is natural and appealing. In other words, a good speaker is likeable.

A brief note about humor. Although humor will usually make a speech more enjoyable for the audience, it is not a requirement. Learning how to be clear and comfortable is the first step for you. As you improve and relax, your sense of humor may wake up. Being interesting is more important than being funny.

Video is Not for Everyone

For many years speech coaches have used videotape as a training tool. This is fine for the experienced speaker who has mastered the basic presentational skills. In that case, video can be an effective tool for finessing a presentation.

However, for beginning and fearful speakers, I do not recommend video. As a matter of fact, I totally discourage students from looking at themselves when they present. When a nervous speaker looks at himself on the screen, he feels self-conscious and embarrassed. I have heard so many stories from students about how humiliating it was to see themselves and all of their faults on video.

If the video camera directs a student's attention to his appearance, it's impossible for him to practice the fundamental steps of the TalkPower training program. The program is based upon a process of inner-awareness that enables a student to pay attention to what he is saying and to stop judging himself. Therefore, the TalkPower exercises direct the student away from the external, or visual, perception of his image (including thoughts about how he is coming across on the video camera).

For the inexperienced or fearful speaker, developing skills of physical control and concentration cannot be learned by watching yourself on a screen. The connections and impulses must initially be experienced in a feeling mode or a sensing mode. We cannot learn to drive by watching a video, and it follows that the same rule should apply to beginning or fearful speakers. Through practice, once the student has mastered the ability to sustain an inner focus, he may find that videotaping his performance is useful.

Using the Podium as a Walker
One last thought. Although there is nothing wrong with putting your hands on the podium, please resist the urge to lean on the podium, placing your weight on your hands or arms. Always stand on your own two feet, supporting yourself with your balance and posture.

Just a note to catch up with you. As you may recall, I was a student last fall in your speaking class. I have continued to work hard on my speaking; with the ongoing support of the techniques I learned, I am pleased to report I have been active in my local Toastmasters club, making five major speeches this spring, and winning "Best Speech" each time! I have also won six ribbons for best impromptu speech, and one for best speech evaluation. The comment I received from our most senior club member after my last major speech was that it was one of the best he ever heard, and that I could easily be a contender in the international speech competition. . . . Most importantly, I am enjoying every minute of the process and so happy to be achieving so much through the spoken word. Thank you.

—Mary Jane Grant, Ontario, Canada

Chapter 8

INTRODUCTIONS AND JOKES

"A Funny Thing Happened on the Way"

If fear of public speaking is the number one phobia, then a man doing a eulogy would rather be the deceased.

—Jerry Seinfeld

If you feel that Jerry is talking about you, then you really need to pay attention to this chapter. Starting with the introduction, you will learn how to manage all of the chaos and turbulence that comes up when you first hear that you have to make a presentation. Here are some basic TalkPower rules to help you take control of the situation.

First let's review the eight parts of the TalkPower Action Formula, paying special attention to the beginning (Introductory Section).

The TalkPower Action Formula

Beginning (Introductory Section)	1) INTRODUCTORY PARAGRAPH 2) Topic Sentence 3) Message Sentence

	4) Background
Middle	5) Menu
	6) Point Section
	Point A
	Point B
	Point C
	Point D
	7) Climax
End	8) Conclusion

The Introductory Section

In the TalkPower Action Formula, the beginning of your speech, which we shall call the Introductory Section, has three parts:

1. The Introduction
2. The Topic Sentence
3. The Message Sentence

Each part has a particular purpose. Let us consider the Introduction, which gives the audience a chance to meet you. When you first begin your talk, the audience looks at you, taking notes about your age, sex, color, height, weight, clothes, voice, accent— even your resemblance to other people. The audience is much too busy to give full attention to anything complex you may be saying. This happens within the first three to sixty seconds of your entrance, so it is not a good idea to begin your talk with long involved sentences or ideas.

Before your talk moves into full swing, start with an introduction (ice breaker) such as a joke, the East-West Introduction (see page 122), a question, a shocking statement, a poem, or a quotation.

The Joke

My favorite type of introduction is a joke. I enjoy telling jokes and I love to listen to them. I am not alone in thinking that engaging the audience with a joke is a good idea. Isaac Asimov, in the wonderful anthology, *Isaac Asimov's Treasury of Humor* (Houghton Mifflin Co., Boston, 1991) says:

> A joke is a social phenomenon, an interaction between people. Like a glass of wine, or a common sorrow, but with fewer side effects and with utter lightheartedness—it breaks down reserve, eases tension and establishes contact.

In a Texas A & M University study on persuading people to contribute money, telling a joke as part of the pitch resulted in contributions that were twice as large as when no joke was told. Also, jokes help to reduce stress. At lunch, at a coffee break, among friends when socializing—on the tennis court, the golf course, on the telephone—you can ease a lot of tension by saying, "I just heard the funniest joke . . ."

What Kind of Joke

Recall a joke that you enjoyed. It probably told a concrete story, followed a logical chain of events, and was easy to understand. If the joke preceded a talk, it probably related to the subject of the talk that followed.

It's not necessary to spend hours looking for the ideal, truly hilarious joke—unless you intend to launch a career as a stand-up comic. All you want to do is initiate a flow between you and your audience. A mildly amusing anecdote or joke usually works well. It gives you a chance to begin your presentation in an easy and friendly manner.

The Introductory Joke

The Introductory Joke or story should be between fifty and 150 words, with a punch line or a strong, clearly conclusive ending. It should be as visual as possible and avoid theoretical or philosophical abstractions. If you have any doubts about the appropriateness or tastefulness of a joke, look for another one.

Once you choose a joke as an opening, dress it up and make it your own by giving the characters in the joke names. Make them your relatives, your colleagues, your friends, your neighbors, your son Billy, your sister-in-law Jenny, your cat Lulu, your boss Mr. Bean or Charles (if it's appropriate). Choose a location that is familiar to your audience.

"My cousin Freddy the lawyer ran into a client at Starbucks on 42nd Street. . ." As you read this you immediately get a picture of the story. Dressing up a joke turns you into an accomplished joke-teller. Lastly, make the joke relevant to your particular audience or work.

Of course, the joke should come across as both humorous and natural, so if you feel uncomfortable telling a joke, don't do it. Not everybody has to be a joke teller. There are other kinds of introductions that will be described shortly. If you would like to tell a joke, but have never done so, here are the steps to take.

Learning How to Tell a Joke

In my workshops, telling jokes as a training exercise is extremely effective. Don't worry about finding a joke at this point. A selection will follow. If you know some good jokes, use one of your own.

The following assignment is carried out in two parts. First, pick a joke from the selection on the following pages. Read the joke aloud; then tell it again, trying to recall it without looking at your notes. Print or type the joke on a 5 x 8 index card, double-spaced so you can read it easily. It should look something like this:

AS A FRESHMAN AT DUKE UNIVERSITY MY

SON PAUL WAS FILLING OUT A

QUESTIONNAIRE DURING ORIENTATION WEEK.

RITCHIE, SITTING NEXT TO HIM,

SEEMED TO HAVE COME TO THE END OF HIS ROPE

AS FAR AS QUESTIONNAIRES WERE CONCERNED.

WHEN HE CAME TO THE QUESTION,

"DO YOU BELIEVE IN COLLEGE MARRIAGES?"

RITCHIE SHRUGGED AND OBLIGINGLY WROTE:

"YES, BUT ONLY IF THE COLLEGES REALLY LOVE

EACH OTHER."

Rehearsing Your Joke (Transitional Mantra)

Arrange several chairs in front of a designated podium, which can be a sheet of paper on the floor where you will be standing.

1. Sit in one of the chairs and hold a paperweight in one hand, and your joke on a card, palms up and hands relaxed in your lap. Do five belly breaths. (Pull your belly in. Exhale through your nose. Hold it to the count of three. Relax your stomach muscles and take in a very small bit of air, and do not move your chest). Repeat five times and count each inhalation and exhalation set as one count.

2. Say out loud, "*I am sitting in my chair . . . I feel my body perfectly balanced.*" (Feel your balance.) Say, "*I feel my hands.*"
(Lift your hands off your lap no more than one inch.)

3. Say, "*I drop my hands to my side slowly.*"

4. Say, "*I get up slowly . . . I take a small step and stop . . . I feel my hands.*" (Do you feel the inner click? Get up and take a tiny step—no more than three inches—in front of your chair. Wait until you feel your hands again.)

5. Say "*I walk slowly to the podium . . . I feel my hands.*" Take as many steps as you need to get to the designated podium. Feel your hands at all times. Say, "*I turn around slowly . . . I face the audience . . . I stop . . . I look straight ahead . . . I stand with my feet comfortably apart . . . I feel my hands.*" Squeeze . . . squeeze . . . squeeze . . . those toes.

6. Read your joke out loud in a normal voice. Don't whisper or strain for volume. Remember to read the first three words with a pause between each word.
7. When you finish reading your joke, say, "*I walk back to my chair . . . I feel my hands.*"
8. Sit quietly while you take ten belly breaths. See how you feel.

Next, put your paperweight away and work with feeling the weight of your hands. Repeat the exercise, including all the steps. Take your time when you do this and try to really get into the feeling of gravity pulling your hands down. This time, tell your joke from memory, without using your card; do it two more times.

If you have any trouble remembering your joke, stop. Wait and concentrate on your hands. Do **not** go back to the beginning of the joke. Continue from the point where you left off.

Learning how to remain in control when you tell a joke to an audience will help you become a good speaker.

Jokes to Get You Started

Every speechmaker should have an anthology of jokes in his library. I like to recommend *Isaac Asimov's Treasury of Humor*. *Reader's Digest* also offers a good selection of jokes that even professional comedians use. Some good resources are *2,000 Sure Fire Jokes For Speakers* by Robert Orbin and *The Best Joke Book Ever* by Wayne Brindle.

Pick one joke, any joke, and tell it to two or three different people—a colleague, your spouse, to a client if it's appropriate. Just say, "I am practicing telling jokes, so listen to this one." Each day, pick a new joke. At the end of the month you will be surprised by how much more comfortable and fluent you are telling jokes.

Following is a small collection of jokes you can practice with:

Grace, a longtime employee, was passed over for promotion. Someone else got the job, and so Grace went to her boss, Harvey, to complain.

Harvey was very understanding. He took the other woman's resume out and said, "Take a look at that, Grace." She read it: it was formidable. The boss said, "Well, do you think I promoted the right woman?"

Grace replied, "Well, if you're going to be swayed by ability . . ."

Margie is a single mom, and she has always wanted to win the lottery. Every night she prays, "Dear God, Please let me win! I've lived a good life; I have been such a good mother to my children. Give me a sign. Tell me that tomorrow I am going to win!"

And a deep voice is heard from above, "Margie, meet me halfway. Buy a ticket."

My neighbor Bill Mack, a very successful businessman, decided to make his new son-in-law, Jerome, a fifty-fifty partner in his business. He said, "Jerome, you are now a partner in a very successful business. All you have to do is go to the factory and learn how it works."

Jerome said, "I hate factories. I can't stand the noise, the confusion."

Bill said, "Well, why don't you work in the office? You can be a manager."

Jerome replied, "No. I don't like office work. I can't stand being stuck behind a desk."

In exasperation, Bill said, "I just made you half-owner of a successful business. You don't like factories; you don't like offices; you don't like desks. What am I going to do with you?"

Jerome said, "Buy me out."

In my psychiatrist's waiting room the man sitting opposite me kept dipping his fingers into his hat and then waving them in the air. Finally I asked him, "Excuse me. What are you doing?"

The man smiled and replied, "I have a supply of anti-tiger dust here. By scattering it all over I keep the tigers away."

I tried to be reasonable. "But there are no tigers within thousands of miles of here!" The man replied smugly, "See? It works."

My cousin Milton doesn't like to get up in the morning. And my aunt Beverly has to struggle with him every day to get him to go to school.

On this particular morning she came into his bedroom at five after eight. He was fast asleep. She shook him, saying, "Milton, Milton, will you get up! You're going to be late for school!"

He said, "Oh, Mom, I don't want to go to school. I don't like it. Let me just sleep here."

She replied, "Milton look, let's talk about it. Tell me why you don't like school, and then I'll try to reason with you."

Milton says, "Oh, Mom, I'm not popular. The kids don't like me. The teachers laugh at me. I'm so unhappy in school. Don't make me go!"

She says, "Milton, you're fifty-five years old. You're the principal. Now get out of bed and go to school before you miss the first period."

The East-West Introduction

If you are uncomfortable beginning your speech with a joke, or if a joke isn't appropriate, another simple and effective way to begin is with a technique I devised for my students and clients. I call it the East-West Introduction. This method provides the audience with two or three simple statements of fact about the subject of your talk. There should be no defense, explanation, or elaboration. Those come later in the speech, during the point section. Following are a few examples:

Sample: Short East-West Introduction

Introduction: Some managers specialize in equity investments. Others offer only fixed-income expertise.

(Squeeze . . . squeeze . . . squeeze . . . those toes.) (PAUSE)

Topic Sentence: Today *(PAUSE)* I *(PAUSE)* am *(PAUSE)* going to talk about the investment strategy at Jones Capital.

Sample: Long East-West Introduction

Introduction: On a single day last month, Office Depot agreed to buy Viking Office Products in a three-billion-dollar stock swap.

On the same day, Nationwide Mutual Insurance Company announced a one-hundred-fifty-nine-billion-dollar hostile tender offer for Allied Group.

Simultaneously, Dillard's, the Midwestern retailer, bought the Mercantile Stores Company for two-point-nine-billion dollars.

(Squeeze . . . squeeze . . . squeeze . . . PAUSE)

Topic Sentence: Today I am going to talk about the high-risk game of corporate mergers.

Variation of the East-West Introduction

Introduction: It was something you wanted to do, at least one time before you died, like hearing Placido Domingo at the Met, visiting the Grand Canyon, hitting it big in Las Vegas. *(Squeeze . . . squeeze . . . squeeze . . . those toes.)*

Topic Sentence: Today I am going to talk about living in Paris. . . .

Or this . . .

Introduction: Everyone I know is in therapy. My boss and his wife go to couples therapy. My neighbors attend group encounter therapy. Even my veterinarian has a pet psychologist who comes in once a week to give emotional support to the patients.

(Squeeze . . . squeeze . . . squeeze . . . PAUSE)

Topic Sentence: Today I am going to talk about my search for the perfect therapist.

The Single Statement or Question Introduction

You can also introduce a speech using a single statement or question, but it must be strong enough to grab the audience's immediate attention.

Introduction: Question: What did the Buddhist say to the hotdog vendor?

Answer: "Make me One with Everything." *(Squeeze . . . squeeze . . . squeeze . . . PAUSE)*

Topic Sentence: Today I am going to talk about how to develop a spiritual practice in everyday life . . . .

The Shocking Statement Introduction

You can also begin with a shocking statement.

Introduction: Thomas McGuane, the author, said: "Almost anyone who was ever questioned about me in high school would agree that I would not amount to anything. Unless I was rescued by a showgirl, a criminal career loomed in the future. . . ."

(Squeeze . . . squeeze . . . squeeze . . . PAUSE)

Topic Sentence: Today I am going to talk about how I became a writer.

Introduction: More people are seriously injured in their own homes than anywhere else. *(Squeeze . . . squeeze . . . squeeze . . . those toes.) (PAUSE)*

Topic Sentence: Today I am going to talk about making your home a safer place.

The Brief Anecdote Introduction

Another form of introduction is the brief anecdote. This works just like a joke.

Introduction: Joan Rivers was interviewing Robert Stack of *Unsolved Mysteries*, and he revealed that when he was a young man, Spencer Tracy was his mentor.

"Oh," said Joan, "Did he give you any tips?"

"Yes," said Robert Stack. "He used to say, 'Don't let 'em rush you, kid. Don't let 'em rush you.'"

(Squeeze . . . squeeze . . . squeeze . . . PAUSE)

Topic Sentence: Today I am going to talk about how to survive in the theater.

Using a Quotation

Using a quotation—from a famous person, from a newspaper article or editorial, or even a well-known line from a movie or play—can make for a snappy beginning to a speech. In general, the shorter the quotation, the better. Avoid complex statements that include too many facts, explanations, or qualifying remarks.

Introduction: When Beatrice Lillie was asked how she cleaned her diamonds, she replied, "Clean them? When my diamonds get dirty I throw them away." *(Squeeze . . . squeeze . . . squeeze . . . PAUSE)*

Topic Sentence: Today I am going to talk about the diamond district in New York City.

Introduction: Sam Levenson once said, "Insanity is hereditary. You can get it from your children."

(Squeeze . . . squeeze . . . squeeze . . . PAUSE)

Topic Sentence: Today I am going to talk about parenting a teenager.

Introduction: In a speech at MIT, where he proposed a twenty-four hour video channel to show the whole earth at all times, Vice President Gore shared his dream: "As Socrates said, two thousand five hundred years ago, 'Man must rise above the earth, to the top of the atmosphere and beyond, for only thus will he understand the earth in which he lives.'"

(Squeeze . . . squeeze . . . squeeze . . . PAUSE)

Topic Sentence: Today I am going to talk about developing a TV channel totally devoted to the earth.

Using a Poem

Finally, a verse from a poem can be useful as an introduction. You have to be careful with poetry though. The verse you choose shouldn't be too abstract or difficult. Choose a simple passage that your audience is likely to understand immediately.

Introduction: "Yesterday is history/Tomorrow is a mystery/Today is a gift: That's why we call it the Present." *(PAUSE)*

Topic Sentence: Today I am going to talk about enjoying the moment, "Carpe Diem."

Whatever type of introduction you chose—joke, humorous anecdote, the East-West method, shocking statement, rhetorical question or quotation—remember, it should not exceed 150 words, no matter how long your speech is.

Note: *If you do not wish to begin your talk with an introduction, but would like to get right into your material, it is perfectly fine to begin your talk with your topic sentence.*

For example:

Topic Sentence: The purpose of my report is to present the final draft of the XYZ proposal.

After a pause, you would follow this with . . .

Message Sentence: I believe that the XYZ version is a great improvement over other approaches we have considered.

Never Introduce an Introduction

If you would like to present yourself in the most professional way possible, keep your introduction clear and sharp. After you have done your three squeezes in complete silence, say the first words of your introduction just as you had planned to say them. Do not, I repeat, *do not* introduce your introduction with a few nervous words like "I would like to say a few words about . . ." or "This is a cute joke that I thought you would enjoy . . ." or "On the way here I was trying to come up with what I would say to all of you folks tonight . . ." No matter how uncomfortable you feel, go right into the first words of your introduction. If you have to thank people or you must say some obligatory opening words, by all means do that. When your thank you's are over, take a pause of three squeezes and go right into your introduction using the exact words you rehearsed with. The audience will move along with you. You don't have to carry them.

When to Write Your Introduction

Work on your introduction last. That's right. After you have prepared all the other parts of your talk. The introduction is an accessory. You don't want to put off developing the main part of your talk as you take precious time searching for the perfect joke or story.

Exercise: Writing an Introduction

1. Write out your introduction on one or more 5 x 8 cards, leaving every other line blank so that you can read the material easily.

2. Be sure to write the words "PAUSE." And "Squeeze three times" after the last word. Keep this card at hand—you will be needing it again shortly. If you wish, pick a joke from the joke section as your practice introduction. Now you are ready for your first rehearsal.

Rehearsal (Transitional Mantra)

Set up several chairs, a designated podium, and a sheet of paper on the floor where you will be standing.

1. Sit in a chair and hold a paperweight in one hand and your introduction card(s) in the other, palms up and relaxed in your lap.
2. Do five belly breaths. (Pull your belly in. Exhale through your nose. Hold it to the count of three. Relax your stomach muscles. Do not move your chest.) Repeat five times, and count each inhalation and exhalation set as one count.
3. Say out loud, "*I am sitting in my chair . . . I feel my body perfectly balanced.*" (Feel your balance.)
4. Say to yourself, "*I feel my hands . . .*" (Lift your hands off your lap no more than one inch.)
5. Say, "*I drop my hands to my sides slowly.*" (Let them hang.)
6. Say, "*I get up slowly . . . I take a small step and stop . . . I wait until I feel my hands again.*" Do you feel the inner click? Get up and take a tiny step, no more than three inches in front of your chair.
7. Say aloud: "*I walk to the podium . . . I feel my hands.*" Take as many steps as you need to get to the designated podium. Feel your hands at all times. Say aloud, "*I turn around slowly . . . I face the audience . . . I stop . . . I look toward the audience.*
8. Squeeze . . . squeeze . . . squeeze . . . those toes.
9. Say THE JOKE or INTRODUCTORY PARAGRAPH. (Squeeze . . . squeeze . . . squeeze . . . those toes.)
10. Say, "*I slowly walk back to my seat . . . I feel my hands.*"

11. Sit down and do five belly breaths.
12. Repeat this entire exercise one more time. This time, do not use the paperweight. Try to feel the weight of your hands.

Note: *Don't worry about breathing correctly once you begin to walk to the podium. If you wish to take a few belly breaths after you face the audience, you may do this at any time.*

Now you are ready to move on to the next chapter, which deals with the Topic and Message Sentences. These elements will complete the beginning section of your speech.

Progress Report

Date	Time	Strong Spot	Weak Spot	Comment	Calm/Nervous (1-10)

Chapter 9

THE TOPIC AND MESSAGE SENTENCE

Speak Now or Forever Regret It

Words matter!

—Senator Robert Torricelli

Now that you know all about how to begin your talk, let us look at the Topic Sentence, the second part of the beginning of your speech.

Beginning (Introductory Section)	1) Introductory Paragraph
	2) TOPIC SENTENCE
	3) MESSAGE SENTENCE
Middle	4) Background
	5) Menu
	6) Point Section
	Point A
	Point B
	Point C
	Point D
	7) Climax
End	8) Conclusion

The Topic Sentence: "Today I am going to talk about . . ."

After a pause (three toe squeezes), the Topic Sentence always follows the last line of your joke or other Introductory Statement. The purpose of the Topic Sentence is to clearly introduce the subject of your talk. It is like the title of a book. When you are anxious about your presentation, a firm statement that says, "Today I am going to talk about . . ." creates a strong lift-off for your talk. It helps you, as well as the audience, to become focused.

Example

Introduction (joke): My neighbor, Bill, a computer salesman, was asked about the food at Jenny's Burgery, a restaurant where he usually has his lunch.

"The food there is terrible," he said. "The fries are cold, the burgers are overcooked, and the brownies are too sweet. Worst of all, they serve such small portions!"

(PAUSE) Squeeze . . . squeeze . . .squeeze . . . those toes.

Topic Sentence: Today I am going to talk about how to choose a good restaurant.

The Topic Sentence is like the title of a book: short. It is a headline, with no explanations. Keeping the Topic Sentence as short as possible adds to clarity.

Let's look at some examples of right and wrong Topic Sentences.

Right

- Today I am going to talk about our move to Long Island.
- Today I am going to talk about traffic congestion in the city.
- Today I am going to talk about global warming.
- Today I am going to describe the new accounting procedures.
- Today I am going to talk about our COVID-19 Vaccination Service Fund Drive.

Wrong

- Today I am going to talk about a subject that is not going to be very popular here, because of all the reasons that were outlined by Mr. Jones last Thursday—and you all must know what I mean by now, and I do mean the move to Long Island, which has been long in coming, and is still rather controversial.

- Today I am going to talk about the most deplorable situation that any city can possibly imagine in the grimmest of dreams, because there has simply got to be some sort of a solution to the dilemma of our traffic congestion.

- Today I am going to talk about one of the most serious ecologically devastating situations that we could possibly dream of, endangering our children and our children's children for generations to come, because of the neglect and lack of interest so prevalent nowadays concerning global warming.

- As you all know, there are some new accounting procedures that many people feel are rather complicated and also costly, as they take a considerable amount of time to understand, but I will try to explain them to you so that there will be a minimum of unfortunate error.

- Today I am going to talk about our COVID-19 Vaccination Service Fund Drive in the hope that all of you will pitch in and lend a hand and be as generous as you possibly can, so that the people who live far away from the vaccination centers can have some sort of transportation available to take them to a place where they will be able to receive a vaccine injection.

The wrong Topic Sentences are all too long, too complicated, and give too much information. A listening audience cannot turn back the page if it has missed something. A listening audience has to absorb what you say as you say it. This is especially important at the beginning of your talk.

Topic Sentences from Jokes

If you are using a joke or a story for your introductory statement, your Topic Sentence should be relevant to your story or joke, as the following example illustrates.

Introduction: Jonathan, a young English author, was due to deliver the first speech of his American lecture tour. "I'm such a miserable speaker," he confessed to his American agent, Arnold. "I know they'll all walk out on me before I finish."

"Don't be silly!" said Arnold. "You are an excellent speaker and you'll keep them glued to their seats."

"Oh, I say!" said Jonathan. "What a wonderful idea! But do we dare?"

Possible Topic Sentences

- o   Today I am going to talk about public speaking.
- o   Today I am going to talk about nervousness.
- o   The subject of my talk is lecture tours.
- o   Tonight I am going to talk about English authors.
- o   I am here to discuss the relationship between agents and authors.

It is not only easy to pull Topic Sentences out from jokes or anecdotes, but it is fun. Try it for yourself with the following joke.

Introduction: My neighbor, Maxwell, told me that when he was at the movies last week he noticed the man sitting in front of him had his arm around a dog. The dog seemed to be really enjoying the movie, laughing at the funny parts, growling at the villain. Maxwell leaned forward and tapped the man on the shoulder. He said, "I can't believe what a smart dog you have."

The man turned around and said, "It kind of surprises me too. He hated the book!"

Possible Topic Sentences

Write four different Topic Sentences derived from the joke, using one of the following to lead into it . . .

Today I am going to talk about . . .
The subject of my talk is . . .
Tonight I am going to talk about . . .
I am here to tell you about . . .

Here are a few possible Topic Sentences you might have found in this little story.

Today I am going to talk about . . . my dog, Bruce.
The subject of my talk is . . . animal intelligence.
Tonight I am going to talk about . . . companionship that a pet can provide.
I am here to tell you about . . . the importance of neutering your dog.

There are at least a dozen other possible Topic Sentences that can be pulled from this one joke. Try to find as many Topic Sentences as possible. But keep them short.

The Message Sentence

The Message Sentence follows the Topic Sentence. It is the third part of the beginning of your speech.

Example

Topic Sentence: Today I am going to talk about decorating your home on a budget. *(Squeeze . . .squeeze . . . squeeze . . . those toes.)*

Message Sentence: I believe that you can have a lovely home without putting yourself in debt. *(Squeeze . . .squeeze . . . squeeze . . . those toes.)*

The purpose of the Message Sentence is to express your point of view about your topic. It comes directly after the Topic Sentence, preceded by "I think . . ." "I feel . . ." "I believe . . ." or any phrase that indicates "This is my opinion."

The Message Sentence is the core idea, the spine of your talk. It serves as a thematic element that frames your talk and holds it together so that it moves in a narrative flow (story telling flow). It appears once in each new point. A short headline, the Message Sentence is your north star, the most important sentence in your talk. Without a message sentence, your talk becomes a series of fragmented pieces of information that makes it difficult for the audience to remember what your talk was about. It helps to motivate or persuade your audience to follow your suggestions.

The Message Sentence acts as the theme of your talk, and is repeated once in each new point you introduce. Guidelines for doing this will be found in the discussion about the point section in the next chapter.

Using a Message Sentence

Let's take a different joke, leading to a different Topic Sentence, and see how the Message Sentence works.

Introduction: An anonymous New York taxpayer sent a letter to the State Comptroller's Office in Albany saying that he had cheated on his income tax ten years ago and had not been able to get a good night's sleep since. He enclosed twenty-five dollars and added, "If I still can't sleep, I will send the balance." *(PAUSE...Squeeze . . . squeeze . . . squeeze . . . those toes.)*

Topic Sentence: Today I am going to talk about the new income tax cuts. *(PAUSE)*

(Squeeze . . .squeeze . . . squeeze . . . those toes.)

Message Sentence: I think that the proposed federal income tax cuts are not in the best interests of the country. *(Squeeze . . .squeeze . . . squeeze . . . those toes.)*

Examples: Topic Sentence/Message Sentence

Topic Sentence: Today I want to talk about visionaries.
(Squeeze . . .squeeze . . . squeeze . . . those toes.)

Message Sentence: I think that if you put nine visionaries in a room, you will get nine different visions. *(Squeeze . . .squeeze . . . squeeze . . . those toes.)*

Topic Sentence: Today I want to talk about the heavy backpacks our children wear to school. *(Squeeze . . .squeeze . . . squeeze . . . those toes.)*

Message Sentence: I believe that heavy backpacks are causing serious injuries to the backs of our children. *(Squeeze . . .squeeze . . . squeeze . . . those toes.)*

Topic Sentence: Today I am going to talk about snowboarding. *(Squeeze . . .squeeze . . . squeeze . . . those toes.)*

Message Sentence: I feel that snowboarding is an important part of the Olympic profile. *(Squeeze . . .squeeze . . . squeeze . . . those toes.)*

Purpose of the Message Sentence

The Message Sentence always appears in the beginning section of your talk because:

- Declaring your position early in the speech helps to build a sense of trust with your audience.
- The Message Sentence is an organizing principle that connects your various points to one another.
- The Message Sentence will help to keep you on track as you develop your talk.
- The Message Sentence helps to reduce or eliminate misunderstandings.
- The Message Sentence communicates your enthusiasm for your point of view.
- When you publicly reveal your personal convictions, you can charge the atmosphere with positive energy.
- If you tell the audience where you are going, they will help you get there.

The Message Statement should be preceded by one of the following phrases:

- I think . . .
- I believe . . .
- I feel . . .
- I am committed to the idea that . . .
- I am of the opinion that . . .
- I . . . *(other)*

Example

Introduction: My college roommate, Donald, sent his mother a very special parrot for Mother's Day. Several weeks later he went to visit his mother. "Tell me, Mom, did you like the bird I sent?"

"Oh yes. I was telling my girlfriend, Frieda, what a wonderful son I have to remember me like that."

"You mean you really, really liked it? You're not just saying that?"

"Well, to tell you the truth, at first I thought he would be small and stringy, but the soup was delicious!"

Donald jumped from his seat. "You ATE it? That bird could speak seven languages!" His mother, equally startled, said, "Well, when he saw me taking out the pot and chopping the carrots, why didn't he say something?" *(Squeeze . . . squeeze. . . squeeze. . . those toes.)*

Topic Sentence: Today I would like to talk about giving an animal as a gift. *(Squeeze. . . squeeze. . .squeeze. . .those toes.)*

Message Sentence: I believe that giving an animal as a gift is not a good idea. *(Squeeze. . .squeeze. . .squeeze. . .those toes.)*

Personal Can Be Persuasive

Some people believe that "I think" is a sign of hesitancy. They prefer to let the facts speak for themselves, relying on charts or graphs or statistics. They feel that giving a personal opinion undermines their credibility. On the contrary, a personal statement about your position is extremely persuasive when that statement is followed by well-researched facts.

Even in a corporate presentation, an expression of personal faith in a policy or a product enhances the strength of the message. If you have any doubts about that, consider the success of famous NBA player Lebron James and his success advertising for Sprite.

Let's see how another opening joke, Topic Sentence, and Message Sentence relate to one another. Here is a joke and a Topic Sentence, with five different possibilities for a Message Sentence. (*Remember, there is only one Message Sentence to a speech.*)

Introduction: A shy young man came into the office of my boss, Marvin. You know Marvin; he's a real go-getter sales manager. The young man timidly approached the desk and mumbled, "You don't want to buy any insurance, do you?"

"No!" was the brusque reply.

"I was afraid not," said the embarrassed man, starting to back toward the door. "Wait a minute!" exclaimed Marvin. "I've dealt with salesmen all my life, and you're the worst I've ever seen. You have to inspire confidence, and to do that you've got to have it yourself. Just to give you the confidence that you can make a sale, I'll sign for a fifty thousand dollar policy."

After signing the application, Marvin said, "What you have to do is learn some good techniques and use them."

"Oh, but I have," returned the shy young man. "I have an approach for almost every type of businessman. The one I just used was my standard approach for sales managers." *(Squeeze . . .squeeze . . . squeeze . . . those toes.)*

Topic sentence: Today I am going to talk about selling.

(Squeeze . . .squeeze . . . squeeze . . . those toes.)

Message Sentence Possibilities

- I believe that a successful selling technique is based on a variety of approaches.
- I think even the most experienced salesman can still learn a new approach.
- I am committed to the idea that it takes more than confidence to make a good salesman.
- I feel very strongly that older competitors should take young salespeople more seriously.
- I am convinced that with the right approach even the most difficult customer can be sold.

Each one of these Message Sentences takes a specific focus that differs from the other four, ultimately giving you five different speeches.

Good Message Sentences

Let us briefly analyze each one of these Message Sentences to see what we can learn.

1. *I believe that a successful selling technique is based on a variety of approaches.* The speaker is talking about the various selling techniques that lead to successful selling. This is probably a training talk.

2. *I think even the most experienced salesman can still learn a new approach.* The speaker is focusing on new approaches, attempting to motivate more experienced salesmen to try new and different selling techniques, asking them not to rely so much on past performance.

3. *I am committed to the idea that it takes more than confidence to make a good salesman.* The speaker will talk about a variety of requirements—psychological, physical, and so on—for becoming a good salesman. This talk would emphasize the personal qualifications necessary in a good salesman, rather than sales techniques. This could be a recruitment talk.

4. *I feel very strongly that older competitors should take young salespeople more seriously.* The speaker will try to make the older, more seasoned salesman aware of the techniques, general enthusiasm, and energy of the new and younger sales competition.

5. *I am convinced that with the right approach even the most difficult customer can be sold.* Here the speaker is focusing on the difficult customer. This talk will concern selling to the difficult customer and reviewing methods that have proven successful with this type of person.

Bad Message Sentences

Here are several Message Sentences that just don't work.

Message Sentence: I believe that successful selling techniques are based on a variety of approaches, because it has been proven time and time again that you can't keep relying on the same old strategies for every single type of customer.

This was fine until we got to the word *because*. Never have *because* in your message. **Don't explain!**

Message Sentence: It seems to me it might be better if even very experienced salesmen made the effort to try new techniques.

This is a very halfhearted approach; a weak, unsure, hesitant way to take a position.

A Message Sentence must be direct and focused.

Message Sentence: I think that the problem of the difficult customer must be dealt with on an individual basis, insofar as it has been our experience that difficult customers, when satisfied with our service and attention, can become our most desirable clients.

This was correct until the word *insofar*. After that word, the impact and strength of the preceding statement was weakened by the addition of another idea.

Idea A: "Difficult customers must be dealt with on an individual basis."

Idea B: "Difficult customers can become our most desirable clients."

Either A or B should serve as the Message Sentence. The second idea can be discussed in the body of the speech.

One Central Idea per Presentation

As soon as you decide upon a Topic Sentence, state a point of view (Message Sentence) so that you have a context with which to conduct your research. There are two important rules to follow to help you develop a Message Sentence.

Rule Number One: A good speech never has more than one central organizing principle. When two or more central messages appear in one speech, you will find the speech pulling in different directions. This makes the speech hard for the audience to follow. You will sense that your speech is not flowing and lose your confidence.

Rule Number Two: Never start your research without a Message Sentence. The absence of a point of view may be appropriate for an encyclopedia, but it is always necessary in a presentation. When a presentation does not have a central or core idea, the talk deteriorates into a series of fragmented pieces of information. When this happens, people tune out and lose interest. Then you will hear rustling, coughing, and whispering in the audience.

Any Message Sentence Is Better than None

It is better to use a Message Sentence that you are not sure about, one that you may later change, than to do your research with no Message Sentence at all. The reason for this is that you must have context for your research. If you begin researching your topic with no context or point of view, you will just be collecting tons of information. As a result, you will have no way to choose which information you need and which information is irrelevant for your purpose in giving the talk. In the process of researching, if you decide upon a different point of view, simply change the original Message Sentence to the new one.

Too Complex?

Perhaps you think that your trouble stems from the complexity of your subject. More likely, you are afraid to state a point of view until you have done enough research. This approach is extremely time consuming, as well as confusing. By accumulating massive amounts of information without a Message Sentence, you will drown in the material. You need the focal point that a Message Sentence provides to keep you moving forward. A Message Sentence is a short headline and should not:

- Explain
- Defend
- Elaborate on the idea
- Give examples
- Develop itself in any way
- Have any words that are not absolutely necessary

To sum up, a Message Sentence is a brief declarative statement that gives the audience your point of view on the topic.

Exercise: Practice Talk

Here are some topics that have come from TalkPower seminars. Since this is a practice talk, and you want to learn the principles of developing a presentation, select a topic that you enjoy working with, one that will not take too much research.

Sports	Diet	Gardening	Your children
A hobby	Music	Art	Building a business
Fitness	Real estate	Health	Internet start-ups
Pets	Dance	Taxes	Cultural diversity
Global warming	Politics	Food	The economy
A vacation	Psychology	Theater	Spiritual experience
Collecting	Space Travel	Fashion	World peace
Travel	Investing	Your school	Other

1. Now write a Topic Sentence.
   Today I am going to talk about _____
   _____.

2. Write a Message Sentence.
   I believe that _____
   _____.

A Talk Is Like a Trip

Suppose you had to drive across country from New York to San Francisco with one week to make the trip. Wouldn't it be smart to get a map and draw up a detailed plan, keeping in mind that your destination is San Francisco? Sounds simple, right?

So tell me, why do so many intelligent professionals totally ignore their destination when they give presentations, using outlines, laundry lists, decks, tons of statistics and facts, research, slides, transparencies, PowerPoint, the kitchen sink (talking so fast to get it all in) and getting nowhere fast, boring us to death?

Where Is this Leading?

My point here is that if you want to create a presentation that takes the audience from their point of view to your point of view before you look up a single fact, you must clarify your topic and Message Sentence. If you do, you will have the perfect underpinnings to accomplish your intention. That is why, in the following section, we are going to spend so much time with only two sentences: the Topic Sentence and the Message Sentence.

Cleaning up the Message

Now look at your Message Sentence.

> A. Is it a headline? Can it possibly be shortened or edited? Do it!
>
> Topic Sentence: _____
>
> Message Sentence: _____

> B. Is it only one message or is it two messages? For example, the sentence *"I think that exercise is relaxing and healthful"* sends out two messages. One message is about relaxation; the other is about health. Choose one as the core theme, and save the other for the body of the speech (to be discussed later), as in *"I think that exercise is important for good health."* Having only one core theme per speech is a crucial principle for thinking logically. It will save you many hours of confusion when you develop your speech.

New Topic Sentence: _____

New Message Sentence: _____

> C. Now that you have edited and clarified your Message Sentence, go back and look at your Topic Sentence. Does your Message Sentence reflect exactly what you say in your Topic Sentence?

For example, a student says (Topic Sentence): *"Today I want to talk about my trip to Italy."*

(Message Sentence): *"I think that Italy is a beautiful country."*

What is wrong with this message? Look at the topic. Isn't it about *". . . my trip to Italy"*? Where does it say *"my trip"* in the message? *"My trip"* is the subject. So, the student has to say something about her trip in the Message Sentence.

For example, *"I think that my trip to Italy was one of the most interesting experiences I have ever had."*

Or, she could keep her original Message Sentence by saying (Topic Sentence) *"Today I am going to talk about Italy."*

(Message Sentence) *"I think that Italy is a beautiful country."* In this case, since Italy is the subject, her Message Sentence is correct.

Fix your Message Sentence or change your Topic Sentence so that they work together.

Topic Sentence: _____

Message Sentence: _____

Your Intention

In the next step, identify your intention. What would you like your audience *to do* after they hear your talk? Identifying your intention is crucial to delivering a successful speech, because your time for speaking is usually limited. Therefore, if you are not fully aware of your purpose in giving your talk, you may begin to drift aimlessly, choosing material that is irrelevant or a waste of time. Here is a list of possible intentions. Choose one for your practice talk.

Possible Intentions
- To close the deal
- To invest with my company
- To buy my product
- To give my agency the account
- To give my company the order
- To act on my recommendation

- To accept my report
- To sign a petition
- To contribute money
- To volunteer
- To vote for my program or idea
- To vote for my candidate
- To give me a promotion
- To unite behind a particular action by forming a committee
- To protest with a particular action
- To respond generously with a commitment of time and/or money
- To be inspired
- To try something new
- To want to know me better
- To write a letter
- To learn how to do a procedure
- To understand a new idea
- To share my experience
- To unite for a particular action
- To feel welcomed
- To have an inspirational experience
- To change their opinion
- To honor an individual
- To begin to exercise
- To eat healthy
- To sign up
- Other

Notice that your intention is always stated with an active verb.

I want the audience **to contribute** money.
I want the audience **to learn** this technique.
I want the audience **to buy** this product.

What Do You Really Want to Say?
On the next few lines, give a brief overall summary of what it is that you want to say in your presentation. Use simple conversational language.

In this speech I want to tell my audience _____

_____

_____

Your Intention Again
Now formulate your intention. Take this from the previous list or develop your own intention.

My intention in giving this talk is to get my audience to _____

_____.

Take a moment to imagine your audience following through on your suggestions.

Sample

Topic Sentence: *Today I am going to talk about making a contribution to City Critters, the animal rescue organization.*

Message Sentence: *I believe that giving to City Critters will save the life of a dog or cat.* (My intention is for the audience to contribute money to City Critters. This last sentence is not spoken aloud.)

Will it Fly?
Look at your Message Sentence again.

Message Sentence: _____

Is your Message Sentence clear and strong enough to help you to realize your intention? If not, fix your Message Sentence. However, remember the rule about one Message Sentence per talk and also that the message must echo the topic.

Topic Sentence: _____

Message Sentence: _____

Rehearsal

You are now ready to start practicing the beginning section of your speech. You have two cards: the first contains your joke or any other kind of introductory statement you choose; the second has a Topic Sentence and a Message Sentence.

Set up several chairs to represent your audience. Sit in your chair, holding a paperweight in one hand and your index cards in the other.

1. Be aware that the right side of your body is perfectly balanced with the left side.

2. Do five belly breaths. Pull your belly in slowly as you exhale through the nose. Hold this to the count of three, 1-2-3. Relax your abdominal muscles. Take a small breath, and do not move your chest. Repeat five times. If you feel that you are not getting enough air, be patient. Eventually you will feel very comfortable and calm when you breathe this way.

3. Say out loud and perform the corresponding action: *"I am sitting in my chair . . . I feel my body perfectly balanced . . . I feel my hands . . . I drop my hands to my sides . . . (Let them hang.) I stand up slowly and take a small step, and stop . . . (Do you feel the inner click?) I wait until I feel my hands . . . I walk slowly to the podium . . . I feel my hands . . . I turn around slowly . . . I face the audience . . . I stop . . . I stand with my feet comfortably apart . . . I feel my hands."*

Note: *At this point you should be standing in front of your imaginary audience.*

4. Squeeze your toes three times. Squeeze, release, squeeze, release, squeeze, release.

5. Give your introduction or joke, and remember to say the first three words with a space between each word.

6. *"Today . . . I . . . am . . . going to talk about . . ."* (squeeze . . . squeeze . . . squeeze)
7. *"I think that . . ."* (PAUSE . . . squeeze . . . squeeze . . . squeeze)
8. Walk back slowly to your seat, saying out loud, *"I slowly walk back to my chair . . . I feel my hands."*
9. Sit down slowly and do five belly breaths. Take a moment to be aware of how you feel. Repeat the entire exercise without the weight in your hand.

Progress Report

Date	Time	Strong Spot	Weak Spot	Comment	Calm/Nervous (1-10)

Chapter 10

THE BACKGROUND

The End of Huff and Puff

All the great speakers were bad speakers at first.
—Ralph Waldo Emerson

Alan, an account executive, is always well prepared for his sales presentations. Although he feels comfortable, his presentations are lackluster. Everyone in the office knows that Alan is a warm and witty person, a likable man in a one-to-one meeting, yet, when he gets up in front of an audience, his personality dissolves and he seems cold.

What is the problem here? Alan doesn't experience the fears or mental lapses that affect so many anxious public speakers. He's very professional and businesslike—too businesslike. That's the problem: Alan never talks about himself or refers to himself in any way. He avoids the word "I." His sales pitch relies solely on facts and figures, with no personal recommendations or opinions. The result is that Alan is so formal his charm doesn't show.

How can Alan convey his warmth and become more personal to his audiences without appearing inappropriate and losing his professional credibility? The answer lies in the background section of the TalkPower Action Formula.

Beginning	1) Introductory Paragraph	
(Introductory Section)	2) Topic Sentence	
	3) Message Sentence	
	4) BACKGROUND	
Middle	5) Menu	
	6) Point Section *Point A* *Point B* *Point C* *Point D*	
	7) Climax	
End	8)	Conclusion

The Background

People need stories.

—Isabel Allende

In the TalkPower model, the Background is the fourth section of your speech. It follows your Message Sentence and provides a context for your talk. It helps you reach out to your audience by telling the story of how you or your company became involved with the topic. Note I said the topic, not the message. The Background Section is not a sales pitch. It is a story about you and your connection to the topic, with no abstractions, theories, or statistics.

As a narrative, the background should have a maximum of 150 words and a minimum of a hundred words, no matter how long the rest of your speech will be. (These word counts are approximate—don't panic if your word count is slightly under or over. Notice the word *slightly*!)

Telling a story about yourself and your topic at the beginning of your speech is a good way to get the audience to relate to you. You may wonder why the audience wants to know about you. The answer is simple. People are interested in other people. They are especially interested in the personal details of those in the limelight, leaders and authority figures. Giving a talk puts you in the limelight, so it's perfectly natural for your audience to want to know something about you.

What you tell your audience about yourself and your topic does not have to be profound. You are the star of this show, and even unimportant information becomes interesting. If you doubt that, consider the press's endless curiosity about who politicians and movie stars date and where they vacation. It doesn't really matter whether a celebrity prefers a Buddhist retreat in the Himalayas or dancing all night at the Rainbow Room. The public likes to know such things. These kinds of details help us to identify with people in the spotlight.

The Background Template

There are some people, however, who find it almost impossible to talk about themselves for more than a sentence or two. With questions, you can draw them out, but when left on their own to reveal themselves, they get writer's block.

In one of my seminars years ago, an engineer was finding it almost impossible to give us a personal story of more than one sentence. I would say, "So how did you get that idea? So who did you bring it to? So then what happened? How did the newspapers hear about it? Tell us, tell us!" It was exhausting.

In this same class, then there is the student who tells us more than we want to know. For example, Bernadette said, "Well, I opened my dancing school because my husband was having a torrid affair with a lady who lived right above. Every night he would disappear, and I found that I was going crazy so I decided to occupy my time by going back to work and that's how I opened my dancing school . . ." and on and on, about her husband's affair. She definitely needed guidelines to help her stay on track about her dancing school.

And so, I developed a template for writing an appropriate personal history that is a fail-safe, guaranteed tell-all framework. Just fill in the blanks! It was an immediate success. Now everyone in my classes, including myself, loves listening to all the stories. We really get to know one another.

Since the template can accommodate only 150 words (or one minute of speaking time), the stories are short, sweet, and filled with interesting information about the people in the workshop. I must say the classes have reached a new level of fun, warmth, and camaraderie as a result.

When you use the Background Template, you too will be able to put together a story, quickly and easily—one that will make it easy for your audience to relate to you and your message.

Name Names

As you fill out the Background Template that follows, may I remind you of an old journalism adage: "Anything specific is interesting; anything general is not." If you are referring to a vacation spot, name the place. For example, "We went on many trips" is not as interesting as "We went on many trips to Chile, Australia, and New Zealand."

I call these references that are not specific "empty references," like an empty picture frame with an explanation underneath but no picture. No matter what you are referring to—a person a place, a child, a husband, a wife, a cat, a college, or a company—always identify it by name. When you flash a familiar name into the consciousness of the audience, this immediately evokes associations, pictures, and meanings that enrich your story. Giving your audience familiar images, by naming names, helps them to better hear your message. We don't just buy a car; we buy a Porsche, a Lexus, a Ford, or a Toyota. Each one of these trade names elicits a totally individual and different value. Each one of these cars gives us a tremendous amount of information about the image of the car and the kind of person who buys it.

Stanislavski wrote, "A word can arouse all five senses. One needs to do no more than recall the title of a piece of music, the name of a painter, of a dish, of a favorite perfume, and so on, and one immediately resurrects the auditory and visual images, tastes, smells, or tactile sensations suggested by the word."

As for you, the anxious speaker, I understand that you do not feel comfortable revealing yourself in public. You like to hide in the background. You don't even like to say "I"! But that was before, when you were a terrified, shaky, panic-attack-waiting-to happen.

Well, those days are over! You're reading the TalkPower book so that you can practice these fabulous breathing and concentration exercises. Soon you are going to speak in public—a situation of high visibility and leadership. Speak to your audience. Tell your story with descriptive words and names woven into your Background Section. Let them see what you see. You can do it—choose to do it!

Templates Make Stories

Stories bring a talk to life. For example, I attended a fundraiser given by an organization that works for peace in the Middle East. The first speaker was a nineteen-year-old student. She told the story of her little village and how this organization had given her the opportunity to study to become a veterinarian. The simplicity and clarity of her story totally charmed the audience.

The following speaker was a diplomat from her small country. His talk was impersonal, filled with generalizations and grandiose huff-and-puff. It took three minutes for the previously warm and alive atmosphere to dissolve. The rustling of the crowd was evident. To tell you the truth, he was boring. High-minded messages, hopes, wishes, and visions are always boring if there are no stories to illustrate the ideas.

As I mentioned before, templates are story guidelines to help you compose the different parts of your talk. The templates that follow will support your imagination so that you will always have a well-developed talk.

Three Different Backgrounds

For the Background section, there are three different kinds of templates: personal, organizational, and historical. On the next page you will find an example of a Personal Background Template. Then on the following page you will see the same template filled in with a personal story.

Personal Background Template

I first became (*select one*) involved with / interested in / concerned about / familiar with _____

about _____ years ago. At that time I was _____

_____

_____

I became aware of the fact that . . . (*PAUSE [one toe squeeze]*) ____

_____

_____

For example . . . (*PAUSE*) _____

_____

And so . . . (*PAUSE*) I _____

_____

_____

I also _____

_____

_____

As a result (*PAUSE*) _____

_____

_____.

Today (*PAUSE*) I _____

_____

_____.

(*Squeeze . . . squeeze . . . squeeze . . . those toes.*)

Note: *In the following TalkPower templates, check to be sure that if you refer to something, you specifically reveal the name of whom or whatever you are talking about.*

The following text is an example of a personal background written by one of my students. Look for the words in **bold**—they indicate the transitional phrases in the template.

> **Introduction:** *Henry Longhurst once said, 'The most exquisitely satisfying act in the world of golf is that of throwing a club. The full back swing, the delayed wrist action, the flowing follow-through, followed by that unique whirring sound, reminiscent only of a passing flock of starlings, are without parallel in sport . . ."*
>
> **Topic Sentence: Today I am going to talk about** *the secret life of a recreational golfer.*
>
> **Message Sentence: I think that** golf *is the most challenging sport available to us.* **Background: I first became** *interested in golf* **about** *thirty years ago.* **At that time I was** *a kid who idealized his dad, who happened to love golf.* **By the end of my first lesson, I became aware of the fact that** *golf is a sport unlike all others.* **For example,** *it is the only sport I know where one attempts to propel an undersized ball toward an undersized target, far in the distance, while staring down at one's feet.* **And so I** *began to swing the golf club. The first ten times I tried to hit a golf ball I missed. On the eleventh try, I dribbled it ten*

yards down the fairway. On the fiftieth try I hit it squarely . . .
and I felt like a God. **As a result,** *through golf I noticed*
I was becoming a better person . . . more patient . . . more
forgiving . . . and, unfortunately, no better at the sport. Over
the years I have read golf books, viewed golf videos, studied
professional golfers on TV, and swapped golf stories with other
fanatics. **Today,** *I do not play golf anymore. With two growing*
children, it takes too much time away from them. But every
so often I play a round of golf . . . in my mind. I strike the ball
with rhythm and grace, far better than I ever could in reality.
I hope that someday I'll return to the golf course, and even if I
never do, I'll always have something to daydream about.

Company Background

In some cases, a personal history may be inappropriate. For example, if an executive is speaking for his company, use of a first-person
narrative may be awkward. Or, if you are a spokesperson reporting
your company's corporate position on a particular topic, the story
should revolve around the corporation.

In that case, a story about the company is called for. The following template, which is called the Company Background Template,
can be used.

Company Background Template

The _____ first
came to our attention [date] _____(PAUSE [one
toe squeeze]). At that time the (*select one*) company / department /
agency / division was

_____
_____. For
example . . . (*PAUSE*) _____
_____
_____.
It was also necessary to (*PAUSE*) _____
_____

As a result (*PAUSE*) _____

_____

In addition (*PAUSE*) _____

_____

As a result (*PAUSE*) _____

_____

Today (*PAUSE*) . . . _____

_____

(*Squeeze . . . squeeze . . . squeeze . . . those toes.*)

Note: *In the following TalkPower templates, check to be sure that if you refer to something, you specifically reveal the name of whom or what you are talking about.*

Example of Company Background

Look for the words in **bold**. They indicate the transitional phrases in the template.

The *new Strips product for asset-backs* **first came to our attention** *about four months* **ago. At that time, the department was** *trying to maximize customers' returns on selling assets.* **For example,** *the Blue Company previously received ninety-nine dollars and fifty cents on their asset/loans when selling their assets. Now with the new Strips product, the customer receives ninety-nine dollars and seventy-five cents on asset sales. It was also* **necessary** *to have the cooperation of the customer so that we could have total access to his assets.* **In addition,** *we worked hand in hand with the customer for three months to receive the optimum price of ninety-nine seventy-five.* **As a result,** *the Blue Company has freed up capital and continues to provide more opportunities for small business to expand.* **Today,** *we advocate the use of Strips in asset-back structures to optimize returns for our clients.*

Historical Background

In the event that you do not wish to refer to yourself or your corporation, here is a third model to follow: the historical background. This is an excellent template for giving a talk to your department, group, or class about the history of the subject that you are discussing. Whichever model you employ, stay within your 150-word budget.

Historical Background Template

The history of _____

_____dates

back to _____

_____.

Originally (*PAUSE [one toe squeeze]*) _____

_____.

As time went on (*PAUSE*)_____

_____.

For example (*PAUSE*)_____

_____.

And so (*PAUSE*) _____

_____.

As a result (*PAUSE*) _____

_____.

Today (*PAUSE*) _____

_____.

(*Squeeze . . . squeeze . . . squeeze . . . those toes.*)

Note: *In the following TalkPower templates, check to be sure that if you refer to something, you specifically reveal the name of whom or what you are talking about.*

Example of Historical Background

The words in **bold** are the transitional phrases in the template.

The history of *the Coalition for Family Justice* **dates back to** *1988 when it was founded by Monica Getz in New York City.* **Originally,** *this organization grew out of the needs of a group of women who were experiencing frustration dealing with the legal system.* **As time went on,** *word about this informal organization spread, receiving local and national attention. Monthly meetings grew in size, help-line calls for assistance multiplied, and a small army of professionals volunteered their services.* **For example,** *family members became educated in regard to defending their rights, and they brought legal family issues to the attention of legislators and the media.* **And so,** *this small nonprofit organization became an important networking resource for thousands of families who could not afford costly legal fees and for those who had been impoverished by divorce and other domestic relations matters.* **As a result,** *the Coalition for Family Justice is now an important agent in the struggle for legal and judicial reform.* **Today,** *the Irvington, New York, headquarters serves as a national model and resource for new chapters across the country.*

Exercise: Presenting a Background

1. Take out the card on which you have previously written your joke or anecdote, your Topic Sentence, and your Message Sentence. Look it over.
2. Select a TalkPower template: personal, organizational, or historical. (Initially, I recommend that you use the Personal Template.)
3. Fill out the template completely. Remember to name names!

Rehearsal

1. Set up several chairs to represent your audience. Sit in your chair, holding a paperweight in one hand and your index card in the other hand.
2. Be aware that the right side of your body is perfectly balanced with the left side.

3. Do five belly breaths. Pull your belly in slowly as you exhale through the nose. Hold this for three counts, 1-2-3. Relax your abdominal muscles. Take a small breath, and do not move your chest. Repeat five times.

4. Say these sentences out loud, and do the corresponding action. *"I am sitting in my chair . . . I feel my body perfectly balanced . . . I feel my hands."* (Wait until you feel your hands.)
   "I drop my hands to my sides . . . (Let them hang.) I stand up slowly and take a small step and stop . . . I wait until I feel my hands . . . (Do you feel the inner click?) *"I walk slowly to the podium . . . I feel my hands . . . I turn around slowly . . . I face the audience . . . I stop . . . I stand with my feet comfortably apart . . . I feel my hands."*
   (You are now standing in front of your imaginary audience.)

5. Squeeze your toes slowly three times. Squeeze, release, squeeze, release, squeeze, release.

6. Give your introduction or joke and remember to say the first three words with a space between each word. PAUSE. (Squeeze your toes slowly three times. Squeeze, release, squeeze, release, squeeze, release.)

Note: *If you are not going to use an Introduction, then begin your talk with the Topic Sentence and pause between the first three words.*

7. **Topic Sentence:** *"Today I am going to talk about . . ."*
   (Squeeze . . . squeeze . . . squeeze . . . those toes.)

8. **Message Sentence:** *"I think that . . ."* etc.
   (Squeeze. . . squeeze . . . squeeze . . . those toes.)

9. **Background Section:** *"I first became . . ."* etc.
   (Remember to look up at the imaginary audience from time to time.) (Squeeze . . . squeeze . . . squeeze . . . those toes.)

10. Walk slowly back to your seat, saying out loud, *"I slowly walk back to my chair . . . I feel my hands."*

11. Sit down slowly and do five belly breaths. Take a moment to be aware of how you feel. **Repeat this entire exercise, this**

time without the paperweight. Try to feel the weight of your hands.

Toastmasters International

The wonderful thing about the TalkPower program is that you can practice and rehearse all of the training procedures at home as long as you need to. Once you feel up to making your public debut, we recommend joining a Toastmasters Club in your area. There you can practice your presentation skills in a supportive environment.

Toastmasters International is a nonprofit organization dedicated to promoting the art of public speaking. Ralph C. Smedley founded Toastmasters in Santa Ana, California, in 1924. Ralph was the director of the YMCA in Santa Ana, and he decided that the young members needed training in public speaking. At that time, the business style of presentation was extremely stilted and formal. He took it upon himself to introduce a new, informal, and conversational style of public speaking—more interesting to an audience and more fun to deliver.

As time went by, more and more people attended his classes. Eventually clubs were formed in other cities and countries, evolving into the hugely popular organization known as Toastmasters International located in Englewood, Colorado. With a worldwide membership of over 180,000 members, You realize of course that there are many more than 180,000 people worldwide who would benefit from membership in a Toastmasters Club. I will give you one guess as to why Toastmasters does not have one billion people in their membership . . .

That's right: fear of speaking in public!

Once you have done some serious TalkPower practicing, you too will want to join this extremely friendly and supportive organization, finding a club right in your own neighborhood. Many businesses sponsor a chapter; so check to see if yours does. You will make new friends, have a chance to network, practice your Talk-Power skills, and have a wonderful time, week after week, as your public speaking skills flourish and grow.

Many Toastmasters are TalkPower graduates. We are pleased and proud to refer our students to this wonderful organization.

Progress Report

Date	Time	Strong Spot	Weak Spot	Comment	Calm/Nervous (1-10)

Chapter 11

THE MENU, POINT
SECTION, AND CLIMAX

Can We Talk?

*If you have an important point to make, don't try to be subtle
or clever. Use a pile driver. Hit the point once. Then come back
and hit it again. Then hit it a third time. A tremendous whack!*
— Winston Churchill

Anita M. is a psychologist at a famous clinic. She and a colleague
were planning to give a series of workshops on communication
skills for enhancing relationships, a subject that Anita specializes in.

Anita contacted me after the first workshop. Her presentation
had been a total failure. She felt embarrassed, and even though she
had committed herself to doing it again, she did not want to continue. Although Anita had planned to use her research in addition to
her collection of clinical case histories—all of which made sense to
her, when she actually gave her presentation, she felt as if she were
going around in circles. Her talk was unfocused, the facts were not
well integrated, and the audience seemed confused. What had gone
wrong? How could we sort out Anita's difficulty?

If we look at Anita's speech in terms of the TalkPower Action Formula, we will discover that although she knew what she wanted to say, her talk was disorganized. Jumping back and forth from theory to case history, there was no logical way to follow all of the material she presented.

What Anita needed was a step-by-step plan for organizing her information into a meaningful talk. She had to learn how to break down her talk into a logical process of reasoning that advanced the progression of her ideas. The Menu Section in the TalkPower Action Formula showed her how to do this.

The Menu

In the TalkPower Action Formula, the Menu Section is the fifth part of your speech. It follows the Background Section. The purpose of the Menu is to give you a method for organizing your information and to give your audience an overall preview of your talk. This Menu is like the table of contents in a book. A Menu is developed by breaking down the topic of your talk into segments called *points*. Each point is then fully developed in the Point Section so that you have a cohesive and logical presentation. This may sound complicated. If you take it step by step you will see how simple and helpful this system is.

Beginning	1) Introductory Paragraph
(Introductory Section)	2) Topic Sentence
	3) Message Sentence
	4) Background
Middle	5) **MENU**
	6) Point Section
	Point A
	Point B
	Point C
	Point D
	7) Climax
End	8) Conclusion

Sample

Let us see how a menu is created, using a topic that was prepared by a student at Hunter College, City University of New York and created in the early 2000s. (In this example, we are leaving out the background section.)

Introduction: In 1899, Charles Duell, the Director of the US Patent Office said, "Everything that can be invented has been invented." *(PAUSE)*

Topic Sentence: Today I am going to talk about how the Internet has changed my life. *(PAUSE)*

Message Sentence: I believe that through the Internet, the world has become more accessible to me. *(PAUSE)*

Menu: In my talk about the Internet, the five topics that I will discuss are:

The intricacies of social media
Buying the latest MP3s
Making new friends online
Great deals on vacation flights
Access to concert tickets

Note: *In this example we are using five items to show you what a menu looks like. A menu can have from two to seven items.*

Brainstorming for the Menu

The question arises: how did the speaker choose these five points? After all, there are literally dozens of different issues that might have been chosen. The answer lies in first using a technique for collecting creative and interesting ideas. This method is called brainstorming.

Brainstorming is a process for coming up with ideas as freely and as quickly as possible in a given time frame, without passing judgment or rejecting any of them.

Remember the sample Topic Sentence on the previous page: "Today I am going to talk about how the Internet has changed my life." Below is a list of possible items that the student came up with in a brainstorming session, using life with the Internet as a spin-off point. Notice how short each point is. Notice that they are not complete sentences, but resemble items in a table of contents.

Ideas from Brainstorming Session
    E-mail
    Access to concert tickets
    The intricacies of social media
    Buying gifts
    Shopping for clothes
    Buying the latest MP3s
    Great deals on vacation flights
    Best prices on household items
    Great value at on line auctions
    Making new friends online
    Finding exotic trends from abroad
    Film and music reviews
    Downloading software and games
    Internet access to short films
    Learning coding
    Designing your own start-up
    The latest news in health
    Online banking
    Research information
    Sharing files with friends

Creating a Menu
By a process of elimination, the menu is created by selecting those
items from your brainstorming list that you wish to develop in the
Point Section. The following example will show how a menu was
created from the previous brainstorming list. *The Point Section will
be discussed later in this chapter.*

Topic Sentence: Today I am going to talk about how the Internet
has changed my life. *(PAUSE)*

Message Sentence: I believe that through the Internet, the world
has become more accessible to me.

Menu: In my talk about the Internet, the five items that I will
discuss are:
    Discounts on required reading texts
    Buying the latest music
    Making new friends online

Great deals on vacation flights
Access to concert tickets

Exercise: Creating a Menu

1) Take out the card where you have previously written your Topic Sentence.
2) Write the Topic Sentence again on the top of a new sheet of paper.
3) Circle the subject of your Topic Sentence.
4) Set your kitchen timer to five minutes.
5) Now do a brainstorming exercise on the subject to create your own list.

_____

_____

_____

_____

The Menu List

6) Now select five items from your brainstorming list. These items will become your menu.
7) Stack the items from the least important to the most important.

Introducing the Menu

The Menu follows your Background section. After you have presented your Background Section, do three toe squeezes, and introduce the Menu with this transitional phrase:

"*In my talk about* (topic) _____ *the five items I will discuss include . . .* or *the five things that I will talk about include . . .* etc.

- • _____
- • _____
- • _____
- • _____

And finally,

- • _____ "

The menu list should be crisp and clear, like chapter headings in a table of contents. When presenting the Menu Section of your speech, do not use numbers such as "the first," "the second," or one, two, three. Silence with a slow squeeze of the toes between each point is all you need for a proper pause.

Before you give the last point, say, "And finally. . ."

These five points constitute the Menu Section. In the next step, we will take each item in this Menu and develop it as fully as possible.

Note: *If you do not wish to take questions during your talk, inform your audience after the last item in your Menu "At the end of my talk we will have a question-and-answer segment. At that time I will be happy to answer your questions."*

Chunking

In the future, when selecting the points for your Menu, do not exceed seven items, including your Climax, no matter how long your speech is. This is not an arbitrary number. It is based on the number of categories that the human brain can absorb at a given time. As Peter Russell writes in *The Brain Book*, immediate memory is limited to about seven chunks of information: "Most people can remember about seven numbers in a row, seven colors, seven shapes, or seven of any other item." If you have more than seven points that you wish to use, I suggest that you chunk them together into complementary headings.

The Point Section

The Point Section is the sixth part of the TalkPower Action Formula. It follows the Menu and is the place where you will develop each one of the items on your Menu.

Beginning	1) Introductory Paragraph
(Introductory Section)	2) Topic Sentence
	3) Message Sentence
	4) Background

Middle	5) Menu
	6) **POINT SECTION**
	Point A
	Point B
	Point C
	Point D
	7) Climax
End	8) Conclusion

Making a Word Budget

If you had to speak for twenty minutes, at 150 words per minute, that would give you about three thousand words. Now take away about two hundred words for your Introduction, Topic, and Message Sentences. That leaves you 2,800 words. Next, subtract the time you will need for your pauses (three toe squeezes between each section plus one toe squeeze between each item in your Menu, which comes to about two minutes). That leaves you a word budget of about 2,500 words. In each point you can use as many words as you like, as long as you do not exceed the total word budget of about 2,500 words.

Templates That End Writer's Block

Now you are ready to flesh out the points in your Menu. To help you do this, I have designed a series of templates to provide support for your thinking and writing process.

Templates are thinking guides for organizing materials into a narrative or story pattern. A story is a framework for information. It helps us to remember discrete facts that we would not normally be able to remember. In the TalkPower system, the templates are made up of transitional phrases that help you arrange your information in each section of your talk in a logical and interesting way. Each template serves as a container for each point on your Menu. These templates are similar to the Background Template. The only difference is that, whereas the Background allows only a limited number of words (about 150), each point can hold an unlimited number of words depending upon your word budget.

This is a very convenient way to organize your material. Each template has its own set of transitional phrases that initiate new ideas and keep you from getting bogged down in detail or suffering from the writer's block that a blank page can trigger. Although each template, as given here in the book, accommodates only about 150 words, you can add as much information as you wish in each one, as long as you adhere to your time limit.

Sample

The following point section, written by Andrea Siegel, author of *Open and Clothed*, for an author's talk she gave at Barnes & Noble, illustrates the use of *Sample Template A*. Look for the words in **bold**, which indicate the transitional phrases taken from this template. If you look carefully, you will notice that Andrea slightly changed the order of the transitional phrases so that they would work for her particular needs.

I had the opportunity *to be interviewed by Trish Hall of the* New York Times *last June.* **At that time** *I was beginning to research my family history.* **It was very interesting to note** *that the article that followed mentioned in passing that Sam Klein, the founder of* S. Klein, *was my great-grandfather. Several women who had worked for him in the 1930s contacted me to tell me their stories.*

For example, *one woman I spoke with was 103. She worked in the mending room fixing damaged clothes. She mentioned how much she enjoyed the annual employee picnics. They went out on a boat on a Sunday to spend the day together.* **Also,** *Eve Finklestein, who was 83, phoned to tell me that in the 1930s when she was in high school, she needed a job, saw an ad in the paper that Klein's was hiring, and went down to the store with her friend Marion to try to get a job. She said to me, "This was in 1932, right after the Depression and I was hired at $8 a week." Eve continued to work in the store for years and eventually worked in the executive offices.*

What I learned from *hearing Eve talk about my great-grand-father was that his idea of beauty did not necessarily conform to* *the societal ideals. Perhaps because of this, his business, which was dressing women in every size, thrived.* **Previously, I had thought that** *my feelings of benevolent love toward dressing all sorts of shapes and sizes of women was my own invention. And my emphasis on this in my book,* Open and Clothed, *was unique.*

And so, *I learned that I come from a family with a history of joyful appreciation of dressing all shapes and sizes of people. And perhaps some of my ideas did not come whole cloth from this noggin.* **My advice to anyone thinking about** *their own life and work is to look at your family history if you want to understand where your values may have originated.*

This is the Template that Andrea used to develop her point. As I mentioned before, Andrea slightly changed the order, which is perfectly fine thing to do if it will improve your talk.

Template A

I had the opportunity to_____

_____

_____ *(state when)* _____.

At that time *(PAUSE)* _____

_____

_____.

It was very interesting to note that _____

_____

_____.

For example, *(PAUSE)* _____

_____

_____.

Also *(PAUSE)* _____

_____

_____.

My advice to anyone thinking about _____

_____

_____.

What I learned from this experience is _____

_____

_____.

Previously *(PAUSE)* _____

_____

_____.

And so, *(PAUSE)* _____

_____

_____.

Additional Templates

On the following pages you will see a variety of template models. Each template can be used to develop one of your points, just as you did with the template in the Background Section. Included are two sales templates and a company policy template.

The purpose of the templates is to give you a structure for the beginning, middle, and end of each point. They are not meant to write your entire speech for you.

This means that although each point template is designed to hold 150 words, you may add as much information as you wish, stretching the borders of each template to accommodate your material. The number of words in each template will depend on the amount of time you have for your talk.

For example, at 150 words per minute, if you have five minutes of information for a point about designing your own website, you can use any one of the point templates, adding as much material as you wish so that it accommodates your entire five-minute point. Using the last transitional phrase in the template for the final words of your point will polish and complete your point in an elegant manner. The templates are enormously helpful for keeping all related material in the same group.

If you wish to change a transitional phrase, please feel free to do so. Also, you may mix and match, or combine templates, if that works well for your talk.

The following is the only Template that has the Message Sentence built into it.

Template B

I believe (*repeat Message Sentence*)_____
_____.

Because *(PAUSE)* _____.
_____.

It is important to understand _____
_____.

And so, *(PAUSE)* _____
_____.

For example, *(PAUSE)* _____
_____.

Frequently *(PAUSE)* _____.

In addition, *(PAUSE)* _____
_____.

As a result *(PAUSE)* _____
_____.

Therefore, we feel _____
_____.

Template C

(*Select one*) The significance of / the importance of (*put in point*)
_____
_____.

has recently become more evident because _____.
_____.

As a result *(PAUSE)* _____

For example, *(PAUSE)* _____

_____

Our *(select one)* position / objective / suggestion / recommendation is:

_____

Frequently *(PAUSE)* _____

_____

For example, *(PAUSE)* _____

_____

This leads to _____

_____

Therefore, I / we *(select one)* feel _____

_____

Template D
It is difficult to imagine _____

_____,

but _____

_____

For example, *(PAUSE)* _____

_____

There remains hope that _____

_____

It is a hope voiced by _____

_____

In fact, *(PAUSE)* _____

_____

Other factors _____
_____
_____.

Still, it is probably true _____
_____
_____.

The fact is that _____
_____
_____.

Finally, *(PAUSE)* _____
_____
_____.

Template E
In any discussion that deals with *(point)* _____
_____,
it is important to note that _____
_____.

Studies tell us / Experience tells us _____
_____
_____
_____.

Furthermore, *(PAUSE)* _____
_____
_____
_____.

This leads us to believe _____
_____.

For example, *(PAUSE)* _____
_____
_____.

Also, *(PAUSE)* _____
_____
_____.

My advice to anyone thinking about _____

_____

_____.

What I learned from this experience is _____

_____.

Previously *(PAUSE)* _____

_____

_____.

And so *(PAUSE)* _____

_____.

If _____

_____.

Template F
Trying to _____

_____,

can be one of the most _____

_____.

I realized this when I was *(state when in time)*_____

_____

_____

_____.

It never occurred to me that _____

_____

_____.

For example, *(PAUSE)* _____

_____

_____.

And so I had to_____

_____

_____.

Also, *(PAUSE)* _____

_____

_____.

It occurred to me that _____

_____

_____.

Finally, *(PAUSE)* I _____

_____

_____.

This resulted in _____

_____

_____.

Today *(PAUSE)* I am *(select one)* happy/glad/sad/thrilled to say that

_____.

Sales Template 1

The most important feature of this product/service/process/instru-
ment/other *(select one)* is _____

_____

_____.

Compare this to other _____

_____

_____.

For example, *(PAUSE)* we have/had a *(select one)* client/customer/
vendor/manufacturer/dealer/distributor/other who needed/wanted/
had to/didn't _____

_____

_____.

We were able to _____

_____

_____.

As a result, *(PAUSE)* _____

_____

_____

_____.

So, *(PAUSE)* if you _____

_____

_____.

You can rest assured that _____
_____
_____ .

Sales Template II
Another example that illustrates our consistent effort to _____
_____
_____ ,

deals with _____
_____
_____ .

In this instance *PAUSE)* _____
_____
_____ .

For example, *(PAUSE)* _____
_____
_____ .

The client _____
_____
_____ .

Our response was to _____
_____
_____ .

And so *(PAUSE)* _____
_____
_____ .

Of course we _____
_____
_____ .

In addition *(PAUSE)* _____
_____
_____ .

Keep in mind the fact that _____
_____
_____ .

Organizational Policy Template

Several weeks/months/days/years ago _____
_____
_____.

The _____
announced that _____
_____.

This caused _____
_____
_____.

In addition *(PAUSE)* _____
had to _____
_____
_____
_____.

As a result, *(PAUSE)* _____
_____
_____.

At the heart of this matter *(PAUSE)* _____
_____
_____.

As we move toward resolution *(PAUSE)* _____
(company name) *(PAUSE)* is committed to _____
_____
_____
_____.

We are proud _____
_____
_____.

The Message Statement

Each time you introduce a new point or category to the audience,
you must restate the original Message Sentence somewhere within

that point. This restated sentence is then called the Message Statement. It reiterates the theme of your talk—the central message that
will motivate your audience to act on your recommendation. It is the
connecting link that joins the various points of your talk.

Inserting your Message Statement into each one of your points is
the final step in writing the point section of your speech. It should be
done each time one of your points is fully developed.

Note: *In Template B, the Message Statement* "I believe that . . ."
*is a transitional phrase that is already built into the structure of the
template. This is the only template that has a specific place for your
message.*

The points in your speech follow one after the other, with a silent
pause in between, in the same order as the points in your Menu.
Remember to squeeze three times with the toes before you begin
each new point.

Rules for Using the Templates

1. When you have completed writing a point, go back and look
    at your Message Sentence. Then find a place within the point
    where you can restate the Message Sentence. You may use
    the same words or other words that have the same meaning,
    but each point must contain some reference to your Message
    Sentence. This new sentence is called the Message Statement.

2. If a transitional phrase in any one of the templates does not
    work well for you, feel free to substitute your own transitional
    phrase.

3. Once you have used a template in your point section, you
    may use it again in the same speech with new information.
    For example, if you use Template C for the first five minutes
    in a twenty-minute presentation, and you use Template D for
    the second point, you can use Template C again for the third
    or fourth point, with different material, of course.

4. Not only can you use the selection of point templates to
    develop your point section, but you can go back and use any
    of the background templates: Personal, Organizational, or
    Historical as a template in the Point Section. This applies,

even though you have used one of them already in the Background Section.

5. Once you use the Background Template as a point template, you do not have to adhere to the 150-word minimum. The word count, in that case, is unlimited, just as it is in all the other point templates. Your word count is determined by your time limitation.

6. Any one of the background templates may also be used more than once in the Point Section, but the rules are the same as stated in Number 1.

7. If you have prepared a twenty-five minute talk, and just before it your boss tells you that you can only talk for eighteen minutes, drop one or two of your least important points and no one will be the wiser.

8. When your speech is complete, organize your points from the least important to the most important, with a pause of three toe squeezes between each one.

Pausing as a Transitional Bridge

The pause is an extremely important means of communication between people.

—Constantin Stanislavski

Traditional public speaking methods utilize transitional phrases called bridges to move on to new ideas. For example:

This leads me to my next point . . .

Following this discussion, I will introduce . . .

And now the time has come to tell you about . . .

I will now discuss . . .

It is not necessary to connect points to one another with these bridges. Ideas need the space that pauses provide. Ideas need time to be absorbed by the consciousness of the audience.

Instead, use a simple pause of three seconds to make a real transition. This pause can be timed correctly if you squeeze your toes three times as described earlier in this book. Silence is the real transition that creates the dynamic excitement of a well-developed speech. Your audience is perfectly able to follow you if the transition is logical. You do not need to hold their hands as you shift from one topic to another.

Sample

In the following example written with a template by a TalkPower student, you will see what one fully developed point looks like. Look for the words in **bold** that indicate the transitional phrases of the template; in this case, *Template F.*

Note: *The topic and message sentences are included to give you some orientation to the point.*

Topic Sentence: *Today I am going to talk about planning a wedding.*

Message Sentence: *I believe that planning a wedding need not be a stressful experience.*

Background . . .

Menu: *The five items that I will discuss are:*

Choosing a type of wedding

Keeping costs down

Planning a ceremony

Planning a reception

Making sure no one's feelings get hurt

Point 2: *Keeping costs down*

Trying to *keep costs down while planning a wedding can be an overwhelming experience. It's right up there with buying a house or planning a family.* **I realized this** *last June* **when I was** *looking for a place to hold our reception.* **It never occurred to me that** *all of the little extras that create atmosphere are never included.* **For example,** *at one catering hall I was shown an ice sculpture in the shape of a wine rack with bottles in it, priced at eight hundred dollars. This was very expensive frozen water.* **And so,** *instead of focusing on the little extras, I found a place called Gando's, with such a beautiful view of Manhattan that things like ice sculptures were not necessary.*

Keeping in mind that all of the little things really add up: a thou-sand dollars here, five hundred dollars there, **it occurred to me** *that maybe charging people to come would not be a bad idea. I really needed to look more closely at what we were spending.* **Finally, I made a list of our actual budget, including items such as the caterer, the florist, and the band.** **This resulted in** *tremendous relief when it came time to sign a contract because I knew how much we could spend.* **Today I am happy** *that we stayed within our budget because . . .* (Message Statement): **It made our preparation as stress-free as possible.**

Message Statement

No matter what the point is about, the Message Statement must always appear in some part of the point. In other words, if your point is about keeping costs down, and your Message Sentence says, "I believe that planning a wedding need not be stressful," then there must be one sentence in your point where you say something about the relationship between keeping costs down and keeping stress down. (See example of how a Message Sentence was used on page 182.)

Exercise: How to Connect Your Message Sentence to a Point

Choosing one point from your menu list, pick a template and develop that point within the template. Select any one you like. When you have completed this exercise, you should have a Topic Sentence, a Message, a Menu, and one of your points from the Menu fully written out in a template.

1. Take your card with the fully developed point written on it (150 words or more) and read it over carefully. Now go back to your Message Sentence and read that again.
2. Look for a place where you can insert the Message Sentence so that it makes sense. You may use the same words, or different words, as long as you retain the meaning of the Message Sentence.
3. Insert your Message Sentence so that it reads well and blends in with the rest of the information.

Sample Speech

The following example shows how Ann B., one of my students, developed a point for a talk about downsizing. I am including the topic, message, background, and menu sections so that you can see how they all work together. Notice how the transitional phrases, in **bold** type, promote the flow of information. (Squeeze . . . squeeze . . . squeeze . . . those toes.)

Topic: *Today . . . I am going to talk about . . . downsizing in corporate America.* (Squeeze . . . squeeze . . . squeeze . . . those toes.)

Message: *I think . . . downsizing must be done in a way that minimizes adverse reactions.* (Squeeze . . . squeeze . . . squeeze . . . those toes.)

Background: I first became involved *with downsizing in an organization about six years ago.* **At that time** *I was consulting to a management team in their efforts to reduce operating costs by five million dollars—a mandate they had received from their upper management, because of delayed new product introductions. . . .* **I was aware that** *they were planning to eliminate staff as part of their budget-reduction process since salaries and benefits represented a significant portion of their overhead.* **For example,** *the average senior professional earned, with benefits, one hundred fifty thousand dollars a year; the typical middle manager, two hundred thousand dollars a year;* **and so** *I worked with them to identify fifteen positions out of three hundred that, if eliminated, would amount to more than fifty percent of their budget reductions. I also worked with them on ways to achieve the remaining budget reductions.* **As a result,** *the recommendations were presented to, and accepted by, their upper management . . . and quickly implemented. However, for that organization, a staff cut of five percent to save more than two million dollars, ended in costing them much more because of the chaos that followed.* **Today,** *I realize that the implications of downsizing in corporate America must be thoughtfully planned and implemented, if the very life of an organization is to be maintained.*

(Squeeze . . . squeeze . . . squeeze . . . those toes.)

Menu: *The five items that I am going to discuss about downsizing in corporate America are:*

The philosophy of downsizing in an organization
The actual selection process; how to approach it
Planning support activities for laid-off employees
Dealing with the feelings of survivors
And finally, the most critical element, rebuilding the organiza-
tion. (Squeeze . . . squeeze . . . squeeze . . . those toes.)

Point: (For this point, the student used Template E.)

In any discussion that deals with *downsizing,* **it's important to
note** *that the implications of downsizing or layoffs do not conclude
with the actual departure of the staff. Rather, this is the time when
they start . . . .*

(Restatement of the Message Sentence): **For example,** *failure on
the part of management to acknowledge the need for, and actually plan out, a rebuilding process for survivors will compound the
trauma of the event.*

Studies *done in organizations that had a well thought out rebuilding process showed that they returned to . . . at least the same, if not
higher levels of productivity far more quickly than those who either
ignored or insufficiently focused on this issue.* **Furthermore,** *these
organizations attended to the physical environment—quickly clean-
ing up impacted work areas.* **This leads us to believe** *that they were
concerned with the feelings of survivors.* **For example,** *they created
forums for them to express and cope with their feelings. They also
reviewed all projects and subsequently got rid of all noncritical
work. Critics raised the question of the long-range viability of the
organization. The company responded by increasing communications between and across groups, thereby addressing the employees'
questions—whether stated or silent.*

Here you see an excellent example of how Template E on page
175 was used to develop a point. This piece is brief, well edited, logical, and it covers the item in the menu: "Rebuilding the Organization." In an actual talk outside the workshop, if the student had a
longer time allotment, she could have included many more pieces of
information and research relating to that point within the structure
of the same template.

Restatement of the Message Sentence

If you look back to the beginning of this student's point, you will see that the original Message Sentence was: "I think downsizing must be done in a way that minimizes adverse reactions." Can you see how the restatement of the Message Sentence echoes the original statement?

"For example, failure on the part of management to acknowledge the need for, and actually plan out a rebuilding process for survivors, will compound the trauma of the event."

This Bears Repeating

Because the Message Statement is a major theme and is stated in each one of your points, your Message Sentence must be limited to one idea. For example, one of my students was preparing a sales presentation for her agency. Her Message Sentence was: "The most important thing about selling is the ability to listen, and to have a proactive follow-up plan."

When it came to developing the body of her speech, she ran into problems. On one hand, her organizing principle was the ability to listen. On the other hand, her organizing principle was proactive follow-up. Which was the major theme? She had to choose one idea. Her choice: the ability to listen is the most important element of selling. Only after she made this choice did her thinking become clear.

Completing Your Points

1. Go back to your Menu. Working on one point at a time, fill out a different template for each one. Include your Message Sentence in each point.

2. If you cannot find a place in the point where your Message Sentence belongs, it means that you have strayed too far away from your topic. In this case, scrap the point, go back to your Menu, and work on another point that relates to your topic.

Again, the most profound transitions always happen in a state of silence. This means that if you squeeze your toes three times, there will be a natural shift from your last point to the next new idea. The audience will follow you. The feeling of continuity comes from the repetition or restatement of the Message Sentence in each point.

Putting Your Points in Order

When you have finished developing each of your points in turn, gather all of your papers or cards together and read them through. Make certain that they are arranged in a dynamic order, from least exciting to most exciting, and number them from 1 to 5. Now you are ready for a rehearsal.

When you rehearse your speech, you will need to pause with three toe squeezes between each point. Remember to insert this pause at the end of each point. Write *"PAUSE . . . squeeze . . . squeeze . . . squeeze"* in big letters on your card.

Pre-Talk Routine (Transitional Mantra)

The setup here will be several chairs and a designated podium. Put a sheet of paper on the floor where you will be standing. If you wish to use a podium, use a music stand (if you have one) or invert an empty wastepaper basket on a table or a desk and use that as a podium. Now you are ready to work without the paperweights.

1. Sit in a chair holding your speech in one hand, palms up and relaxed in your lap.
2. Do five belly breaths. (Pull your belly in. Exhale through your nose. Hold it to the count of three. Relax your stomach muscles. Do not move your chest.) Repeat five times, and count each inhalation and exhalation set as one count.
3. Say out loud, *"I am sitting in my chair . . . I feel my body perfectly balanced."* (Feel your balance.)
4. Say, *"I feel my hands."* (Feel the weight of your hands as you lift them off your lap no more than one inch. Wait until you feel your hands. Do you feel the inner click?)
5. Say, *"I slowly drop my hands to my sides."* (Let them hang.)

6. Say, "*I get up slowly . . . I take a small step and stop . . . I wait until I feel my hands.*" (Get up and take a tiny step, no more than three inches in front of your chair.)

7. Say, "*I walk slowly to the podium . . . I feel my hands.*" (Take as many steps as you need to get to the designated podium. Feel your hands at all times.)

    Say, "*I turn around slowly . . . I face the audience . . . I stop.*"

    Say, "*I look straight ahead . . . I stand with my feet comfortably apart.*" Say, "*I feel my hands.*" (Squeeze . . . squeeze . . . squeeze.)

8. At this point you are facing your imaginary audience. Run through your entire presentation, remembering to squeeze three times with the toes after every section and point. Remember to look up at your imaginary audience from time to time.

9. When you finish the last word of your speech, squeeze three times and say, "*Thank you.*"

10. Then, "*I walk slowly back to my chair . . . I feel my hands.*"

11. Sit down. Do five belly breaths. Be aware of how you feel.

Repeat this entire rehearsal. Try to be aware of the feeling of the weight of your hands.

The Climax: Your Last Point

Beginning	1) Introductory Paragraph
(Introductory Section)	2) Topic Sentence
	3) Message Sentence
	4) Background
Middle	5) Menu
	6) Point Section
	Point A
	Point B

	Point C
	Point D
	7) **CLIMAX** (the last point)
End	8) Conclusion

The last point in your Menu is called the Climax. It follows the rules of all the other points, and precedes the Conclusion. Since this is your final chance to get through to your audience, to convince or persuade them, it is your last opportunity to voice your message sentence to support your intentions. I call this last point the Climax because it is the high point of your speech.

A Talk in Three Acts

The dynamic structure of the TalkPower Action Formula is modeled after a traditional three-act play. The first act of the play introduces the characters and the plot conflict, the second act develops the story up to the climax or the high point (called the cliff hanger), and the third act resolves the conflict and brings the play to an ending. Since the climax/high point of a three-act play usually falls at the end of the second act, the high point of your talk should be at the end of your point section. In other words, your last point should be the high point of your speech, not the conclusion.

Example of a Fully Developed Climax Template

Next is an example of a Climax. You can see from the descriptive language and the positive suggestions how this Climax would persuade people to consider vacationing at the retreat. This example is based on Template A. Using approximately 150 words, it is a good illustration of how you can use the templates for sales presentations.

(Look for the words in **bold**. They indicate the transitional phrases of the template.)

Topic: *Today I am going to talk about the Sivananda Yoga Retreat.* (PAUSE) **Message:** *I believe that the Sivananda Yoga Retreat in the Bahamas offers a great opportunity to vacation in a* *spiritual community.* (PAUSE) **Point in Menu:** *The Healing Quality of Sivananda.*

Climax

I first had the opportunity *to experience the healing quality of the Sivananda Yoga Retreat* **about** *fourteen years ago.* **At that time** *I had never meditated or done yoga and was looking for a way to begin a regular spiritual practice. Previously, I had experienced off-again-on-again attempts to find a connection with a higher power.*

Before I left, I must admit that I was concerned that I might find a group of people who were very different from me. To the contrary, **it was very interesting to note that most of the** *guests were professionals, artists, entertainers, therapists . . . all looking for the same thing.*

For example, *the young woman who shared the charming beach hut with me was an economist from Virginia, now working in Poland. Her mother, who had chosen to take a room by herself, was a psychoanalyst and had been coming to the retreat for many years.* **Also,** *the ecumenical nature of the retreat (it was Christmas when I first went) offered Christmas, Hanukkah, and Hindu celebrations.*

What I learned from this experience *is that no matter how old you are, you can do yoga and learn to meditate at your own pace. The beginners' yoga teacher was a seventy-five-year-old man named Irving Fingerhut. Since World War II, he had been crippled as a result of a horrible airplane accident, in which he broke every bone in his body. After nine years of lying on a gurney, through intensive yoga, he totally regained his physical health and could do the most amazing postures. As an expert in bad back problems, Irving continued teaching until he passed away at eighty-five years of age.*

Previously, *I had vacationed at manicured resorts or traveled to Europe, and although those vacations were restful and interesting, they could not compare to the feeling of well-being and healthfulness I experienced when I came home from Sivananda.* **And so,** *each year for the past fourteen years, I return faithfully to the Sivananda* *yoga retreat in the Bahamas, either at Christmas and Hanukkah, or Easter and Passover for my yearly mental, physical, and spiritual rehabilitation. My quality of life has been inordinately improved by the gift of Sivananda.*

My advice *to anyone interested in going to a spiritual retreat is to start with Sivananda in the Bahamas—delicious vegetarian food including exotic Indian dishes, heavenly weather, beautiful beaches, and wonderful people who are attracted to the spiritual values that Sivananda offers. Bring your suntan lotion, but leave your cigarettes, alcohol, and caffeine at home!*

Strengthening the Climax

Go back to your speech and look at your five points. Take your last point and dress it up, dramatizing it so that it becomes even more exciting. This can be done by using dramatic language, visually colorful descriptions, active verbs, or a dramatic story. If you feel your last point is just not salvageable as an exciting climax, then substitute a new point, either an anecdote or a piece of information that can serve as the high point of your talk. Be sure that your Message Statement is included in your Climax and that you write *"REST PERIOD—SQUEEZE THREE TIMES WITH THE TOES"* at the end of the point.

Now you are ready for a full rehearsal. Turn to page 187 and do a complete rehearsal. Notice how the frequent rehearsals give you a feeling of confidence and comfort when you stand up and speak. In addition, as the material becomes more familiar to you, you will not need to look at your notes so often.

Using Newspaper and Magazine Articles for Your Climax

Example A: News about a Scientific Discovery

Here is an example of an excerpt from an article in the *New York Times* used as a Climax in a speech about the controversy surrounding funding our space program.

Topic Sentence: *Today I am going to talk about the controversy surrounding the funding of our space program.*

Message Sentence: *I believe that funding space programs is vitally important for ensuring our superiority in the race to conquer space.*

Climax: *A recent* New York Times *article tells us that the latest detection made this month by American astronomers is of a planet about twice the mass of Jupiter that is orbiting the star, Gliese 876, one of the sun's nearest neighbors, at a distance of only fifteen light years. The discovery of Gliese 876 adds another element of surprise and surmise to the continuing quest for other planetary systems. The large object is orbiting a small star, a red-dwarf class star less than one third the mass of the sun.*

Dr. Stephen P. Maran, an astronomer and spokesman for the American Astronomical Society, said this was one of the most significant discoveries since the first detection of planets around other stars, beginning in 1995. "If red dwarfs have planets, there must be a vast number of planets in the galaxy," he said. "It's also important because red dwarf stars have very long lives, which means more time for life to have a chance to evolve on any planets where conditions are favorable to life."

Message Statement: <u>*This discovery certainly points to the importance of continued support for our space program, if we wish to maintain a competitive edge.*</u>

Notice that in this short climax, only the article was used. If the student had more time, he could have included the article plus Template A, filling it out as indicated.

Example B: A Profile of a Famous Personality

Here is an example of another excerpt from an article in the *New York Times* used as a Climax in a speech about cultural values, featuring the singer Celia Cruz who passed away in 2003.

Topic Sentence: *Today I am going to talk about the significance of traditional art forms.*

Message Sentence: *I believe that honoring traditional art forms will create a line of cultural continuity for future generations. Quoting from the* New York Times:

Climax: *Many Americans have never heard of her, yet she has a nonstop schedule of sold-out concerts, a Grammy, and a street* *named after her in Miami. She speaks little English, but she has an honorary degree from Yale, a star on Hollywood Boulevard, and a medal from the National Endowment for the Arts. She is Celia Cruz, the Cuban-born salsa singer, whose inventive improvisation, intoxicating rhythms, and trademark shrieks of "Azucar" (sugar) have enchanted fans for half a century. Ms. Cruz, who sings only in Spanish, has never attempted to cultivate a non-Hispanic audience.* (**Message Sentence**) *<u>a testament to the profound gift of continuity Ms. Cruz' traditional music brings to new generations of the Hispanic population.</u> Ms. Cruz began singing full-time with Cuba's most popular orchestra, La Sonora Matancera, in 1950. On one endless bus tour after another, through big cities and small towns, Ms. Cruz began to cultivate her international public. Some seasons, she said, she gave five performances a day, every day. "But my voice never gave out," she added. "The more I sing, the better I get."*

Example C: An Anecdote of Dramatic Intensity

Here is an example of an anecdote used for a Climax in a speech about the importance of reporting suspected child abuse.

Topic Sentence: *Today I am going to talk about reporting suspected child abuse.*

Message Sentence: *I believe that all adults have a responsibility to report a suspected case of child abuse before it is too late.*

Climax: *Bob Gannon was a tough kid from a tough neighborhood. He joined the US Navy at seventeen, where he became involved in an amateur boxing program. Bob got married at twenty and stayed active in the Golden Gloves and other amateur boxing events. He had grown to five foot nine and 159 pounds. One particular night in May, 1998, Bob Gannon faced his antagonist and stepped forward. He threw two punches, the second of which landed on his rival's head. His opponent dropped, never to rise again. Bob's opponent, his eight-year-old son, was dead—another victim of child abuse.* (**Message Statement**) *<u>Surely this was not the first time that Bob Gannon had abused his son, and yet not one person came forward until it was too late.</u>*

Example D: A Quote from a Magazine Article

Here is an example of an excerpt of a *New York Magazine* article used for a Climax in a speech about alternative medicine.

Topic Sentence: *Today I am going to talk about the growing popularity of alternative medicine.*

Message Sentence: *I believe that it will not be long before alternative medicine enters the mainstream of medical practice.*

Climax: *Let me quote from a recent* New York Magazine *article. Two of the city's most prestigious institutions:* (**Message Statement**) *Beth Israel Medical Center, Columbia-Presbyterian Medical Center, have announced ambitious plans for integrative or complementary programs that promise to feature mind-body medicine. Although some doctors on staff are actively skeptical, an increasing number seem to be asking a different question altogether. "What took so long?" The medical world's reluctance to endorse these alternatives baffles some scientists. "It's considered radical to send someone to a modified Dean Ornish cardiac program," marvels Stephen Josephson, an assistant professor of psychology at Cornell Medical College, "but to crack their chest open, to do a bypass, that's considered conservative."*

The important thing here for all hospitals—and I think Beth Israel has realized it earlier in a more aggressive way—is that these services are going to be driven by the consumer, the patient, asserts Beth Israel trustee William Sarnoff, former chairman of Warner Publishing. "They're going to demand it, as time goes by, because it does work."

Progress Report

Date	Time	Strong Spot	Weak Spot	Comment	Calm/Nervous (1-10)

Chapter 12

THE Q&A

The Audience Has a Turn

I have the answer. What was the question?

—Gertrude Stein

After years of critiquing speakers, including excellent and fearless ones, I realize that the real conclusion to most speeches happens not when the speaker makes her concluding remarks, but when the Q&A is over.

In the final moments that follow the answer to the last question, when the speaker, slightly dazed from the energetic give-and-take of the Q&A, mumbles her farewell, moving away from the podium, she is relieved—the ordeal is over. This type of exit is so abrupt, so lacking in style that I have often said to myself, "There must be a more elegant way to depart, more fitting for the role of leadership." There is! I suggest that instead of asking for questions after the conclusion, you do it before the conclusion.

Yes, you read that correctly! Do your Q&A before you do your conclusion. This gives you the last word, allowing you to regain any points you may have lost during the Q&A. Even if you were challenged by some members of the audience you still have another chance to voice your ideas during the conclusion. This is how.

Before I Conclude, Are There Any Questions?

1. Say the last words of your climax point. Squeeze your toes three times.
2. Say, "*Before I conclude, are there any questions?*"
3. Answer as many questions as you have time for.
4. Near the end of your Q&A time, say, "*We have time for one more question.*"
5. Answer the last question . . . Squeeze your toes three times.
6. Say, "*In conclusion . . .*"
7. Do your conclusion.
8. Say, "*Thank you.*"
9. Squeeze your toes three times.
10. Walk back to your seat with style and confidence, saying to yourself, "*I slowly walk back to my seat . . . I feel my hands.*"
11. Sit down . . . Do ten belly breaths (reenter the group).

The Real Purpose of the Q&A

The purpose of a question and answer segment is to add variety to your presentation by giving members of the audience a limited opportunity to participate. When responding to their questions, your objective is to project likability, present yourself and your point of view as calmly, smoothly, and credibly as possible, and hold on to your position of leadership.

Some participants of my TalkPower seminars feel more comfortable with the Q&A because it feels like a conversation and it gives them a chance to respond directly.

Yes, But . . .

The other seventy percent dread it. Here are the reasons:

"I will not know the answer and I will look foolish or stupid."

"I am afraid I will have thought-blocking and just stand there like an idiot."

"I will not be able to articulate a good answer on the spot."

"I will feel out of control."

"I am afraid that it will be a question that I will not want to answer."

"I am afraid that I will get a hostile question, and I will just shut down."

"I feel I will be exposed and everyone will realize how little I really know, and then they will know that I am not as smart as they think I am."

All of these responses speak to the past, when you had no tools to deal with your loss of confidence and fear. Using the TalkPower method to maintain concentration under fire will significantly change the way you handle questions in the future. In addition, the following discussion will help you through this very threatening and potentially dangerous section of your talk.

You're the Boss
Since this is your presentation, you make the rules. If possible, keep the following points in mind:

- Call on as many different people as possible.
- Limit each member of the audience to one question.
- Keep your answers brief. You don't have to tell everything you know. Choose one thing you wish to emphasize. (See pages 279-280 on thought-blocking during the Q&A.)
- Try not to get into a discussion with a member of the audience. If you do, the rest of the audience will be left out, and the discussion will become a personal conversation in public. The audience is watching you, so if this turns into a power struggle, you may lose your place as the leader.
- Remember, you don't have to come off as the most brilliant person in the universe; you just have to look calm, confident, and able to handle the situation like a leader.

Repeat the Question!
After you have heard the question, take your gaze away from the person asking the question and look directly at your audience. Repeat the question. Always. This is your most important survival technique for dealing with the Q&A because:

- It gives you time to think.
- It allows the audience to hear the question.
- It keeps the attention of the audience on you. When you repeat the question you make it your own by pulling the attention of the audience back to you. Also, by repeating the question—or restating the question in your own words—you can take the bite out of any attack.

Don't React—Repeat!!!

For the insecure speaker, each new question presents the threat of a partial or complete mental shutdown. Therefore, the most important reason for repeating the question is that, dynamically, it gives you time to recover from the shock of the unexpected question. When you absorb the brunt of a question, by repeating it, you create a buffer against the impulse to react immediately with an answer that you might regret. Repeating the question gives you the opportunity to recover your poise and avoid firing off a thoughtless response. Remember you don't want to react. You want to respond.

Just imagine if someone suddenly pushed you and you lost your footing. You could not properly respond to the push as long as you were off balance. Similarly, in the Q&A, a question, especially a hostile one, is experienced as a violent assault to your psyche. When you repeat the question, you regain your psychological footing and can respond from a position of balance. I cannot emphasize enough the importance of developing the habit of repeating the question. It sounds like a simple procedure, but the benefits are profound. There are several ways to repeat a question.

Example

Question: *How can you say that global warming is our most immediate environmental crisis, when destruction of the rain forests presents such a hazard for global equilibrium?*

Suggestions for repeating the question:

- "A question has been raised about the high priority that we give to global warming."

- "The question is: How can I say that global warming is our most immediate environmental crisis?"
- "Global warming as a priority."
- "A question about priorities."
- "Rain forests."

Even a brief response, as in the last example, will help you resist the impulse to react rather than give a thoughtful answer. This is important if you wish to project confidence, maintaining your image of leadership with a friendly, kind, and mature presence.

Repeating the question should become habitual behavior. If you do not cultivate this habit, it will be too late to answer effectively when a difficult, confrontational, or unexpected question suddenly appears.

Questions from Hell
Preparing properly for the Q&A can turn a walk in a mine field into an invigorating jog in a park. After you have finished working on your talk, list five to ten questions (especially the most difficult ones) that could possibly be asked; questions that might make you uncomfortable. Include questions such as:

- What question may prove embarrassing to you?
- What question do you know you do not have the answer to?
- What question refers to your weakest point?
- What question will bring up a past error or omission?

Now write out short, simple answers to each one. Concentrate on the questions that do not have good answers, like "Why did you lose the XYZ account?" When trying to answer these questions, your anxiety may prevent you from coming up with a good response. What to do?

Ask For Help
Call a colleague, your friend, ask your wife . . . what about that smart sister-in-law of yours—say, "How would you answer this

question?" Chances are that since they have no anxiety or investment here, someone will come up with a spin (creative interpretation or angle)—a new way of looking at the question—that sounds reasonable. What you need is an answer you can live with. Such as "Have you ever looked at this from a historical perspective? In 1933 the market was . . . Then in 1961 . . . but then in 1987 . . . And now . . ." Or, "Well, you know XYZ has had six different agencies working on that account in the last eight years. . ."

Remember, you don't need a great answer. There are no great answers for the "What about bankruptcy?" type of question. Still, you want to be prepared; you want to have an answer that will make you look and feel like a reasonably intelligent person.

When you get the answer from your friend or colleague, be sure to write it down. Make your answers short and clear, and then go to the next question. Finally, list your brief but satisfactory responses and rehearse them along with your presentation. Later, when that killer question comes up, you will be able to reply with confidence, thinking "I knew you would ask that question, and I just happen to have the answer."

There is No Such Thing as an Unanswerable Question

Richard B. spent a good deal of his time figuring out strategies to avoid making presentations. He dreaded the thought that he might be asked a question that would put him on the spot. In a private consultation, when I asked him what he was afraid of, he became extremely uncomfortable.

Realizing that this client needed a direct approach, I asked, "Richard, suppose you had complete control over all the questions? Which question would you not allow?"

"I certainly wouldn't want them to ask how far over budget we are," he replied. Now we had to work out an answer for this potential bear trap—an answer that would make sense to a critical audience. Richard contacted a colleague to ask for help. Once he had identified the specific source of his concern, he was able to deal with it by preparing a reasonable response to the anticipated attack. Every question has an answer that will pass as a response from an intelligent being . . . you just have to figure out in advance how to do this.

Questions Your Mother Might Ask
- What question would you love to be asked?
- What question will show you off to your best advantage?
- What question refers to your strongest point?
- What question would you ask yourself after listening to your talk?
- What question refers to a past triumph?

These questions may not be asked directly, but you certainly should be able to fit the answer to one or two of them into your response to another question. Formulate several of these advertisements for yourself into specific questions and then write out triumphant answers. Rehearse these along with your presentation; chances are you will be able to make use of them.

Farming Out and Planting Questions
Another technique for adding variety to your presentation—or for getting you off the hook—is to pass a question on to a colleague. If you know that your colleague has the answer, you can say, "Janet, would you like to answer that?" However, a bit of caution is suggested: You don't want to be upstaged by someone who is more articulate than you.

Planting questions is also a good idea if these questions will give you the opportunity to talk about your strong points or an important achievement. Make up two or three questions that you would love to have the opportunity to answer. Give them to several friendly colleagues requesting that they ask these questions during your Q&A. Please WRITE OUT the questions or you may be in for a big surprise when you hear a totally different question—one that you are NOT prepared to answer.

Rehearse and Be a Star

It is said that Abraham Lincoln drove his aides crazy, rehearsing his presentations again and again. Nevertheless, his Gettysburg Address, though only three minutes long, is one of the most famous speeches in history.

When you rehearse you must practice reading the questions and answers out loud as part of your presentation because rehearsals are the key to all performance success stories. Actors say, "As you rehearse, so shall you play." As a matter of fact, in one of my recent seminars, an insurance attorney came up to me after the Q&A part of the training and said, "That's why I failed when the presentation did not go well at the mock trial last week. If I had prepared the questions in advance, I would never have had a problem."

Public speaking is really show business, as every politician, official representative, and statesman knows very well. Professional speakers would never think of taking center stage without a set of rehearsed answers. Before any presidential news conference, White House aides spend hours preparing briefing books full of possible questions and appropriate statements for important events so that the president can prepare in advance. For example when President Biden was making his speech about the George Floyd verdict, he said, "Again, as we saw in this trial from the fellow police officers who testified, most men and women who wear the badge serve their communities honorably. But those few who fail to meet that standard must be held accountable, and they were today."

Diplomacy

Another good strategy for taking you out of the combat zone is to reply to an inflammatory remark with apparent sympathy. For example, you can say, "Now that is a very interesting piece of information," and then add something else that you would like your audience to remember.

Last year, one of my clients, a public figure, was interviewed on TV and responded with great defensiveness to many of the questions. We later discussed the interview, and I suggested a more strategic way of handling this kind of frontal attack.

Much to my delight, at his next news conference, when a reporter said, "Do you mean to suggest that this is a scandal being uncovered?" my client replied, "I can see that you are quite concerned. I, too, am quite concerned and appreciate your interest." This response caught the reporter totally off guard and served to defuse the inflammatory tone of the encounter.

By All Means, Interrupt!
Sometimes a member of the audience will challenge you by attempting to make a speech of his own. When a question becomes a long dissertation, by all means, interrupt. Don't wait for the speaker to finish. Count to three and force yourself to say, "Would you be so kind as to ask your question?" If the questioner persists in monopolizing the floor, count to three, interrupt again, and say, "Thank you for your contribution. May I have the next question?" Of course this is not a smart approach if the questioner is a client or your boss.

Most members of the audience will be delighted with your assertiveness. They, too, dislike moves made to upstage the speaker. The longer you allow a member of the audience to monopolize the floor, the more impatient the audience will be for you to regain control. Remember, this is your time on stage! You are the star. You have the right to interrupt any person who tries to take the audience's attention away from you.

What! No Questions?
What if you ask for questions and there is total silence? To prevent the embarrassment of such a scenario, have several of your own questions ready for the time when you ask for questions and no hand is raised. For example:

You: *Are there any questions?*

Audience: (Silence)

You: *A question that many people ask me . . .* (Fill this in) *Any other questions?*

Audience: (Silence)

You: *Another question that people ask is . . .* (Fill this in) *Thank you for your questions.*

(Squeeze . . . squeeze . . .squeeze . . . your toes.)

In conclusion . . .

Even if there are no questions, always say, "Thank you for your questions." It's a gracious way to end the Q&A.

Not Knowing the Answer

Invariably, one of my students will ask, "What if you really do not know the answer to a question?" Although there is nothing wrong with saying "I don't know" when indeed you do not know, the only people who seem able to do this with confidence are specialists and experts. For the beginning speaker, or the nervous speaker suffering from low self-esteem, to make a public confession of ignorance is humiliating.

Remember the purpose of your presentation. Your objective is to present yourself and your point of view as calmly, smoothly, and credibly as possible. Your goal in the question and answer period is to hold on to your position as the leader of the group. If you are going to be upset or worried about having to say, "I don't know," then don't say it. Instead, say one of the following:

- That is a very interesting question. As a matter of fact, we are in the midst of gathering that information, and I will be glad to get it to you as soon as I have it myself.
- I would like to check my figures very carefully before I rattle them off here. I will be glad to send you a memo when I get back to my office.
- That information is not available at the present time, but I will be happy to get back to you as soon as I have it.

A Word to the Wise

Once again, may I remind you that rehearsals are crucial to a successful performance. Of course, you need accurate, up-to-date information, but do not overestimate the value of lots of facts. So be prepared to back up every statement you make. The key to a successful presentation is the overall image of confidence you project. How you handle yourself, your likability, your clarity, your warmth, and your ability to bring meaning to the facts with the power of your personal belief, is always developed in rehearsal.

Fudging

Politicians often avoid answering a question, if they do not like it, by giving a prepared answer to a different question. If that works for you, by all means use it, but you have to be careful. That technique is extremely transparent and can be irritating to the audience. Certainly, working out an answer in advance for an unwanted question, no matter how embarrassing, is a better way to go.

On the other hand, there are times when fudging the question can save your life. In that case, decide what is in your best interest. Your job is to project likability and to hold on to your position of leadership. Standing your ground is crucial to maintaining an image of leadership. Don't be afraid to repeat the same answer several times if elaborating on an answer will get you into trouble. Even if the audience feels that you are being indirect, the alternative, a discussion about the messy details that makes you look really bad and that they will remember and even quote, is not recommended.

This technique is effective even if you have nothing to hide but do not wish to go into details about some personal matter. For example, in a TV interview, Larry King asked Steven Spielberg four times, in a variety of ways, why he chose to adopt African American children. Spielberg calmly replied four times, "We chose the children, not the race." Finally King gave up.

Semi-Fudging During an Interview

So we agree that you do not necessarily have to answer the exact question that has been asked. I once heard bestselling novelist Gore Vidal discuss his technique for dealing with the questions of talk show hosts. (Often, hosts or their assistants will discuss the points you want to cover before the interview.) If they stray from your agenda, just say, "Yes, that's interesting," and then state the point you were going to make. Don't let others take control of your interview. How can you learn to do this? It's like any other kind of skill. You have to practice at home before you master the technique, but it can be done if you prepare in advance. For a detailed discussion see chapter 19, *Other Performance Situations*.

At the Risk of Repeating Myself

Thoroughly preparing for unwanted questions, as well as wanted ones with good answers, will enhance your image no matter what the circumstances. Even when you do not have the best answers, if you are able to respond with confidence, the audience will come away with a good impression. Looking and sounding good is just as important as having all the answers.

The Abusive Question or Remark

When you speak in a public forum, you may be challenged by a very hostile or argumentative member of the audience, perhaps someone who is not totally responsible for what he or she is saying. Even though you are the recipient of an insulting or abusive question, you remain the most highly visible person. How you handle the situation will affect the way your audience perceives you. In the case of an abusive questioner, the best strategy to adopt is to never try to reason logically with your antagonist. A verbal assault cannot throw you if you refuse to participate in the give-and-take of such an exchange.

What can you do? First, let us discuss the strategy; then we will look at an example. When you face any verbal abuse—regardless of whether it is in the form of personal insults, accusations about the integrity of your organization, or other forms—the following strategy is recommended.

1. Center yourself . . . feel your balance . . . squeeze three times.
2. Repeat the question. Speak slowly in a relaxed voice.
3. Define who you are. Look at the audience.
4. Define your purpose in making the presentation.
5. Explicitly refuse to enter into any personal debate. Stick to your refusal by concentrating on your balance. This will set up an inner boundary that separates you from the person asking the abusive question.
6. Focus your attention on yourself—not your antagonist.

Below is an example of an excellent response given by a Talk-Power client, a psychiatrist, during a presentation in a public forum. A member of the audience asked her an insinuating question in reference to her fees.

"I am a trained professional (defining her role) *with many years of experience. I am here to share with my audience information* (defining her purpose in being there) *and my point of view about the issue. I believe that . . ."* (she went back to her Message Sentence). Then she said, *"Next question please."*

You really have to rehearse this strategy for at least ten minutes in order to be able to pull it off.

If He Is Out to Get You
A doctor in one of my workshops remarked about the peculiar pleasure that certain individuals in the medical profession (I'm sure this applies to many professions) derive from boning up on the most esoteric aspects of the speaker's specialty and then bombarding him or her with impossible questions intended to humiliate. She said the best response she had come across when asked an impossible question was to say, "I don't know. Next question," in a rapid-fire staccato manner, dismissing the question as one would wave away a mosquito.

Perhaps you feel that if you were the recipient of an abusive remark, you would be too nervous to handle the situation with the same kind of aplomb. In that case, additional practice is necessary so that you are in control during a Q&A. The sense-memory imaging rehearsal, beginning on page 210, based on a combination of acting techniques and behavioral training methods, is extremely effective when preparing for a difficult Q&A.

Losing Your Cool
Becoming angry or upset in the middle of a Q&A can be just as embarrassing to the experienced speaker as it can be to the beginner. Of course, the experienced speaker is much less likely to let it show. However, even seasoned politicians can give the media something to

harp about for days if they become impatient, bitter, or just down-right angry with their opponents, journalists, or an annoying question. So, how do you keep your cool when your blood pressure, or the issues, or both, become overheated? Please don't say *"Take a deep breath"*—not at this stage of the book.

First of all, a good healthy pause of three long toe squeezes, before you respond or answer a question, will work wonders to restore your self-control. This will give you emotional distance from the irritant. Most speakers do not do this. For example, several of our recent presidential candidates displayed extremely defensive styles when asked confrontational questions. Not being able to resist the impulse to speak without first thinking carefully about what they wanted to say, their reactive behavior gave them the appearance of immaturity—a lightweight quality that made them seem impulsive and weak.

On the other hand, the speaker who is able to take the small pause and ground himself before he answers, appears thoughtful, strong, and responsible.

Pausing

No matter how high the lift-off for the speaker, when she begins her talk, she must know how to pause. This is especially true during the Q&A segment. If you take a pause to focus within and make contact with the pull of gravity, you will be able to resist the impulse to rush ahead.

The way to do this is to have several places in your speech where you pause and focus your attention on your body balance. In this way, you drop your attention down into your body for a mini-second and rest, before you begin the next high moment. These pauses must be written into the Q&A section of your script (like stage directions) along with the written answers you prepared for your anticipated questions. Be sure to include the pauses when you rehearse your presentation out loud. Follow these instructions and your Q&A will be a resounding success!

Rehearsal for Questions from the Floor

Visualizing will not change or correct a phobic or a highly nervous response, because in order to visualize successfully, you have to have a certain degree of concentration. The anxious speaker is generally too out of control to do this properly. However if you can squeeze your toes for three quick squeezes, you may be able to take control. At any rate, once you have completed the TalkPower training, you will have the skills to benefit from the following visualization routine.

Exercise: Preparation for Q&A Practice on Tape

1. After you have completed and rehearsed your talk, make a list of ten questions, wanted or unwanted, that you think may be asked, and write out a strong but *brief* answer for each question (preferably *fewer* than fifty words).
2. Record the visualization that begins on page 212. Repeat the instructions and voice your questions into the tape recorder with a soft voice—slowly and clearly. Take enough time to answer each question. Follow the instructions for imagining a positive response and do the approval out loud. Pause for three toe squeezes wherever ". . ." appears in the text. Then go on to the next question.

Now you are ready to practice the visualization.

Exercise: Q&A Practice on Tape

1. Sit in your chair. Close your eyes. Center yourself.
2. Take ten belly breaths, pulling in your belly and blowing out through your nose, then relaxing your belly. Count each exhalation and inhalation as one breath.
3. Imagine that you have given your talk. Try to see the room you are in—see the light in the room. Feel yourself sitting in the particular chair you will be using or standing where you will be standing.

Note: *This exercise will not work if you visualize any disapproval from your imaginary audience. This exercise may be uncomfortable—even nerve-wracking—at first. The more you rehearse, the easier it gets, as long as you do your belly breathing between each question. The belly breathing smooths out your tension and trains you to stay calm under stressful conditions.*

Visualization for Q&A

I am sitting in my chair . . . My eyes are closed . . .

I am now centering my body . . .

Focusing inward, sensing that my body is perfectly balanced between my right and left buttock . . .

My head is centered between my right and left shoulder . . .

My stomach is relaxed . . .

I will now take ten inhalations and exhalations, breathing in through my nose and exhaling through my nose and counting as I do this . . .

I now imagine that I have just given my presentation and have asked for questions from the floor . . .

I am standing or sitting, ready to answer questions.

I see the room I am in.

I am trying to see the light in that room.

I see the clothes that I am wearing.

I look down, and I can see my shoes or my boots.

I see the people who are in the room with me.

I see several individuals I know.

I see what they are wearing.

I try to hear any kind of sound that is in the room or outside of this room. I am breathing comfortably. (Take three slow belly breaths.)

I feel pleasantly excited.

Now the first question is asked . . . (Fill in here with your first question.) *I see the person who is asking the question.*

I am breathing calmly. (Take three slow belly breaths.)

I am now repeating the question out loud . . .

(Repeat the question aloud. Pause. Give your answer.) *My answer is exactly what I would have wanted to say. I am pleased at how well it came out.*

I can hear the murmur of approval from my audience.

I can see them nodding in my direction.

I feel the pleasant vibes that I am getting from my excellent response.

I hear the next question . . . (Fill in here with your next question.)

I see who is asking this question.
I am breathing calmly. (Take three slow belly breaths.)
I repeat the question out loud. (Repeat the question aloud.)
I answer the question thoughtfully. (Answer out loud.)
I am pleased with my answer.
I see the approving faces of my audience looking at me.
I feel that I am accepted and understood.
I bask in a feeling of success.

Continue asking your questions in this manner . . . breathing . . . repeating your questions . . . answering your questions . . . noting the approving responses to your answers . . . until you have gone through all of your questions.

"Are there any questions?"
"Yes, what's the capital of North Dakota?"

—Groucho Marx

Progress Report

Date	Time	Strong Spot	Weak Spot	Comment	Calm/Nervous (1-10)

Chapter 13

THE CONCLUSION

Having the Last Word

Begin at the beginning . . .
and go on till you come to the end: then stop.
—Lewis Carroll

Remember the speaker who suddenly, out of nowhere, uttered an abrupt "Thank you" and left the stage with the speed of a frightened rabbit? Or the times we were forced to listen to a speaker's "final remarks" endlessly summarizing his point. Why is concluding such a problem?

The lack of understanding about how to say good-bye when speaking in public is curious. After all, most people know perfectly well how to conclude a business letter or telephone call. The explanation lies in the unfamiliarity of the public speaking situation. This seems to trigger a kind of passivity or paralysis on the part of the speaker, making him unable to initiate an ending. Knowing the rules about how to conclude will help to make a strong exit.

What Is A Conclusion Anyway?

The purpose of the conclusion is to prepare the audience for your departure, just as the introduction to your talk gives the audience the opportunity to meet you. In the TalkPower model, the conclusion contains a brief review of your main points and the repetition of your Message Sentence.

This is all you need for your audience to experience a sense of closure. If you do this skillfully, you will impress your audience with your authority. Let us see if we can streamline the conclusion so that it has the same impact and "verbal graphics" value as the rest of your presentation.

The Conclusion

Beginning	1) Introductory Paragraph
(Introductory Section)	2) Topic Sentence
	3) Message Sentence
	4) Background
Middle	5) Menu
	6) Point Section
	Point A
	Point B
	Point C
	Point D
	7) Climax
End	8) CONCLUSION

No matter how long your speech has lasted, keep your conclusion to 150 words or less. However, don't be too abbreviated in your closing, or it will seem abrupt. My rule of thumb is to construct a conclusion that is between seventy-five and 150 words.

The exception to the 150-word limit is a really great story that echoes the idea behind the Message Sentence. Even here, be careful not to stretch out your conclusion so that it becomes tedious (with the audience silently saying, "I know, I know . . . !").

Easy Does It

Talk low, talk slow, and don't talk too much.
— John Wayne's advice to Michael Caine

Your conclusion should be calm and smooth. Avoid bombastic or shocking endings. They confuse and agitate the audience, as well as yourself. A TalkPower conclusion lists your previously stated main points and never gives any new information. Do not introduce new facts or ask for anything that has not been mentioned in the body of the speech.

For a foolproof, consistently successful conclusion, use the following Conclusion Template. It is brief and clear, and even after a grueling Q&A it helps you to bounce back by allowing you to restate your point of view.

Conclusion Template

In conclusion *(PAUSE)* I would like to *(circle one)* remind / ask/ suggest / recommend / appeal / share / leave you with the thought that

_____

_____,

because *(PAUSE)* _____

_____.

I feel confident in saying that you will be very *(circle one)* pleased / surprised / happy / enriched / rewarded / gratified _____

_____

_____.

(Stop talking and do three squeezes.)

In my discussion of . . . *(topic)* I have tried to familiarize you with:
(List all the points in your Menu—no more than seven!)

   1. *(PAUSE [one toe squeeze])* _____

   2. *(PAUSE)* _____

3. *(PAUSE)* _____

4. *(PAUSE)* _____

5. *(PAUSE)* _____

6. *(PAUSE)* _____

7. *(PAUSE)* _____

But above all *(PAUSE)* imagine how _____

_____

_____

_____.

(Squeeze . . . squeeze . . . squeeze . . . those toes.)

Thank you.

Four Types of Conclusions

A) Use the TalkPower template to review the main points of your talk.

B) Conclude with a poem, or song, and tie it into your Message Sentence at the end of your Conclusion Template.

C) Conclude with an anecdote or story that drives your point home. This will be similar to the type of story you may have used in the introduction.

D) Conclude with an appropriate quote at the end of your template. Instead of saying "But above all, imagine how . . ." just go right into your quote. Be sure that it is not too long.

Examples of Conclusions

A) TalkPower Template: The following is an example of a conclusion written by Leo Simon with the Conclusion Template. Notice the words that are in **bold**. They represent the transitional phrases of the conclusion.

In conclusion, *I would like to remind you of the magnitude of Stephen Curry's contribution to the game of basketball.* **Because** *this impact has soared above and beyond his spectacular mastery of the game* **I feel confident that** *you now have a greater appreciation of the phenomenon, which may never again be equaled in our lifetime.* **In my discussion** *of the effect of Stephen Curry, when he played and won versus the Oklahoma City Thunder 121 to 118 in overtime,* **I have tried to familiarize you with** . . .

- *Stephen's inspiration to the game of basketball*
- *His draw to tourists*
- *His status as a stellar role model for children*
- *His boost to the game of basketball*
- *And finally, his positive economic impact on the Warriors*

But above all, imagine how *the spirit and the fortune of the game of basketball has soared along with Stephen Curry's illustrious career.*

Notice how the speaker restates the Menu, reminding the audience of the main thrust of his speech.

B) Poem: A short poem is an effective ending to a talk. You can insert it at the end of your template. For example, when I gave a talk at a conference about the effects of the pandemic upon creativity, I ended my talk with this poem:

One Year of Silence
    By: Natalie H. Rogers
    Like living the same day
    Over and over
    Days of silence
    Wrapped in puffs of weighted air
    Stillness, Inhospitable and cool
    Gives no invitation for examination
    Not one word of why

    I thirst for a single drop of sound
    Even a bare sigh
    Only quiet greets me
    Quiet, stuffed in my mouth
    My throat my ears
    Choking the sanity out of me
    I attempt a strategy
    For survival
    Cheerfully I think

What sounds will tomorrow bring
What yesterday sounds can I recall
And I remember
Loud happiness
Laughter bouncing
Against the walls
The whoop and holler
Of past exultations
This sudden memory
Brings comfort

Or was it a dream
A dream
Has it come to this
Do I doubt the sounds of my past
Do I dare to question
How my lips trembled
As I spoke my vows
Are memories fading?

What is happening to me
Let me save myself
With one hopeful thought

A thought
To be my Mantra
Till sound returns

"What then is this silence
If not some beautiful sound
Waiting to be born"

C) **Story:** An inspiring story is always a favorite with the audience because it is uplifting as well as entertaining. In this Conclusion, the Message Sentence expresses the importance of determination. It is illustrated by this story that tells us that no matter how daunting a stuttering problem might be, if one has a powerful willingness to overcome, miracles can happen.

> *When President Joseph Biden was a young boy he developed a serious stuttering problem. Young as he was Joe wanted to do something about it. And so he decided to try to read poetry out loud. He put aside the time and every day after school he would slowly read several Shakespearian sonnets out loud. This was a very long and arduous process, but Joe was determined to fix his "problem" and to speak normally just like the other kids. No matter how difficult it became, he would not give up his practice. As much time went by, his stutter began to diminish until after several years of consistent practice his speech sounded perfectly normal. Although it is true that on rare occasions when President Joe Biden is stressed or exhausted a very slight trace of a stutter might appear, for all practical purposes that stutter is gone. Of course his effort was certainly well placed because being president of the United States gives him the perfect venue for showing his uplifting speeches and talks.*

D) Quote: Often, a quote will tie a presentation together as nothing else can. You must select the quote with great care so that it does not diminish the impact of your talk. For example, George Bernard Shaw once said

"Martyrdom is the only way a man can become famous without ability."

Here, the conclusion reflects the Message Sentence: "I believe that the mystique of celebrity clouds our ability to distinguish between our heroes and our wannabes." People worry that by repeating the Message Sentence in the Conclusion, they are becoming too repetitious. This would be true in a conversation; in a presentation the Message Sentence drives home the main thrust of your intention. It is a thematic element that gives style to the design of the talk through repetition.

Exercise: Conclusion

Look at the Conclusion Template and write a brief Conclusion for the speech that you have been working on. Include your Message Sentence. Does your Conclusion give you a sense of closure?

Remember Your Intention?

In chapter 9, I asked you to identify the intention of your talk, stating what it was you wanted your audience *to do* after they hear your speech. Now that you have written your speech, go back and check to see if you have supported your intention by asking: Is my Message Sentence strong enough to motivate the audience to take the action I recommend?

Bernice A., in a presentation to persuade the Davis Company to sponsor a summer camp for disadvantaged children, said, "I believe that children are the future." When she completed her speech, she realized that "children are the future" is too general. She needed a more direct Message Sentence to support her intention. Therefore, she changed her message to: "I believe that we must all pitch in financially to make this program a success."

Notice that she did not have to change anything else except to substitute her new Message Sentence for her old Message Sentence in each one of her original points.

Note: *Remember, although you do not have to use the same words that you used in your Message Sentence, the meaning of the Message Sentence must appear in each one of your points in the form of a Message Statement.*

In a speech that Sally T. had prepared for her local block association, she used the Message Sentence, "I believe that traffic lights are important for pedestrians as well as drivers." Well, of course traffic lights are important. Who would disagree? The point that Sally wanted to make was that broken traffic lights should be reported immediately and repaired. When she changed her Message Sentence to "I believe that a broken traffic light is a hazard to the community," her speech became stronger. She was more effective in motivating her audience to form a permanent watchdog committee for reporting broken traffic lights.

The following exercise will help you determine whether your Message Sentence helps you to realize your intention.

Exercise: Checking Your Intention

1. Go back to the speech you've been working on and answer the question: "Ideally, what is it that I would like my audience to do after they hear my talk?"

   I would like my audience to _____.

2. Please write in the Message Sentence that you used in your speech:

   _____
   _____

   Is your message stated in such a way that it will really help you to bring about your intention? ❑ Yes ❑ No
   Is you message clear? Important? Energetic? Strong? As specific as it can be? ❑ Yes ❑ No
   If all the answers above are *Yes*, leave the Message Sentence alone. If any answer is *No*, what can you do to improve your Message Sentence?
   New Message Sentence: _____
   _____

Let's Go Over This One More Time

The overview on the following pages will give you a total picture of how a speech is put together using the TalkPower Action Formula. In the left hand columns you will find a brief description of each section. On the right hand side, the self-talk column will give you a thought-by-thought narration that fully reviews the intentions of the speaker.

The TalkPower Action Formula: How it Works

Part I: The Introduction
DESCRIPTION OF SECTION
1. Introduction

The introductory remark serves to introduce you to the audience. It can be a joke, a shocking statement, rhetorical question, quotation, etc. It should have no more than 150 words (one minute of speaking).

2. Topic Sentence

The Topic Sentence introduces the subject of the speech. It follows the last line of the introductory remark and is one sentence long.

3. Message Sentence

The Message Sentence introduces your central point of view about the topic. It follows the Topic Sentence and is also a single declarative sentence.

A joke, a shocking statement, or a question, or a quotation, etc.
(PAUSE)
"Today I am going to talk about . . ."
(PAUSE)
"I think . . ." "I feel that . . ." "I believe . . ."
(PAUSE)
SELF-TALK
"This introduction will help the audience focus attention on me."

"Now that the audience has had a chance to meet me, I am going to direct their attention to the subject of my talk."

"Now I need to share my point of view about the topic so that the audience will be able to follow my thinking. The Message Sentence will help me to persuade them to buy my product . . . vote for me . . . take my suggestion, etc."

Part II: The Body
DESCRIPTION OF SECTION
4. Background

The background answers one of three questions:

1) Why am I talking about the topic? *(Personal approach)*
2) Why is my company interested in this topic?
   (Professional approach)
3) Why is this topic interesting? *(Historical approach—a brief summary of the topic)*

The background has a maximum of 150 words and a minimum of seventy-five words.

SELF-TALK
"Now I need to share something about myself or my company. The more they know about my connection to the topic, the more credibility I will have. I do not have to defend my point of view here."

5. The Menu
The menu is a list of the points you will discuss in your point section. This section looks and sounds like a table of contents.

"In my talk about "I will list one to seven . . . the issues or items. I will keep each things that I will item short and crisp and discuss include . . . have a small pause before Finally, . . . " each item instead of a *(the last item)* numerical designation."

DESCRIPTION OF SECTION
6. The Point Section
The Point Section is where you develop each item in your Menu.

Point A

This is the first Point on your Menu. Choosing a template you will develop this point in 150 words or more, depending on how long you wish to speak.

Point B

The second point is a little more exciting than the first point. Once again, remember to include your Message Sentence wherever it works.

Point C, D, and so on

Depending on your allotted time, you will have a maximum of seven points.

SELF-TALK

"I am beginning to develop the flow of my talk through a step-by-step or point-by-point procedure. Now I can begin to introduce more complex ideas. Of course, repeating my message in each point will help to drive my intention home. "

(PAUSE)

Second Point: "I will now discuss the next aspect of my topic. When I repeat my Message Sentence, it acts like a theme, becoming more familiar to my listeners."

"The Point Section helps me to present all the information that is relevant to my topic in a logical or story form, so that the audience can get as full a picture as possible. Now the pieces all fit together and they can see the reasoning behind my message."

DESCRIPTION OF SECTION
7. The Climax
This is the high point of the talk. Although this climax has all of the characteristics of a point, since this is your last point—it must be as dramatic and exciting as possible.

SELF-TALK
"The climax will really help to motivate my audience. This is my last chance to drive home my message. I will make this as colorful as possible. I want my audience to act on my intention and remember me." *(PAUSE)*

[Q & A] "A reminder: I must re- peat each question so that I feel grounded and in control and give a responsive, not a reactive, answer."

Part III: Conclusion
8. Conclusion
This is the very last section and gives closure to the talk. You are preparing to leave by reviewing the main points of your talk or by using one of the other forms for saying good-bye. Use no more than 150 words in the conclusion unless you have a concluding story that takes a few more words.

"My conclusion is telling the audience that my speech is practically over. I feel a sense of closure. I have done my very best to share my message in an interesting and informative way."

Fifteen Foolproof Steps for Preparing the Best Speech You Ever Gave
Note: *For maximum efficiency, if you follow these steps, you will arrive at your destination in the shortest time, unruffled, and with a minimum of chaos and frustration. My students find it hard to believe how simple this is.*

1. The Introduction is an accessory: work on it last, after you have completed all the other parts of your speech.

2. Decide on a Topic Sentence. *"Today I am going to talk about . . ."*

3. Establish your Message Sentence. *"I think/feel/believe that . . ."* You must have a Message Sentence before you begin your research, even if you are not sure about it. (You can change it later.)

4. Choose a background template and fill it in (approximately 150 words).

5. Brainstorm the subject in your Topic Sentence. (Give yourself five minutes to do this.)

6. Pick two to seven points from your brainstorming list for your Menu. The number of points depends on your time allotment.

7. Do your research and flesh out each point in your Menu, using one template for each point as a jump start.

8. Make your last point (the Climax) as dramatic as possible.

9. Check to see if you have included a Message Statement in each one.

10. If there is a Q&A, prepare your list of possible questions and answers.

11. Select the type of Conclusion that you are going to use (150 words maximum) and complete this part.

12. When your speech is finished, write the Introduction using the East-West introduction, an anecdote, a shocking statement, a joke, a quote, or a question. Do not get hung up looking for a great joke. If you like it, then almost any appropriate joke will kick off your speech with panache.

13. Count the number of words to be sure you don't exceed your time allotment.

14. Insert the words "REST PERIOD—SQUEEZE THREE TIMES WITH THE TOES" at the end of each section.

15. Be sure to number your pages. At the end of your Menu Section, remember to tell the audience that you will answer questions during the Q&A.

Exercise: Organizing a Complete Speech

Let's imagine that you have just been assigned a talk, either by your boss, your organization, or your club.

1. Pick your topic. Here is a selection of topic possibilities:

- Fitness
- Social Media
- Your job
- Parenting
- Spiritual theme
- A great vacation
- A training talk
- Investment
- A how-to
- Your Favorite Sports Team

- The importance of religion in your life
- Your point of view about the economy
- A Sales Talk
- A recruitment talk
- Budgeting
- A work-related issue
- A controversial subject
- Health
- Your Pet

Using the TalkPower Action Formula, organize a complete speech about a topic you are very familiar with.

Rehearsal

Now you are ready to prepare for your debut in the real world. From here on, you will perform the Transitional Mantra, silently speaking the instructions to yourself. Set up several chairs and a designated podium. Place a sheet of paper on the floor where you will be standing. If you wish to use a podium, use a music stand (if you have one) or invert an empty wastepaper basket on a table or a desk and use that as a podium.

1. Sit in a chair; palms up and relaxed in your lap. Work with the feeling of the weight of your hands. Lift your hands up subtly so as not to be obvious to others.

2. Do five belly breaths. (Pull your belly in. Exhale through your nose. Hold it to the count of three. Relax your stomach muscles. Do not move your chest.) Repeat five times. Count each inhalation and exhalation set as one count.

3. Say to yourself, *"I am sitting in my chair . . . I feel my body perfectly balanced."* (Feel your balance.)

4. Say to yourself, *"I feel my hands."* (Lift your hands off your lap, no more than one inch.)
5. Say, *"I drop my hands to my sides slowly." (Let them hang.)*
6. Say, *"I get up slowly . . . I take a small step and stop . . . I wait until I feel my hands."* (Do you feel the inner click? Get up and take a tiny step—no more than three inches—in front of your chair.)
7. Say each of the following to yourself: *"I walk slowly to the podium . . . I feel my hands."*
   Take as many steps as you need to get to the designated podium. Feel your hands at all times.
   "I turn around slowly . . . I face the audience . . . I stop . . . I look straight ahead . . . I stand with my feet comfortably apart . . . I feel my hands."
8. You are now standing at the podium.
   Squeeze . . . squeeze . . . squeeze . . . those toes, and begin your talk.
   Remember to squeeze between each section.
   After you have said the last word of your conclusion, say, *"Thank you."* Squeeze three times with the toes, and say, *"I walk slowly back to my chair . . . I feel my hands."*
9. Sit down. Do five belly breaths. Be aware of how you feel.
10. Repeat this entire sequence.

What If I Don't Feel Nervous?

Mark was doing so well in the workshop. He was pausing, taking his time, well on his way to developing an excellent presentation technique. However, in his final presentation, he did not pause and he rushed through his talk. "What happened?" I asked. "You seem to have given up all of your concentration techniques."

"Well," said Mark, "When I was sitting there doing my breathing, I felt so good. I was absolutely not nervous, so I just walked up to the podium without doing my pre-talk routine. Once I was up there and I looked at the audience I started talking and I lost control. I just started racing. I realized that it was too late to pause so I tried to get it over with and that's what happened."

That reminds me of the ballet dancer who does not do her pre-dance stretching because her legs don't feel stiff. And then she injures herself. Well, perhaps Mark needed that awful experience to learn that he must never get up in front of an audience without first doing his inner-awareness work.

No matter how calm you feel as you wait for your name to be called, once you stand up to face an audience, if your attention is not focused in your hands, you will have no way of controlling your inner acceleration. It's like driving eighty miles an hour on an icy street and taking your hands off the wheel. No matter how calm you feel before you begin your talk, never skip your pre-talk routine of focusing on the weight of your hands.

Enough! Enough! Stop Writing Already!

For that important presentation, stop all writing five days before the day of the talk. You must rehearse for five days with a complete, unchanged script, one that you have a chance to become familiar with. Changing your talk at the last minute can get you into a lot of trouble.

Be rigorously disciplined. No matter how great an idea you have, save it for the next talk. Slipping and sliding with new material, that you have not had the proper time to rehearse, is a foolish way for you to act out your anxiety. Please take this very seriously. Remember, a successful presentation is not about being a genius. It's about projecting likability, confidence, and being in control! You can only do this if you are familiar with your material.

Team or Group Presentations

The TalkPower Action Formula is an excellent model for any presentation that is a collaboration of two or more presenters. Decide upon a topic, a message, and a menu, and have each member of the team take one or more points in the menu. The Organizational or Historical Background Template work best here. You will find that the entire presentation holds together with a sense of continuity and flow, in a minimum of preparation time.

What If You Can't Use the TalkPower Formula?

Often I present the TalkPower seminar at a company where a deck, laundry list, or other type of organizational structure is used, or a client may have his presentation written for him. In both cases, he cannot use the complete TalkPower Formula.

If this is your situation, you can greatly enhance your talk by inserting a Topic and a Message Sentence in the beginning of your talk, and then restating your Message Sentence whenever you come to a new major subject. The repetition of your message will give your talk continuity and flow, even though the basic structure bounces you willy-nilly from subject to subject. This is a very skillful and simple way to get rid of the sense of fragmentation that so many presentations inflict upon the audience.

For example, do your Introduction or whatever it is that you begin your talk with.

When that part is finished, pause and squeeze . . . squeeze . . . squeeze . . .

Topic Sentence: Today I am going to talk about

_____.

Squeeze . . . squeeze . . . squeeze . . . your toes.

Message Sentence: I think . . . I believe . . . I feel

_____.

Then go back to your original script and insert or repeat the Message Sentence with each new major subject. Use the same words or other words that capture the original meaning of your Message Sentence. You will not believe how much more compelling your talk will become if you adhere to this simple procedure. Naturally, your rehearsal will be done with the Transitional Mantra, and your pre-talk routine remains the same, no matter what kind of a structure you are using. Right?!!!

Part III
THE POLISH

Chapter 14

SHOW AND TELL

Visual Aids

*Paul likes all the lights to be out with his slide machine on,
before he can relax and think and really talk. . . . Then he turns
into a really wonderful speaker.*

—Diane, wife of the president of
a computer products company

If you are planning a talk that will run five minutes or more, consider using visual aids. Visual aids (or visuals) are any pictures, objects, artifacts, flip charts, illustrations, transparencies, or projections that you show your audience in the course of a talk.

Some people think audiovisual bombardment will cover up a poor performance. It can't. Imagine the president's annual State of the Union Address written, produced, and presented by Walt Disney Studios. Then imagine what your reaction would be to a stammering leader who could do no more than point at the Disney production material. Hiding behind visual aids fools nobody. Your anxiety is relieved, but you will not sell yourself, your product, or your ideas effectively.

Ask the High-Tech Maven

This book is primarily a mind-body approach to public speaking. When it comes to high-tech aspects of your presentation, I suggest that you refer to other experts for specific information on voice production, voice-overs, videos, video computer presentations, video recording equipment, video digitizers, three-dimensional models, transparencies, slides, sound recorders, show boards, scanners, presentation graphics, overhead projectors, lectern attachments, microphones, and chalk boards. An excellent reference book on all aspects of the more technological components of visual aids is *The Complete Guide to Business and Sales Presentations* by Malcolm Bird (Van Nostrand Reinhold).

Low-Tech Talks

Although corporate and government presentations utilize the most sophisticated state-of-the-art technological wonder-gimmicks, all around the world thousands of people are giving demonstrations and presentations without fancy equipment. These include sales pitches, presentations at clubs and organizations and classrooms, training talks, PTA meetings, Rotary Club speeches, lectures, Toastmasters, and cultural talks in the fields of art, music, literature, dance, politics, the Internet, and many other subjects.

Let us consider the matter of visuals from a modest perspective. The purpose of visuals is to add variety to your talk and to illustrate and enhance your point of view. If your visuals are handled badly, or if they detract from your personality by hiding you—as a slide projector in a dark room can do—they become a hindrance.

Do-It-Yourself Visual Aids

What is it that makes a visual aid usable? Pictures and posters must be large enough for your audience to see. An effective technique is to tape the poster to a blackboard, then cover the poster with a large piece of paper that can be pulled off easily when you want to display it.

One of my students, in a talk on escalating CEO compensation, used a large chart with CEO salaries, bonuses, and stock options in successive vertical strips an inch wide. Each strip represented one year's package. He taped an inch-wide strip of paper over each column. As he moved from year to year, he dramatically pulled off each strip of paper to reveal the escalating expense of executive compensation. His technique was very effective and illustrated his message in a new and creative manner.

Handling Your Visuals

When you handle visuals, you are still in a performance mode. Therefore, the way that you pick up objects, how you hold them in front of an audience, and the speed at which you move a pointer across a screen or a map must be slower than it would be in a casual social situation.

This is important when using graphs and maps so that the audience can see and absorb what you are trying to show them. If you are using slides or a video use a pointer or a long pencil. Never use your finger or your hand. If you use handouts, do not pass them out during your talk. People will begin to read in your face, and you will lose your audience.

Most important—you must rehearse your visual section in the same way that you rehearse the other parts of your talk. If you do not have the slides or transparencies at home, walk through the verbal part with sheets of paper that you turn over to represent the various slides or transparencies.

Electronic Aids

You are the star of your show. Not your visual aids. They are accessories to your speech. Slides, films, PowerPoint presentations, and visual or audiotapes make a talk or speech more alive—if they are used sparingly. Such materials are wasted and create confusion if they are not directly connected to the point you are making. If you are using slides, use them judiciously and only when they enhance the presentation. Remember, you do *not* have to use every single slide and transparency that your team has prepared for you!

The Use of Video

A five-minute video can greatly increase the impact of a twenty- to thirty-minute speech. Often, though, videos are shown at the wrong time. If the video is intended to be the high point of your speech, the beginning of your talk is not the right place for it. The audience will not have enough information to understand the significance of the video, and you will not have had the time to engage them with your own personality.

Following a video is awkward even for the most experienced speaker. When the audience has to focus on you in contrast to the glamour and electronic wizardry of the video, it may be difficult to recapture their interest.

A video makes a greater impact if it is shown at the end of a speech. It serves as your climactic point, followed by your Q&A and then your conclusion. The impact of your image combined with the dramatic placement of the film leaves the audience with a heightened sense of your personality.

Handling Equipment

Advance preparation and rehearsal time are necessary to ensure that slides are in order and not upside down, the PowerPoint is typo-free, the video isn't blurry, and the correct spot on the audio is cued up. Careful advance planning is a must for a smooth performance.

If you are bringing your own computer, projector, video equipment, or a music player, you know how it works. If the group you are addressing is providing such equipment, arrive with enough time so you are able to practice. If someone else is going to be running the computer or music player, spend time explaining what you want beforehand. In addition, the person running the visual presentation needs a copy of your speech, with cues to change the PowerPoint slide or play the video clearly marked.

Never attempt to use electronic aides if you have not had the time to make the preparations to rehearse, using the aides as fully as all the other parts of your presentation. I repeat: Come early enough to handle the specifics of the equipment. However, don't get so involved in the mechanics that you do not have time to prepare yourself (belly breathing, Transitional Mantra, etc.).

Audio-Visual Infatuation

A word of caution: Many speakers become obsessed with the audio-visual preparation and leave no time for their personal rehearsal. Avoiding the spoken part of the presentation is the result of anxiety, covered up by an immersion in the audio-visual. Now that you have been practicing the TalkPower self-calming techniques, I hope you will not ignore the need to rehearse your presentation and the Q&A part.

The video will not be remembered; you will be. It is better to have a sparsely equipped audio-visual section, with an interesting and personable talk, than an Oscar-winning special-effects demonstration with you as a nonentity.

The Demonstration Talk, or How-to

One of the best ways to develop confidence for a demonstration talk is to do a "how-to" test run at home. The how-to presentation is one of the most popular events of my seminars because it gives students the opportunity to hear other students describe and demonstrate a hobby or a skill.

This talk becomes a working model for any other demonstration or teaching presentation, and is especially helpful for technical talks. The key is to break down the information so that it is easy to listen to, not to use jargon, and to make a story out of it.

Here is a list of some of the how-to's presented by my students and clients.

- How to service a brokerage client
- How to calculate investment performance results
- How to get stock market information
- How to raise bees as a hobby
- How to convert rental property to a cooperative
- How to hunt wild geese
- How to watch a football game

- How to find an apartment
- How to organize a vacation tour
- How to find a name for a baby
- How to get rid of clutter
- How to change a flat tire
- How to make wine
- How to start a meet-up
- How to pass the bar exam
- How to have a happy marriage
- How to have a successful dinner party
- How to bring up an adolescent
- How to sail a seventy-foot craft
- How to make forty tiny cherry cheese tarts
- How to run an orientation meeting for a group of new salespeople
- How to begin a Zoom group
- How to collect fossils
- How to do an astrological chart
- How to fix up a loft
- How to do your own income tax forms
- How to find the right dating website
- How to prepare for a tax audit
- How to set up a food cooperative

These are just some of the numerous how-to topics that have been presented in my seminars. As you can see, they do not call for complex research. They are good practice topics for learning the principles of putting together an excellent talk.

Example of a How-to
The how-to speech begins, like any other talk, with a topic, message, background, and menu sections. However, you don't have to use the point templates because the body of your speech is composed of instructions for your "how-to." Just follow the logic of your "how-to," step by step, and use the Conclusion Template for your ending.

The following how-to will demonstrate this lesson. (Again, items in **bold** indicate the transitional phrases that appear in the Background and Conclusion templates.)

Introduction: *In the time of the pandemic, meetings as we knew them before were no longer possible. It was not considered safe or healthy for people to gather together in person, so a new venue for people to meet together had to be created, Zoom.* (Pause)

Topic Sentence: Tonight I am going to talk about *how to create a Zoom meeting.* (PAUSE)

Message Sentence: I believe *that knowing how to create a Zoom meeting is a valuable skill.* (PAUSE)

Background: I first became interested *in creating a Zoom meeting during the 2020 pandemic.* **At that time** hanging out with my friends in person was no longer safe. **I became aware of the fact** *that using Zoom was one of the safest ways to stay in touch with my friends and help me feel less isolated during the lockdown.* **For example,** *during the first week of the pandemic I was invited to four Zoom meetings with my friends.* **And so,** *I decided to learn how to organize my own Zoom meetings in order to create a poetry group.* **Also,** *I thought that organizing my own zoom meetings would help me better stay in touch with my clients.* **As a result,** *I followed an online tutorial and mastered the art of creating my own Zoom meetings.*

Today *I host at least four Zoom meetings a week.* (PAUSE): **In my talk about how to create a Zoom meeting, the three items that I will discuss include:**

- Opening the Zoom application
- Creating a Zoom account
- And finally creating a Zoom meeting

It is difficult to imagine how anyone could keep in touch with their friends during the pandemic if they did not know how to create a Zoom meeting.

The first step to creating a Zoom meeting is opening the Zoom application on your computer. You can do this by finding the blue camera on the bottom bar and clicking twice.

If you don't have the Zoom application already installed, you must download the application from the Zoom website. You can do this by clicking on the blue download button on the Zoom website.

The second step to creating a Zoom meeting is creating a Zoom account in the Zoom application. (If you already have a Zoom account, you can skip this step.) To do this simply press "create an account" when you first enter the Zoom application and fill in your email, password, and name.

The third step to creating a Zoom meeting is making sure you are signed in to your Zoom account. To do this, make sure you see a picture with your name on it on the upper right hand corner of the Zoom screen. If you do not see this, you are not signed in and you must press the big blue "sign in" button on the bottom and enter your Zoom email and password you created in step two.

The final step to creating a Zoom meeting is pressing the big orange "New Meeting" button. After you press the orange button you will automatically be entered into a new Zoom meeting.

Congratulations! You have successfully created a Zoom meeting.

My advice to anyone thinking of creating a Zoom meeting is: don't hesitate and don't be afraid of the technology, because the rewards, having a connection with the outside world, are invaluable.

What I learned from this experience is how easy and satisfying creating a Zoom meeting is. I will definitely continue to create Zoom meetings even after the pandemic is over.

In conclusion, I would like to suggest that if you have not yet created a Zoom meeting, that you do it as soon as possible because your social life will greatly improve and your feelings of lonliness and isolation will disappear. **I feel confident that** *you will be very surprised at how easy it is to create a Zoom meeting.* **In my discussion of** *creating a Zoom meeting, I have familiarized you with:*

- *Opening the Zoom application*
- *Creating a Zoom account*
- *And finally Creating a Zoom meeting*

But above all, imagine *how happy you will be now that you're able to not only hang out with your friends but attend game nights, weddings, birthday parties, and a host of other activities that you could never imagine yourself attending because of the lockdown.*

Exercise: Practice How-to

The next assignment involves a how-to demonstration where you will have the opportunity to work with visuals. The purpose of this exercise is to help you discover a new and simple way to present complex technical material. Once you have put together a how-to with a hobby, skill, or professional procedure, you will see how easy it is to develop any talk that demonstrates a product, a method, or a technical system.

The How-to Talk

1. Select a hobby or skill that you know well and would like to talk about.
2. Write a complete eight-minute talk, using the TalkPower Action Formula as a guide. As with previous speeches, your how-to will have an Introduction, Topic Sentence, Message Sentence, Background section, Menu, Point section, Climax, and Conclusion.
3. Assemble your visual aids (from one to four should be enough), and decide where you are going to use them. Usually visuals are shown in the point section. If you only have one visual, the climax might be a good place to put it. Those are just suggestions. Put your visuals wherever they will be most effective.
4. Arrange your visuals at the place where you are going to give your talk.
5. Now go through a complete rehearsal of your talk.

Rehearsal

Set up several chairs and a designated podium, with a sheet of paper on the floor where you will be standing to practice speaking.

1. Sit in a chair with your palms face up and your hands relaxed in your lap. Work with the feeling of the weight of your hands.

2. Do five belly breaths. (Pull your belly in. Exhale through your nose. Hold it to the count of three. Relax your stomach muscles. Do not move your chest. Repeat five times. Each inhalation and exhalation set is one count.)

3. Say to yourself, *"I am sitting in my chair . . . I feel my body perfectly balanced."* (Feel your balance.)

4. Lift your hands off your lap no more than one inch so that no one else notices. Say to yourself, *"I feel my hands."*

5. Say, *"I bring my hands to my sides slowly."*

6. Say, *"I get up slowly . . . I take a small step and stop . . . I wait until I feel my hands."* (Do you feel the inner click?) Get up and take a tiny step (no more than three inches) in front of your chair. Stop.

7. Say, *"I walk slowly to the podium . . . I feel my hands."* Take as many steps as you need to get to the designated podium. Feel your hands at all times. Say, *"I turn around slowly . . . I face the audience . . . I stop . . . I look straight ahead . . . I stand with my feet comfortably apart . . . I feel my hands."* Now begin your introduction without reading from your cards. When you come to your background section, you may read from your cards, but look at your audience from time to time.

Go through your entire speech, remembering the instructions given in this chapter for the slow, precise handling of all visual material. Sections of your speech that call for the use of visuals should be familiar enough so that you do not have to read from your cards. (You may need both hands free in order to demonstrate an object or a technique, and in the case of slides or film, the hall will be darkened.)

8. When you finish your talk, say to yourself, *"I walk back to my chair . . . I feel my hands."* Sit down in your seat. Do five belly breaths.

Progress Report

Date	Time	Strong Spot	Weak Spot	Comment	Calm/Nervous (1-10)

Chapter 15

SELF-ESTEEM

I Have the Right to Speak

*My father always used to say, "If a fish woulda
kept his mouth shut, he wouldn'ta got caught."*
—Michael Quinn, executive

It makes no difference whether your fearfulness and avoidance comes from a history of shame and humiliation or a traumatic stress reaction, twenty five years of observation tells me that a fearful reaction to speaking in public is always accompanied by feelings of low self-esteem. This manifests as thoughts and self-perceptions such as "My ideas are foolish. I do not have the right to take up other people's time. In other words, what I have to say is of no value."

How Does One Develop Low Self-Esteem?
Exploring this question with my students, I am struck by the number of times the word *support*, or rather, *lack of support*, appears in the discussion.

"I never could interest my father in anything I did."

"My brothers always laughed at anything I had to say at the table."

"My mother was so depressed, I didn't dare ask her to listen to my stories and poems."

How does the word "support" figure into all of these stories?

Support

The dictionary defines support as keeping something going . . . to hold up . . . to vote for . . . to keep from losing courage . . . to advocate, champion . . . to defend one who is too weak to advocate for his own cause (as in championing the rights of children). When I think of the word "support" I think of the fragile stem of a Morning Glory, climbing up and around a trellis. I see an expression of interest on a mother's face as she listens attentively to her little girl explaining how she made the sculpture that she brought home from school. I see a teacher applauding a student for his original thinking when he disagrees with the consensus of the class. I see more yes than no in a family.

I often ask my students, "Did you get support at home from your parents? I know you were loved. Someone had to love you very much; otherwise you could never have reached such levels of achievement. But did they give you support? Did they listen to you? Give you their time and attention? Express interest in what you were doing or thinking? Did you feel respected? More than 65 percent of the time, the answer, I'm sorry to say, is no.

"Don't get too big for your britches" was the national anthem in our home.

> *And so here I am, still feeling ashamed about wanting to be a leader . . . as if I had done something wrong . . . especially when I stand up in front of my staff, I feel as if I am showing off . . . I get so embarrassed . . . I hear my mother and father saying to me, "Maureen, who do you think you are, standing up there, talking to those people?" I cave in . . . I lose my confidence and start to shake and stammer. It's a nightmare.*
>
> —Maureen, sales manager

Expecting Audience Disdain

When you speak, do you expect the audience to react with the same disdain and dismissal, lack of interest, criticism, shaming, or punishment that your mother, father, or teacher reacted with? Is that why you feel so worthless? So powerless up there? Is that why you cannot support yourself or your ideas when someone asks you a confrontational question?

Learning to Feel Less Than . . .

It's important for you to recognize that because you were actually trained—by parents, teachers, or peers—to expect to be dismissed, ignored, attacked, or punished for your thoughts and ideas, you have learned to place little value on yourself. What started as a lack of interest or the admonitions of parents, teachers, or friends became internalized. And now you are self-governed by a complex, invisible "police state" in your mind that denies you the right to express yourself.

Several weeks ago in a workshop, a student giggled hysterically just before she had to do her presentation. My intuition told me that she had experienced a great deal of shaming in her childhood. Later, a scene flashed painfully in front of her. She was seven years old, playing the flute in school at a concert. Suddenly all the sheet music fell off the stage. She hastily retrieved the music and as she put the flute to her lips, she happened to look up to see her father at the back of the hall, shaking his head back and forth with his arms on his hips and a look of disgust on his face. In that moment, she said she felt totally worthless, wishing that the floor would open up and swallow her. Certainly this memory, which the student revealed as if it had happened that morning, played a major part in reinforcing her feelings of embarrassment when she had to get up to speak in public. Although this woman was the president and owner of a chain of children's toy stores, she never felt confident enough to accept an invitation to speak at sales conferences.

Your Secrets Keep You Ashamed

In the first chapter, *Born to Speak*, I discuss how people with this problem are mystified as to why they have this strange inability to speak in public. Forgetting or dismissing the emotional abuse they had to endure as children, they blame themselves. In this chapter, where we are dealing with the role that low self-esteem plays in reinforcing the fear of public speaking, the abuse you may have experienced as a child is certainly worth looking at again.

By confronting your truth, you can start to process and heal the expressive child within you. The purpose of the list that follows is to sweep out from under the rug the toxic debris you may have been exposed to. Now you can have clarity about where your low self-esteem began.

What They Said That Makes You Feel Worthless

- ❑ A 95 test score? . . . What happened to the other five points?
- ❑ Never disagree with your mother or father.
- ❑ Never draw attention to yourself.
- ❑ Children should be seen and not heard.
- ❑ You get a Gold Star for being quiet.
- ❑ You are so full of yourself. I'll cut you down to size!
- ❑ Your answers are stupid.
- ❑ What a disappointment you've turned out to be.
- ❑ You'll never amount to anything.
- ❑ Why can't you be like your brother?
- ❑ You are so stupid.
- ❑ You're crazy.
- ❑ What a dummy!
- ❑ You don't know what you're talking about.
- ❑ I can never take you anywhere. You always embarrass me.
- ❑ You are so ugly.
- ❑ You are so fat.
- ❑ You look like something the cat dragged in.
- ❑ You have a big mouth.
- ❑ Go stand in the corner so everyone will know what a dunce you are.
- ❑ You are a lazy, stupid child.
- ❑ Only an idiot would think the things you come up with.
- ❑ Why was I cursed with a kid like you?

❑ Why can't you be like your cousin Fred?
❑ You act like an idiot . . . just like your father.
❑ You'll never be the man your father was.
❑ If you say that again, I will wash your mouth out with soap.
❑ Go to your room without supper.
❑ What a worthless kid you are turning out to be.
❑ Zipper your mouth.
❑ Spoiled brat!
❑ You're a slob . . . just like your mother.
❑ You retard!
❑ You are bad!
❑ God will punish you.
❑ Shut up!
❑ Don't break your arm patting yourself on the back.
❑ You make up ridiculous stories.
❑ I don't have time to listen to your stupid stories.
❑ You always talk nonsense.
❑ What is wrong with you?
❑ Go away and don't bother me.
❑ If you don't stop crying, I'll really give you something to cry about.
❑ Add you own . . .

You may say, "What's done is done. Can I undo the past?" The answer is YES, you can begin to undo the past.

In the preceding chapters we focused on TalkPower techniques to help you establish the performance and speech writing skills necessary for overcoming public speaking phobia. Now that you have a firm foundation of physical control plus a solid system for thinking and writing, we can work on the third and final element of the Talk-Power program—a plan to develop your self-esteem.

Healing the Expressive Child within You
The purpose of the exercise on the next few pages is to reconnect you to the expressive child residing within. That child who was blocked from expressing himself freely and now suffers from low self-esteem

is still alive. By sending loving energy and attention to that small inner voice, you can develop the neural pathways that will encourage your expressive impulses to release themselves.

Note: *The effectiveness of the following exercise will be determined by the effort you make to work the complete TalkPower program.*

Exercise: Expressive Child
Part One—Preparation

Setup: Record the following exercise in a soft voice on your cell phone or laptop. Speak slowly and clearly and pause for three toe squeezes wherever three periods (. . .) appear in the text. After you make the recording, sit in a chair or lie on your bed, listen to the recording and follow the instructions on the tape.

I am sitting in my chair . . .

My eyes are closed . . .

I am now centering my body . . .

Focusing within, sensing that my body is perfectly balanced between my right and left buttock . . .

My head is centered between my right and left shoulder . . .

My stomach is relaxed . . .

I will now take ten exhalations and inhalations, breathing out through my nose and inhaling through my nose and counting as I do this . . .

Part Two *(Please remember to use a gentle voice)*

You are going to the family album.

It is on your lap and you begin to turn the pages back, back to long ago.

You are looking for a photo from the past.

You are looking for a picture of yourself as a little boy or a little girl or a baby picture.

Take your time . . .

When you see a photo that interests you or that seems to jump out at you, stop.

That is the picture you will work with.

Take your time . . .

Once you select your picture, put it on a big television screen in your mind . . .

Look at it . . .

See where the light is coming from . . .

Are you in a house or outside?

Try to focus on what surrounds the figure or figures in the picture.

What do you see? . . .

Now, if there are other people in the picture, look at them . . .

What are they wearing? . . .

How have they combed their hair? . . .

Now look at yourself . . .

Do you feel close to or distant from this child? . . .

Take the time to answer, please . . .

What are you wearing? . . .

How is your hair combed? . . .

Look at your face . . .

What kind of expression do you have on your face? . . .

Look into the eyes of this child . . .

What does this child need from you? . . . Take some time to answer this question.

Put your hand on your chest . . .

Imagine that your heart is a small golden sun . . .

Imagine that this golden sun is beaming out rays of light, from your heart to the expressive child within you . . .

See the rays of light making a bridge between you and the child you are visualizing . . .

See all that love . . .

All that compassion . . .

All that admiration . . .

All that kindness . . .

All that patience . . .

All that sweetness . . .

Glowing from your heart to your expressive child, surrounding and inundating him/her with endless adoration.

Take a pillow and hold it in your arms . . .

Hold it close to you . . .
Feel what it feels like to be one with that expressive child within . . .
Sit like this and talk to the expressive child within . . .
Whisper all the loving things that this child needs to hear . . .
You could say something like this:
I have been away from you for a long, long time . . .
Now we are together again and I want to be close to you . . .
I want to be your best friend . . .
I will protect you . . .
I will stand up for you . . .
I will listen and really try to hear you . . .
I will be there for you . . .
You will never be alone again . . .
I will always love you . . .
No matter what you do or say, I will always love you. . .
I will always be your very best friend . . .

With the pillow in your arms, feel what it feels like to be inundated with the energy of love . . . to be one with the expressive child within. Sit this way until you feel complete. Do this exercise each night, sitting up or lying down in your bed, before you go to sleep.

Cognitive Restructuring
Another effective procedure is to identify specifically which messages reinforce your fear of public speaking. In this way you can build upon the feelings of self-worth you developed in the previous expressive child exercise and extinguish the negative messages by not using them. (Use it or lose it.)

To help you accomplish this attitudinal shift (changing the way you think) let us look at the process of cognitive restructuring. This is a behavioral approach for changing our negative attitudes and values by changing the disapproving messages we give ourselves into words that are positive and encouraging. In other words, you can look at cognitive restructuring as a new way of thinking that will give you the right to speak and the right to express yourself, even though you previously thought these rights were not available because you felt so worthless.

Entitlements Test

Do I believe that . . .	Yes	No	Unsure
I have the right to express myself?			
I have the right to my own point of view?			
I have the right to ask others to listen?			
I have the right to inform or teach others?			
I have the right to try?			
I have the right to grow?			
I have the right to achieve?			
I have the right to make mistakes?			
I have the right to fail?			
I have the right to try again?			
I have the right to feel anxious and uncomfortable at first?			
I have the right not to know everything?			
I have the right to stand in front of a group?			
I have the right not to know?			
I have the right to be a leader?			
I have the right to my speech time?			
Others have the right to their points of view?			
Others have the right to disagree with me?			
I have the right to disagree with others?			
I have the right to be different?			
I have the right to try something new?			
I have the right to take a risk?			
I have the right to feel vulnerable?			
I have the right to reveal my point of view in public?			
I have the right to reveal my achievements?			
I have the right to try to persuade people?			

Look at the Entitlements Test and check off the specific beliefs that reflect your attitude toward yourself and public speaking. This exercise will examine the various rules and regulations that are a part of your private censorship bureau. When you answer the question "Do I believe that I have the right to express myself?" don't answer with the obvious intellectual response of "Of course I believe I have the right to express myself."

Instead, go to the emotional or gut response and discover what inhibiting messages have become a part of you. Look at each statement carefully and then fill in yes, no, or unsure.

If your responses indicate you do not feel that you have the right to express yourself or the right to make a mistake, it follows that you would be anxious about accepting an invitation to speak. In a performance situation, your responses may include:

- Forgetting what to say or think about an important issue *(thought-blocking)*
- Thinking several contradictory things *(confusion)*
- Feeling sure that you are thinking the wrong thing *(self-denigration)*
- Feeling that you are being criticized or condemned *(self-condemnation)*
- A feeling that you are really a fraud and will be exposed *(doubt in one's authenticity)*
- Making self-demeaning facial expressions or gestures *(nonverbal signs of self-denigration)*
- Humiliation, embarrassment, shame *(an automatic physical/psychological response to high visibility)*

If you answered every question on the Entitlements Test with a "yes," then you have already adopted a Bill of Rights for yourself. For those of you who have answered "no" to one or more of these questions, let's turn the questions into statements and look at them more closely. We'll begin by establishing a Public Speaker's Bill of Rights.

The Public Speaker's Bill of Rights

1. I have the right to express myself.
2. I have the right to my own point of view.
3. I have the right to ask others to listen.
4. I have the right to inform or teach others.
5. I have the right to try.
6. I have the right to grow.
7. I have the right to achieve.
8. I have the right to make a mistake.
9. I have the right to fail if I try.
10. I have the right to try again.
11. I have the right to feel anxious and uncomfortable at first.
12. I have the right not to know "everything."
13. I have the right to stand in front of a group.
14. I have the right to be a leader.
15. I have the right to my speech time.
16. Others have the right to their points of view.
17. Others have the right to disagree with me.
18. I have the right to disagree with others.

The value of the Public Speaker's Bill of Rights is that it shows you how to identify your rights so that you have permission to express yourself freely. This is not merely a matter of "positive thinking." The examination of specific rights is a behavioral training technique. If you work on them systematically, in conjunction with the expressive child exercises plus the basic TalkPower training program, over time it will change the way you think about yourself. Eventually you will be able to feel good about expressing yourself.

Take Back Your Rights

Choose three or four rights that you have particular difficulty owning, and write them out on the back of a small card. Put those cards in your wallet, and tack them up around your home. If you don't want them in plain sight, attach them to the inside of some private place like your dresser drawers, your bathroom cabinet, or other places where only you will see them regularly. Each time you come across one of the cards, repeat the message silently to yourself: "I have the right to make a mistake," or "I have the right to express myself."

Jane S., one of my students, believed that she had to know everything about a subject before she had the right to talk about it. Jane tormented herself with doubts and apprehensions about her qualifications for doing a presentation. Keeping a low profile in her career, she missed countless opportunities to demonstrate her level of expertise and be seen as a leader.

Analyzing her reactions to the Public Speaker's Bill of Rights, Jane realized that she had denied herself the right not to know "everything." This insight helped her develop a new perspective. Now when preparing a speech, if she starts worrying about not having all the facts, Jane repeats to herself, "I have the right not to know everything. I have the right to make a mistake. I have the right to fail. I have the right to try again." Combined with her newly acquired performance skills, the permission to express herself allows her to make presentations with increasing comfort and confidence.

Exercise: The Worry List

Some people report that repeating self-affirming messages to themselves, whether silently or out loud, is not enough to overcome the obsessive worrying that precedes a presentation. For such people, I recommend "The Worry List." This technique is extremely effective when you use it in conjunction with belly breathing, inner-awareness, and speech-crafting practices.

Before a presentation, make a written list of all the things that you are worried about or that you think will go wrong. Then separate them into two lists:

1. Concerns you can't do anything about, and
2. Concerns you can do something about.

The next step is to take the concerns you can't do anything about and put them on ice. That's right. Imagine yourself opening your freezer and putting all those concerns away. Now let's take the concerns you can do something about and find solutions for them.

Example: Michael is a publicity man for a major rock group. In two weeks he will have to do an important presentation to the West Coast sales reps. This is a major event, and although he has done other presentations before, he is quite nervous about this one. Here is his worry list:

1. He will oversleep on the day of the presentation.
2. The meeting will be canceled.
3. The group's new recordings have not been shipped to stores on time.
4. His nervousness will show.
5. He will not handle the Q&A well enough.
6. He will leave his notes at home.
7. The storm in Texas will flood the roads to the airport.
8. Traffic will be terrible that day and he will be late.
9. The overhead projector will blow a bulb.

Next, we will take out all the items over which Michael has no control:

1. The meeting will be canceled.
2. The roads will be flooded.
3. The overhead projector will blow a bulb.
4. Recordings have not been shipped to stores on time.

Obviously Michael cannot control these things, so we will put them on ice. Sitting in a chair, just imagine that you have put these four items in a paper bag, opened up the freezer, and put the paper bag inside.

Now we will find practical solutions to the concerns that Michael can still have some control over.

Sample Worry List		
	Problem	**Solution**
I.	*I will oversleep*	I will call a phone service to wake me up, plus set two alarms.
2.	*Terrible traffic*	I will start a half an hour earlier than usual.
3.	*Nervousness will show*	I will do a very thorough rehearsal, plus my breathing practice for several days before the presentation and also just before my talk. I will be very disciplined about rehearsing.
4.	*Afraid of the Q&A*	I will make an inclusive Q&A list and answer and rehearse all of the questions beforehand several times.
5.	*Leave notes at home*	I will make sure to have an extra copy that I will put in my briefcase the night before so I know it will be there.

Planning effective solutions will go far to ease your worries. Of course, you must do the breathing and concentration work, and have a well-organized talk with plenty of rehearsals in order to receive maximum benefits from this technique.

The worry list exercise is not a major panacea, but it can calm your mind by finding practical solutions for specific worries.

TalkPower for Women

I was taught that women had to be nice, kind, and pleasant and that if you smiled people would like you . . . that women who wore serious expressions, or disagreed with or challenged men, would be criticized as being too pushy and not feminine.

—Sally, designer

Many women find it difficult to assert their right to speak. In an article for the *Sunday New York Times*, Colette Dowling, author of the book, *The Cinderella Complex*, takes note of this problem.

> *In a survey of 200 students training to become psychoanalysts at the William Alanson White Institute in New York, Ruth Moulton, a senior training analyst there (she is also on the faculty of Columbia University) found that fifty percent of the women tested were unable to speak in public, as compared with twenty percent of the men. For some women, the anxiety was so overwhelming it produced attacks of dizziness and fainting.*
>
> *In trying to state their positions, some women become confused, forget what they wanted to say, can't find the right word, can't look people in the eye. Or they blush, stutter or find that their voices quiver the minute someone disagrees with them.*

These findings corroborate my own observations. When it comes to public speaking, women have the same difficulties as men plus an additional handicap. There are many reasons for that handicap.

Second Class Rose

- The importance of body image has become so exaggerated that many women are not comfortable standing up in front of an audience. A self-critical voice denigrates their physical appearance—feeling too fat, breasts too small or too large, too short or too tall.
- Many women traditionally have been overprotected and disrespected. Thus it is especially difficult for them to take on the adult role of leadership.
- There may be a handicap in that, at times, women as well as men feel that a woman must prove herself. In spite of the progress that women have made in many professions, prejudice against women still exists. Ginger Rogers said "A woman can do the same work as a man but walking backward in high heels."

- Women are socialized with conditioned "feminine gestures" that do not allow others to take them seriously. Examples are head bobbing, looking around for approval, touching the hair and body, and smiling excessively and giggling.
- Many women are not clear about the difference between assertive, aggressive, and cutesy complaint behavior in a leadership role.
- High visibility is often extremely anxiety provoking for women because of their learned traditional position in a support role rather than a leadership role.
- Women tend to be overly self-critical and not trust their own abilities.
- Some women in leadership positions feel they must be overly aggressive in imitation of the masculine power profile.
- Many women believe that "acting like a lady" does not include speaking up. This adherence to the "feminine role" undermines their ability to speak in public.
- Many women who are subject to sexual harassment, bullying, teasing, and other intimidating experiences that occur in the workplace by aggressive bosses feel intimidated about speaking out about them. Although since the advent of the "Me too" movement, women are beginning to come forward.

My mother would always say a good Asian woman does not have to talk.

—Elizabeth, psychiatrist

Growing Up

Using the cognitive restructuring model, women can now change passive, self-demeaning behaviors to more assertive behaviors. For example, one of my clients, Grace, was vice president of a civic organization. She was the only female member of this important organization, made up of 125 of the eastern seaboard's most powerful corporate executives and board chairmen. Because of her performance anxiety, Grace declined to run for the organization's presidency, even though she certainly was qualified and longed for the status and prestige this office would give her. Whenever she tried to talk, her mouth became dry, her heartbeat accelerated, and Grace would lose her breath. The TalkPower seminar, and the practice Grace did afterwards, gave her the tools to accept herself as a leader in this predominantly male setting. She gave herself the right to have her own point of view by identifying her fear of looking too aggressive or unfeminine if she disagreed or had her own ideas.

The basic cognitive restructuring techniques helped Grace transform her fearful thoughts into self-supporting affirmations. Eventually she became an excellent speaker with great personal charm. Today she enjoys the position of being one of the only women presidents of this kind of civic organization in the United States. It is a position Grace calls "a dream come true."

Chapter 16

PLANNING MAKES PERFECT

'Twas the Night Before Showtime

Speak the speech, I pray you, as I pronounced it to you,
trippingly on the tongue; but if you mouth it, as many of your
players do, I had as lief the town-crier spoke my lines.

—Hamlet, William Shakespeare

Any good manager will tell you that successful productions are envisioned, planned, and scheduled with records, goals, and deadlines. So, when you have to give an important presentation, you must become your own producer—transforming what began as a stack of facts and a rapid heartbeat into a beautifully polished performance. Most of the time you are on your own, and so your management skills play a very important role in the success or failure of your presentation.

The Myth of Spontaneity
A young lawyer specializing in real estate law contacted my office for an emergency consultation. It was the day before he was to appear on TV for a five-minute presentation. Not only was Jeff nervous, but

he knew there were going to be three other panelists, one of whom was highly critical of his position. We scheduled a meeting.

When I asked him to discuss what he intended to say, Jeff replied in a furtive manner, "Well, I don't know exactly what I am going to say. You see, I want it to be spontaneous . . . when I get there and I hear the others I will know what I want to say. I don't want to spoil the spontaneity of it all. I have my notes here, and I have to go over them with you."

It took us two hours to figure out what it was that Jeff wanted to say in this five-minute presentation—two hours so that he would be on target, to the point, and come across as a professional who knew his business. We did the very best that we could, and his presentation went as well as it might have under the circumstances. However, it certainly would have made more sense if he had worked on his talk one week ahead of time, avoiding all of that misery and fright. This was a great opportunity, so didn't he deserve to use it to show himself off to his best advantage?

The Overnight Disaster

When people tell me they work best under pressure, I tell them that it is impossible to plan, write, and rehearse a well-thought-out presentation one or two days before a scheduled appearance. A hurriedly assembled talk, with no time for rehearsals, or corrections, is a big mistake, especially for people who have a problem with public speaking. That mistake is compounded by the fact that many people suffer from anticipatory anxiety, a severe form of anxiety, for days or even weeks before a presentation. It may take the form of sleepless nights, with constant worry and dread that the presentation will turn out to be a catastrophe.

As many studies have shown, anticipatory anxiety is usually associated with avoidance behavior. A person fearing a task will put off working on it until the last minute. As the deadline draws closer, your chances of coming up with a first-rate presentation grow dim and your anxiety and avoidance increases. A wonderful opportunity to show how smart and special you are is lost in a lackluster performance.

Rescue Remedy

The best way to overcome anticipatory anxiety is to get to work immediately. There is something about breaking down a task and making a detailed schedule that relieves anxiety as nothing else can. So the best way to overcome anticipatory anxiety is to get to work immediately

On the following pages, various charts and rehearsal schedules will help you plan, write, and rehearse your presentations. Copy them and use them each time you have to do a talk. The TalkPower game plan will prove invaluable for mapping out your basic organizational work in one or two pages.

The TalkPower Game Plan (Anti-Denial Strategies)

Step 1

Whenever you have to do a presentation, fill in all of Part A (below) before you begin to write your talk. This little overview can work wonders in reducing anxiety and giving you just the jump start you need to begin working on your talk.

Part A

Type of assignment _____

Date assignment received _____

Date assignment due _____

Number of preparation days _____

Number of minutes for speech _____

Place _____

Who will be present _____

_____

Topic _____

Intention *(I would like my audience to . . .)* _____

_____

_____

_____

More Game Planning *(More Anti-Denial Strategies)*

Step 2

Now begin to write your talk on your 5 x 8 cards. Whenever you have completed a section, fill in the appropriate information in Part B of the game plan. (Remember, the game plan is no substitute for your speech. It is simply an overview or map of where you are going.)

Part B

Number of minutes for speech _____

Type of Introduction *(leave for last)* _____

Topic Sentence _____

Message Sentence _____

Type of Background _____

Menu

    Point A _____

    Point B _____

    Point C _____

Point D _____

Climax _____

Q&A *(List of possible questions)*_____

Type of Conclusion _____

Choice of visuals *(optional)* _____

Look at your intention again and review your Message Sentence. Did you do what you set out to do? ☐ Yes ☐ No

Places People, Places

There are two ways to make the transition from the privacy of your office to the public forum. You can plunge in directly once you have completed the program we have outlined here, or you can go about it gradually.

Let us assume you feel ready to confront an actual audience in a public situation.

We will follow that with a more gradual transition process.

Finishing Touches

Your talk is completely prepared, and you have rehearsed it twice each day for one week. Be sure that you have your cards numbered and in order.

1. The night before your presentation, choose what you will be wearing. For women the safest bet is a suit with an attractive blouse, or a blazer and a skirt. There are certain industries where other styles are more correct. Use your own judgment. Make sure that your outfit is perfectly clean, with no wrinkles.

Note: *The nicotine in cigarettes and the caffeine in coffee both affect the sympathetic nervous system, stimulating adrenaline production. To avoid activating your fight or flight response, try not to drink any coffee or tea in the twenty-four hours before* *your talk. Or, reduce the amount of caffeine you consume. If you smoke, make an effort to cut down on the number of cigarettes you smoke by putting yourself on a cigarette budget the day before your talk.*

2. Go to bed at a reasonable time. Do the belly breathing exercise, counting up to fifty inhalations and exhalations. The breathing will help you fall asleep. If you find that you cannot fall asleep, get up and run through another rehearsal.

3. In the morning, follow your normal routine. Be sure to give yourself enough time to do everything, so that you do not have to rush. Rushing is disastrous for the nervous speaker. Eat lightly and slowly. Listen only to soft, relaxing music. It is not a good idea to stay home to rest for the presentation. This causes you to obsess about it. Go to work as you always do. But take it easy during the day.

4. I know it's difficult, but try to keep a slow pace. When you realize you are moving quickly, stop what you are doing and feel the weight of your hands for a moment and reduce your speed whenever possible. Picking up a cup of water or holding several books and being aware of the weight of the object can help to slow you down. Do not walk quickly. Do not get involved in long, complicated discussions, or (heaven forbid) arguments or confrontations. You don't want to become agitated or stressed. Keep an air bubble of space around you. Do some of the body awareness exercises in chapter 2 during the day.

5. Do what good actors do on the day of a performance:
   - Talk less.
   - Eat less.
   - Don't rush.
   - Go to work as usual.
   - Treat yourself with special love and care.
   - Don't go around telling people what is happening to you.
   - Be very private.
   - Try to follow a simplified mode of behavior.

6. Before you speak, walk slowly to your meeting room or wherever your talk will take place. If it is in your office, take a stroll down the hall, concentrating on your hands, and then return to your office.

7. In your meeting room, don't get involved with the hustle and bustle. Stay inwardly focused. If you must respond to others, keep it short. Sit in your chair and center yourself. Begin calm belly breathing and counting.

Save It for Your Entrance

A politician consulted me about his hyper image on a television program. He insisted that he was doing his breathing and pre-talk routine correctly, yet he was still tense when the TV interview began. I accompanied him to the next talk show. He did his breathing exercises in the car en route to the station; but as soon as he got into the studio, he became involved in a heated discussion with the other guest on the show, right up to the last moment before his appearance. He told me that he thought this would give him the sense of being "up."

"Aha!" I said. "The mystery is solved. You say you are following my instructions, but you are really not. Next time, no debate until the show begins."

What a difference it made in my client's next TV appearance. The producer came out after the show to greet him, remarking on how warm and sympathetic his performance had been, especially in light of the controversial subject he had been discussing. My client was delighted and now always tries to relax quietly before his public appearances.

Another client, an attorney who was on President Ronald Reagan's team, recounted to the class how the president always came to his speaking engagements early and would go into a room all by himself for a half hour before his talk. I'm sure that this period of seclusion contributed to the warmth and confidence so evident in President Reagan's presentations. Remember: No actor worth his salt ever socializes with friends before a performance. Actors don't do it and neither should you.

When Your Name Is Called and It Is Time to Speak

1. You have been sitting in your chair doing your belly breaths, pulling your belly in, exhaling through your nose, relaxing your belly, and not moving your chest.

2. Say to yourself, *"I am sitting in my chair . . . I feel my body perfectly balanced."* (Feel your balance.)

3. Focus on your hands as if you held those paperweights; your palms facing up, and your hands lying relaxed in your lap.

4. Lift your hands off your lap no more than one inch, so that no one else notices.

5. Say to yourself, *"I feel my hands."* (Wait until you feel your hands.)

6. Say, *"I drop my hands to my sides slowly."* (Let them hang.) Say, *"I get up slowly . . . I take a small step and stop . . . I wait until I feel my hands."* Do you feel the inner click? Get up and take a tiny step (no more than three inches) in front of your chair. Stop.

7. Say to yourself, *"I walk slowly to the podium . . . I feel my hands."* Take as many steps as you need to get to the designated podium. Feel your hands at all times. Say, *"I turn around slowly . . . I face the audience . . . I stop . . . I look straight ahead . . . I do not scan the room . . . I feel my hands."* Now you are centered and ready to speak.

Not Quite There Yet?

If you need more time before you feel ready to speak in public, this section is designed to guide you gradually through the transition.

For a test run, you need one or two people to create the audience. Recruit a friend, co-worker, spouse, or other relative. Once you have decided on your preview audience, make a definite appointment for a specific time and place. The more formal you are about this, the better it will be.

Compose a complete eight-minute talk, using the TalkPower model. Be sure to choose a topic of interest to your audience, one that you are well informed about. A how-to provides an excellent subject for a first talk.

Make a list of questions you may be asked and work them into your rehearsal. Be prepared to repeat the question and then to respond briefly. Be sure to stick to your time limit by using the word budget allowance for an eight-minute talk. Count your words in each section, and cut if you are seriously over your allowance. Rehearse your talk at least once each day for five days before your run-through, including the day of your presentation.

When the day of your run-through arrives, take it as seriously as a real presentation. Keep a slow pace, eat lightly, don't drink any beverages that contain caffeine or alcohol, and dress as if you were really going to be seen by the most important people. This approach will show you how to prepare for a real presentation.

Was I Good?

Let us assume that you have already presented your practice talk. Do not ask your audience how they liked it. Here are two questions you may ask if you wish to benefit from constructive feedback:

1. Was I clear: Did you understand what I was talking about?
2. Were you comfortable listening to me: Was I too fast, or did I show any annoying mannerisms?

Explain to your audience that these are the areas that you would like them to comment on. You want to avoid the kind of feedback that might be critical and negative, at the expense of your confidence. Suggestions about what you might have said, what the real priorities of the issues are, or complaints that you didn't convince them are irrelevant. If you were clear and your audience felt comfortable listening to you, you are ready to do a serious, "real world" presentation. If your audience reports that you were not clear, try to find out what the problem is.

Examine the structure of your talk: Check your Message Sentence. See if it appears in each of your points. Ask your critics what you could have done to clarify your talk.

If your audience says that they were not comfortable because you rushed, used nervous gestures, or distracted them with annoying mannerisms, such feedback should be taken seriously. Did you do a breathing warm up, did you walk up to the front of the room with heavy hands, did you squeeze your toes after the Topic and the

Message and after each one of the other sections? Work on correcting the problems as you continue to practice. Set up another trial run for a second presentation with the same material. Do the same one again until you get it right.

With Such Friends, You Don't Need . . .

It sometimes happens that a well-meaning friend, spouse, or other person close to you can be overly critical or negative. Their standards may be so impossibly high and unrealistic that you are left with a terrible feeling of inadequacy, even though the same performance might be perfectly acceptable in a professional setting with your peers and boss as your audience.

If you sense that the reactions you are getting are overly negative, this is not the right audience for you. Do your talk for someone else. Get a second opinion. Even a third or fourth opinion can be helpful, because it gives you the chance to practice in front of yet another audience. Use the same talk.

At the end of these trial runs, if you still feel nervous about making a professional presentation in the "real world," perhaps you might like to participate in a TalkPower: A Panic Clinic For Public Speaking workshop. Or else, once again, I recommend the Toastmasters International speakers club. Many graduates of the TalkPower seminars have joined Toastmasters to practice and polish their newly learned presenting skills. See page 161 for more information.

Promises, Promises

Unrealistic or inappropriate expectations can wreak havoc with your morale, even after the best training programs. Here is a list of constructive, realistic expectations that will help you to cope and grow:

Nervousness: Expect to feel a bit nervous, but not afraid. Remember, if you have followed the TalkPower plan, you may feel nervous, but you will look calm and in charge, like a polished professional.

Control: Expect to feel 100 percent more in control than you have in the past.

Enjoyment: Please, please do not expect to enjoy giving your presentations in the beginning of your training. If you do, you will be setting yourself up for a big disappointment. It really is not realistic to expect to enjoy something difficult that you are learning to do, especially if you had a lot of anxiety about the activity in the first place. There are so many unfamiliar things to think about and to manage. When you first use the TalkPower program, just expect to feel much more in control of yourself and to sound really good. So be grateful.

Confidence: Do not expect to feel confident. Confidence comes from an accumulation of successful experiences. You don't necessarily have to feel confident to perform in a poised, confident looking manner.

Perfection: Do not expect to be perfect. Nothing that is alive is ever perfect.

Self-esteem: Expect to feel a surge of self-esteem after your talk.

Improvement: Expect to improve your performance with each presentation. Promise this to yourself and you will not be disappointed.

Progress Report

Date	Time	Strong Spot	Weak Spot	Comment	Calm/Nervous (1-10)

Chapter 17

FROM BUTTERFLIES TO BASKET CASES

Survival Kit for Public Speakers

Would you believe it? I was afraid of my own wedding.
                                        —Tom, physician's assistant

Fears and phobias always present a challenge to our courage and ingenuity. This is particularly true for people who suffer from the fear of speaking in public. This chapter will coach you so that you can zero in on and eliminate all of the absolutely horrible and unmentionable things that could possibly happen to you before, during, and after you get up to that podium. Of course, if you take three weeks to work the entire TalkPower program first, the following procedures will feel like a day at the beach. Train with these techniques one day at a time and you will definitely conquer the aggravating public speaking anxiety that rears its ugly head whenever you have to share your thoughts in front of a group.

Oh No! Thought-Blocking Again

Whenever you speak to a group, in a formal presentation or at a meeting, there is an obvious physical as well as psychological distance. The comfort of the one-on-one conversation is gone because you are in a performance mode and everyone is looking at you. It's important to note here that the thinking part of your brain is divided into two hemispheres: the right brain, which makes all the adjustments to spatial relationships and houses feelings and creativity; and the left brain, which deals with words and language and logic.

So, when you blank out as you begin to speak, you are experiencing a left brain/right brain malfunction. I believe this happens because your nervousness and anxiety cause an interference with the complex process of thinking and talking (left brain function) while the right brain is making adjustments to the unusual distance you are standing away from the audience, and you probably are not used to lots of people looking at you. As a result, the normal left brain (word-recall function) stops working.

Therefore, if you have difficulty remembering the first words of a talk, the best way to get you thinking is to concentrate on your body balance. When you feel that inner click, there is a shift into right brain activity, freeing up your left brain. Wait for several seconds by squeezing your toes three times and the words will come. Thousands of my students have found that practicing this Talk-Power technique can prevent thought-blocking. Another way to get immediate help when you forget the first words of a joke or story is to try to visualize the place where your joke or story begins. See the scene where it happens: in a garden or in a courtroom or in a classroom. Then begin telling your story or joke as you had planned. Once again, this works because when you visualize you activate the right brain and free up the left brain, the part of the brain that was previously stuck.

Following is an example of how you would begin to tell a story with words that suggest pictures. First, I'll include the story with abstract-type words and then the story with picture-type words.

Introduction: Abstract Word Story

A man was with his child, and the child was misbehaving, causing a scene. Amazingly, the father remained very calm and kept saying, "Michael, take it easy, control yourself, Michael."

Finally, a woman approached the distressed man, and said, "You know, I am a teacher in a special education school, and I must say I admire your self-control. I might add that you have a fine-looking lad. Is his name Michael?"

"No," the father answered. "His name isn't Michael. I happen to be Michael. This is Johnny."

Topic Sentence: Today I am going to talk about parenting.

By changing the first sentence you can make it easier to remember how your story begins.

Introduction: Picture Word Story

"A father was taking a walk with his little boy in Central Park. The child was kicking, screaming, and carrying on so much so that there were people staring at them."

Can you see how "little boy," "Central Park," "kicking, screaming and carrying on," and "people staring," is so much more visual than what we had in the first version? By simply imagining the scene in Central Park and the child kicking and screaming, you will activate your right brain functions, so that the words to your story can follow fluently. Whenever you are stuck and cannot remember a thought, picture the action behind the thought. You will have a much better chance of recalling what it is you want to say.

Thought-Blocking During the Q&A

Sometimes when the Q&A begins, you become so filled with anxiety that the usual remedy for thinking clearly (repeating the question) is not enough to give you the ability to think. As a result, you can become speechless. Your brain seems to jam up and close down.

This usually happens when you have a great deal to say in response to a question; the pressure causes you to become overwhelmed and to lose the ability to organize your thoughts. The best way to cope with Q&A thought-blocking is to immediately break down the answer into several parts. After you repeat the question, tell the audience that there are two or three or even four parts to the answer. You must rehearse this technique quite thoroughly days before your presentation. Just make up a few questions to ask yourself and break them down into two, three, or four parts and answer each one out loud. I repeat: you must do this out loud if you expect it to work when you stand in front of your real audience.

Example: This example comes from a Q&A that took place at a community board meeting. My client, a police officer, was giving a talk about community safety.

Question: How can we protect ourselves in the street?

Answer: There are three important precautions that you must always remember.

1. Avoid dark streets. When you walk down a street, be sure that the street is well lit. And be sure your car keys are in your hand.
2. When you walk at night, always choose streets where other people are walking and where stores are open. Walk briskly.
3. Late at night, no matter how upscale the neighborhood, if you are alone, you are vulnerable to a predator. Take a cab to your door and ask the cab driver to wait until you open your door.

This is a good example of how to break down a question, so that you can organize your thinking and avoid thought-blocking.

Here is an excellent example of an organizing model suggested by a well-known New York matrimonial attorney.

Question: If a woman is involved in a divorce action with her husband and she also owns a business with him, should she communicate with him about the business directly, through an intermediary, or not at all?

Answer: In answering a legal question of this nature, the lawyer must analyze the situation in light of three areas:

1. The legal ramifications and consequences.
2. The psychological ramifications and consequences.
3. The business ramifications.

In answering this question, we must factor in the consequences inherent in each one of these areas.

From a legal perspective, . . . *(give answer)*

From a psychological perspective, . . . *(give answer)*

From a business perspective, . . . *(give answer)*

This method, of setting up the answer by breaking the question down into three parts, gives us a very clever thinking system for handling the question. Not only is it a good model when answering a legal question, but it also can be used in any situation, no matter how technical or complicated the question.

Dry Mouth

Dry mouth is a sign of speaker anxiety. Just as the digestive tract does not manufacture digestive juices when we are upset, the production of saliva is also inhibited by fearful thoughts. This condition is common and certainly no cause for alarm, as long as you have a glass of water near you when you speak. However, drinking gracefully from a glass of water in front of an audience is not as easy as it would seem and requires practice at home.

The most important thing to remember about drinking from a glass of water during your talk is that you must take your time. Rushing intensifies your self-consciousness and will destroy the flow of your address.

Exercise: Sipping Water at the Podium

1. Do the complete belly breathing, Transitional Mantra/pre-talk routine.
2. Stand near a desk or table that has a glass of water resting on it.
3. Put your hand around the glass, and as you lift it off the table, focus your attention on the weight of the glass of water. Feel the inner click.

4. Continue concentrating on the weight of the glass as you slowly carry it to your mouth.
5. Take a few sips and return the glass to the table. (You will notice when you do this that your mind blocks out thoughts about what is around you. This will also happen in the real world when you face an audience and focus on the weight of a glass. As long as you focus on the glass and move slowly, you will learn to feel quite comfortable.)
6. Continue practicing until the glass is empty.
7. Never try to drink while you are talking.

Note: *In the real world, if you practice by taking a sip or two in this slow way, worrying about dry mouth will be a thing of the past.*

Um and Ah . . . Nonverbal Fillers

Instead of stepping away from the audience to stop and think in silence, the person who says "uh" or "um" has the nervous habit of making a sound to fill the pause. That is why this is called "a nonverbal filler." This may comfort the speaker, but it drives some people in the audience wild. The use of these nonverbal fillers such as "er," "ah," and "umm," can be a problem for the experienced as well as the inexperienced speaker. People who use fillers feel extremely uncomfortable when a half-second of silence passes as they stand in front of an audience. It is as if the person must be connected to the audience at all times by talking or making a nonverbal sound. Often one who says "um" and "ah" is not even aware that he or she is doing it.

In most cases, graduates of the TalkPower program recover from this habit because elimination of nonverbal fillers is a natural result of the training. The focus on body-awareness brings on the sense of being grounded that allows the speaker to pause and think in silence. In addition, the speech-writing formula, with its deliberate pauses, also trains the speaker to feel comfortable with a beat of silence.

If you feel that nonverbal fillers are a problem for you, use the following technique adapted from the behavior modification repertoire.

The point of this technique is to make you so acutely aware of this habit that you begin inhibiting the tendency automatically.

Exercise: Eliminating Nonverbal Fillers

You will need a tape recorder, a pencil, and a piece of paper for completing this special exercise.

1. Make a recording of yourself doing a brief talk. Include a Q&A.
2. Play the recording back. Every time you hear yourself say "er" or "umm," or any other nonverbal filler, mark an x on your paper.
3. Now repeat the talk without the recording, while standing up as though addressing an audience. Every time you hear yourself making an unnecessary verbal noise to fill a pause, make a mark on your paper. You will probably find that at first you are using more nonverbal fillers than ever. This means that you are becoming fully aware of making the sound.
4. Repeat the procedure for five days, using the recording, and then going through the talk two more times without it.
5. After five days, the number of marks you make on your paper will have decreased significantly. Try to be aware of using "umms" in your conversations. Continue the exercise for a second week, working on it every other day. After several days of practice, you will find that you have the impulse to say "uh" but now you are aware of it and able to resist the impulses. At this point you are well on your way to getting rid of this annoying habit. The procedure can be repeated for a third week, but is seldom necessary.

Another technique you can use is to hold a paperweight in one hand while you give your talk out loud. Concentrate on the weight of the paperweight at all times. The "umms" will quickly disappear. In the real world, if you are still saying "umms," concentrate on the weight of your hand, keeping it free at your side. This technique will give you the grounding necessary to eliminate the nonverbal filler.

The Bobbing Head Habit

A sure sign of loss of physical control is a head that bobs up and down during a presentation. A bobbing head not only distracts the audience, but it also diminishes the speaker's image as a leader. If you have any doubt about this, just stand in front of a mirror and watch yourself make a statement as you bob your head. Then do the same thing holding your head still. The most serious effect of a bobbing head, however, is that when your neck muscles tense up and your head begins to move about with force, your stomach and chest clench up like a fist. You stop breathing normally, and cut down on the amount of air that you are taking in. This causes a gasping breathlessness that seriously interferes with your performance.

Here is an exercise that I have designed for students who wish to break the bobbing head habit. Do the exercise for five minutes once a day for four weeks. At the end of the four weeks, rest for one week and begin again if the condition is still not under control. Usually four weeks will do the job.

Exercise: Anti-Bobbing Head

This should only take about five minutes.

1. Stand with your back pressed lightly against a wall.
   Say, "*I feel my head against the wall.*" Say, "*I feel my shoulders against the wall.*" Say, "*I feel my buttocks against the wall.*"
   Say, "*I feel myself perfectly balanced between my right foot and my left foot.*"
   Say, "*I feel my arms hanging at my sides.*"
2. Hold a page from a newspaper in front of your eyes and read one article out loud as you press your head against the wall. Read slowly. Do not move your head. The point is to focus

on your head as it presses against the wall while you read. Do not forget to breathe normally.

If you have to do a presentation, rehearse your talk in this way. You may feel stiff and zombie-like; but remember, this is a training device. You are trying to break the habit of bobbing your head.

As time goes by, keeping your head still will become more and more a part of your normal behavior and you will no longer feel stiff, but poised and comfortable.

Making Faces

Dorothy had a really terrible habit. Whenever she spoke before a group, from time to time she would roll her eyes, stick out her tongue, squint her eyes shut, and stretch her mouth in a mock smile with her mouth closed while she shrugged her shoulders.

Dorothy was not fully aware that she did this, but one day a young man in the audience grimaced back at her. She was shocked, mortified, and enlightened all at the same time.

"Oh my God," she said. "He just made a face. It's like me! That's what I look like. Oh, it's so tacky."

What could she do to put an end to this unattractive habit?

Even after Dorothy told us this story, she punctuated her last words by sticking out her tongue, squinting her eyes, and moving her head toward one shoulder. "Oh, look at that. I did it again," she said with an embarrassed laugh.

"Okay, okay," I said. "Just center yourself and see what you feel."

"I feel a wave of shame sweeping over me," she said.

"Just relax and feel the feelings," I replied.

About . . . Face

1. The first step to eliminate making faces is to be very aware of your face whenever you speak. This will make you feel very self-conscious and inhibited at first, but the results are worth the trouble.

2. When you do catch yourself making a face after you have done it, relax and feel the feeling that sweeps over you.

Exhale and do five belly breaths, letting the shame pass out of you.

3. Center yourself, feeling that the right side of your body is perfectly balanced with the left side of your body.

4. When you rehearse your talk, speak slowly and clearly and be aware of your face as you speak.

5. In conversations, try to remain aware of your facial gestures, keeping your face as relaxed as possible by slightly parting your lips. You will find that very soon you are not making as many faces, and then, none at all.

What If You Lose Control?

The beginning speaker often experiences a general sense of loss of control at some point during his speech. As a result, rapid speech, thought-blocking, rapid heartbeat, trembling voice, cracking voice, or waves of anxiety may occur.

Experience tells me that when this happens, it is because a negative thought like: "Oh my, I sound boring and awful," has triggered your fight or flight response, producing a wave of anxiety. Sometimes when the speech is going very well you may think, "Oh, it's so quiet. They are really listening." This is so unfamiliar it can also produce a rush of anxiety. The thing to do is stop talking, take a pause of three or four seconds by squeezing your toes three times and focusing your attention on your body balance. In doing this, you deactivate the left side of the brain (where negative thoughts originate) and connect with the right side of the brain.

The minute you stop talking and concentrate within, the right brain connection causes an inner stillness that is immediate, reliable, and effective. It's like putting your foot on a brake to make a car slow down or stop. As soon as you feel yourself losing control, you must take that pause. If you wait too long, the progressive loss of control will make it difficult for you to regain your composure. To practice this at home, read a paragraph from a book, stop suddenly, and squeeze your toes three times. Do this five times.

Here is a step-by-step breakdown of this technique. Let us assume that you are in the middle of your talk. Your heart is beginning to beat very quickly, or you are starting to breathe in a gasping manner.

1. Stop talking at the end of the sentence and immediately concentrate on your toes.
2. Begin slowly squeezing and releasing them.
3. Feel your body balance as you do this, and look in the direction of your audience. Not only will you feel calmer, but you will be able to continue talking. Resume from wherever you left off.

Nervous Gestures and Pacing

> *How agreeable it is to see an actor on the stage where he exercises restraint and does not indulge in these convulsive cramped gestures. We see the pattern of his part emerge distinctly because of that restraint.*
>
> —Constantin Stanislavski

Flapping Hands/Nervous Pacing

In addition to speaking too quickly, the untrained speaker often moves his hands and his body about nervously. Pacing back and forth, flapping and waving awkwardly are extremely distracting. When you begin speaking, stand still and keep your hands at your sides during the minute it takes to tell your joke or anecdote. "But I'm used to moving my arms. Isn't body language good?" you say. You may even feel more comfortable moving your arms and gesturing with your hands. You may feel, as many of my students put it, "like a zombie," with your arms hanging at your sides. But you won't look like a zombie. If you keep your arms at your sides, you will look calm and collected. Practice this as part of your rehearsal.

"But aren't I supposed to feel comfortable?" you may ask. "Isn't this 'body language'?" Feeling comfortable, yes; acting out your nervousness, no. There is a distinct difference between involuntary movements and expressive gestures (*body language*). Involuntary movements like spastic jerks, tics, hand waving, pacing, and so on, have nothing to do with the meaning of what you are saying. These movements are simply manifestations of uncontrolled nervousness. Expressive gestures are hand, arm, facial, or body movements that further express your message to the audience. Expressive gestures enhance a talk, and the ability to use restraint and move skillfully comes from much experience. So when you first begin your training, speak slowly and try to keep your body still until you overcome your impulse to make uncontrolled movements. Beginning speakers are advised to keep their movements as simple as possible. Eventually you will learn to feel comfortable being still. Then you can begin to discover what expressive movement is all about.

Shaky Voice and Wobbly Knees

Very often in a workshop, when I ask a speaker how he feels about standing up in front of the group, he will say that his knees are shaky or that his voice is wobbly. In many instances, there is no visible indication of this. What you are probably feeling is some tiny submicroscopic nerve vibrating, making you aware of a shaking sensation or a wobbling or cracking voice. Although you may feel nervous and shaky, if you are using body-awareness techniques, keeping your body still and under control, none of the nervous symptoms you experience will be obvious to your audience. As a matter of fact, you will look calm and pulled together. As for that wobbling or cracking voice—most of the time when the class is asked about it, they say they can't hear it. Neither can I. If you continue to practice with the TalkPower program, all traces of the shakiness will gradually disappear.

Are You Swaying Again?

Many people sway when they speak in public. Usually they are not aware of it. The audience, however, sees the speaker rocking back and forth, and this causes a sort of wavy interference between them and the speaker, like fuzz on a photo. When a speaker sways, his speech does not come from a firm clearly focused "instrument," as we say in the acting vernacular. You know how annoying it is to watch a television program if the picture sways back and forth or up and down.

Have you ever seen an actor who was not supposed to be playing an intoxicated person swaying back and forth as he speaks? Never! You never see an actor sway because acting training develops physical concentration. You, too, can have physical concentration.

If you are a swayer and wish to break the habit, the first thing you must do is become aware of your swaying. Ask a colleague, "Am I swaying when I do a presentation?" If the answer is yes, here is the training program for you.

Exercise: Anti-Swaying

1. Stand with your body (head, shoulders, back, butt, legs, heels) pressed against a wall as close as possible, with a short newspaper article in your hand.
2. Say out loud, *"I feel my head against the wall . . . I feel my shoulders . . . my butt . . . my heels . . . against the wall."*
3. Say, *"I feel my body perfectly balanced, and my arm hanging at my side."* (Notice how still your body becomes even though you feel stiff and robotic.)
4. Hold the newspaper article up and read out loud, feeling your head pressed against the wall.
5. After the last words, step away from the wall and stand stiffly, as you did previously. Read the article again without moving. You will feel tense and zombie-like, but this is the only way to train your body (muscle memory) to stand firmly still without swaying.
6. Do this once every other day for two weeks, and try to be aware of standing firmly grounded, and not swaying when you speak in public.

Standing still helps your anxiety level to go down. You feel calmer, and from the audience's point of view, you are certainly a more attractive speaker. When I teach my students to stand still, they say that they feel much calmer.

Who Said That?

Some of my students report a feeling of detachment when they get up to do their presentations. These people are able to present adequately, but they have a lingering feeling that their words are not connected to their bodies.

What happens is that because of anxiety the normal flow of energy from the brain into ideas, speech, and gestures, is blocked or otherwise irregular. As a result, the following symptoms are reported.

1. Hearing my words outside of me and not feeling they are really mine.
2. An out of body experience.
3. Feeling physically stiff and disconnected.
4. Feeling painfully self-conscious.

Exercise: The Kinesthetic Rehearsal

The kinesthetic rehearsal (a perfect exercise for this problem) is an old acting exercise that will free you up so that you feel connected to your words; you will lose that feeling of being tight and inhibited.

For this exercise you need a setup. Tape your cards to a wall in the room where you are going to rehearse so that you can easily see them in front of you. Read these instructions carefully, and then begin.

1. Sit in a chair. Let go of your tensions by centering yourself. Inhale through your nose and gently blow out through your nose for ten belly breaths.
2. Concentrating on your hands, stand up. Balance your body in place, and then slowly walk to the place where your cards are taped to the wall.
3. Vigorously rehearse your speech, saying every single word silently in mime. That's right, silently with gestures. There are no spoken words in the kinesthetic rehearsal. The entire rehearsal consists of your using your hands, feet, and facial

expressions as vigorously as possible, miming (as in charades) each word in your speech. Vigorous means bobbing your head, waving your arms, stamping your feet, grimacing. Try to communicate as visually as possible the meaning of each word in your talk without speaking.

For optimum benefit, inject energy and force into your movements without saying a word aloud. You'll find that gesturing with exaggerated movements physically frees up your energy so that your ideas flow and you feel in touch with yourself.

When you do this correctly, you feel quite energized.

If you find this exercise difficult or feel inhibited or embarrassed in a room alone by yourself, you can be sure that you really need this exercise to overcome the painful self-consciousness you feel when you speak in public. Although this may be uncomfortable at first, if you force yourself to do this exercise once each day for two weeks (in addition to your regular practice rehearsal), you will put an end to your feeling of detachment.

Students report that after doing this routine faithfully, there is a 75 percent increase of feeling grounded, including a sense of physical comfort when speaking in public.

Note: *The kinesthetic rehearsal should not be done until you go through all of the TalkPower exercises for fourteen days because the violent gestures and motions reinforce all of the jerks, tics, and involuntary movements of the nervous, untrained beginner. First you must bring yourself into a more controlled state with the belly breathing and inner-awareness exercises.*

What Did He Say?

If you find that you begin to race ahead, speaking too quickly and out of control, here is a simple way to learn to slow down. Before your next rehearsal, take your script and put a red dot at the end of each sentence. You can also circle the commas if you feel that you are talking very fast and you can't wait to get it over with.

In your rehearsals, when you read from your script and you come to a red dot, stop talking and pause for a fast toe squeeze and release.

This practice will eventually train you to slow down to a moderate speed. You will feel much more comfortable and in control, and the audience will be highly appreciative!

Anticipatory Anxiety? That Will Keep You Humble

Anticipatory anxiety (worrying, negative thinking, panic about an upcoming presentation) can occur from the time you agree to do a presentation up to the day of the speech. Even if the scheduled talk will not happen for six months or you are chosen as the keynote speaker for your organization for the following year, anticipatory anxiety can attack, making your life secretly miserable.

An overwhelming feeling of dread, of certain failure, humiliation, disaster, prophetic visions of catastrophe, and dark foreboding define this horrific condition: anticipatory anxiety.

Of course, you are not going to discuss this with anyone. You? A successful, intelligent achiever? Worried about a talk? If it will give the reader any comfort, I have spoken to trainers, teachers, and salespeople (including professional speakers), and many report that they are subject to attacks of mild to severe anticipatory anxiety. Even one of our most world-famous superstar singers cancels event after event due to the unbearable pressure of anticipatory anxiety.

The main complaint that all report is an unrelenting feeling of helplessness, not only in public speaking, but also in regard to every other type of performance situation.

Even Stars Get the Jitters

Anticipatory anxiety is a universal experience. Actors get the jitters; even our Olympic gods and goddesses the ice skaters fall prey to the ravages of anticipatory anxiety. As previously mentioned, the prescription drug Inderal has been the dreadful magic potion for many musicians who suffer from performance anxiety before concerts, especially when they are working with a tough conductor.

The best way to put anticipatory anxiety behind you is to begin to assemble your talk as soon as you get your speaking assignment. I mean *immediately*. I stress the time factor because the minute you begin worrying about your presentation, a feeling of helplessness and paralysis envelops you, and avoidance—under any circumstances—becomes the behavior of choice. Any excuse will do as long as it allows you to put off working on the dreaded assignment. Procrastination breeds more anxiety. "Oh, I have four months to work on the darn thing. Plenty of time."

Oh, four weeks? A piece of cake . . .

Two weeks? Well!!!

Five days? Ugh!!!

Oh, I can knock that together the night before . . . ! Getting up early?

What a mess!! I think I'm going to be sick. . . .

Good News about Anticipatory Anxiety!

You can defuse the habit of anticipatory anxiety forever by completing the written part of your talk and beginning a schedule of weekly rehearsals as soon as you get the assignment. By this I mean full, stand-up rehearsals as soon as you know what your talk is about, how long it is going to be, and who is going to be there. (See chapter 16, *Planning Makes Perfect.*)

This bears repeating: If you feel that it is not necessary to begin rehearsing because your talk will not happen for many months, well, it's up to you but I suggest that you tackle the presentation as soon as possible. Get it out of the way. Compose it and file it until you need it. Enjoy the peace of mind that happens when you don't have to worry about it. That's right. File the completed script—but be sure to print out a hard copy, just in case. We do not want to have any horror stories. When you have the written speech in your hands and are rehearsing it, your anticipatory anxiety will surely be much easier to handle As soon—and I mean the moment—you have your first anticipatory anxiety attack, even a mild one, you must pull out the speech. Be sure that the pages are numbered properly. Take this TalkPower book and walk yourself through a full stand-up rehearsal. Even if you wake up in the middle of the night having a nightmare where you cannot find your speech and you are standing in front of Hollywood's elite, rehearse (with good long belly breaths first, if you please).

Do this every time you get an attack of anticipatory anxiety, and you will see how those demons of negativity and fear beat a hasty retreat. No longer are you helpless . . . you are taking action. You are empowering yourself, with the tools of performance, a script, plenty of rehearsal time, and state-of-the-art techniques for feeling calm and in control.

When you take action by rehearsing, you reframe the fearful and negative idea of helplessness that triggers the panic. You have the written script prepared, and that empowers you. Your script is concrete evidence of your ability to meet this challenge.

In addition, the new wiring system in your brain will strengthen due to the rehearsals, giving you a calm, slow, entrance, a well-paced talk, and enough control for a grand finale in your conclusion.

Giving yourself plenty of time to sort out your ideas, to edit and re-edit, to find those funny stories, and to get those audiovisuals in order (if there are any) means that you have done everything you can to eliminate the threatening aspects of this event. Guess what? Eventually, you may even enjoy the preparation.

Anticipatory Rumination

Often people who have anxiety about an upcoming presentation will ruminate about (dwell on) things that could go wrong: imagined catastrophes, accidents, mistakes, and a general feeling of impending disaster take over. The worry list exercises in chapter 15, together with the previous anticipatory anxiety exercise, are very effective for gaining a sense of control.

Shame

I once heard a therapist say that shame is like an electric bulb that suddenly glows with greater intensity—an intensity triggered by a perception, thought, or memory about a perceived humiliation. For the public speaker who suffers from the effects of shame before, during, or after a talk, this reaction of extreme blushing or heat, or feeling of embarrassment, is a painful sign that you believe that others see you as being not worthy, lower than the lowest, less than nothing.

To fight the feelings by avoidance only increases this devastating reaction. When you practice the TalkPower mind/body program regularly, plus the following anti-shame exercise, you can eliminate the shame reaction after six months of weekly rehearsal. The peace of mind is certainly worth the effort.

Exercise: Getting Rid Of Public Speaking Shame

When you stand in front of a group—better yet, when waiting to speak—make up your mind not to fight or resist your shame reaction. Embrace your shame. When you feel it coming over you, stay in touch with the feeling, exhale, and do your belly breathing. Breathe and relax with the shame. Breathe it in and out, letting it swell and grow inside of you. Breathe and surrender to the reaction of shame. Try to tolerate the feelings of shame by breathing into them. At the same time, it's important to be aware of any pictures, memories, or thoughts that come up for you. Try to rehearse this technique at home privately until you feel that you can do this in front of an audience. For example, think of a really embarrassing thing that happened to you and try to feel the shame. Then relax and allow yourself to really feel it.

Make a commitment to work on your shame. Whenever you feel even a tinge of self-consciousness, immediately exhale, begin breathing, and relax into the sensation. Let the shame pass through you and out of you. At first this exercise is incredibly uncomfortable. Do a little bit each day. After several weeks you will find that the intensity of the shame sensation begins to diminish, and finally, disappears, as the exercise rewires your brain with new neural patterning for self-esteem. Read the instructions for getting rid of anticipatory anxiety. The practice programs are similar.

Stuttering

A few of the people who come to my seminars have a mild stuttering problem. Some of them have been in treatment with specialists; others avoid speaking because their stuttering problem activates when they speak in front of a group.

These students are integrated into the regular TalkPower program and do exactly the same exercises. The only modification in their training is that when they begin to stutter during their talk, I place a lightly weighted object (a paperweight) in each hand and ask the student to concentrate on the weight of the object as he or she speaks before the group. In every case, the stuttering stops as if by a miracle. The effect is so obvious and immediate that at times there are gasps in the class at the fluent speech of a previously stuttering student.

Later, these same students no longer hold the weighted objects and are told to concentrate on the weight of their hands. This has to be done carefully, because if one only pretends to concentrate on the weight, the exercise will not work. With real concentration—really sending attention into the weight of the hands so that one genuinely "feels" them resist the pull of gravity—the previously stuttering student can maintain his clarity of speech.

I advise people who would like to try this exercise to use a paperweight or a small can of tuna fish. Spend two to four weeks working with the actual weights before giving them up to concentrate on the weight of each hand.

Stuttering Testimonial

I have been stuttering since I was twelve. At first, it was difficult to read aloud, and gradually developed to the point where I couldn't speak in public. In the end, even talking with people became more and more difficult. Over the years, stuttering has caused me great suffering. Since my youth, in order to overcome this shortcoming, I have tried almost every method I can understand, including receiving stuttering correction, but to no avail. Until near middle age, I finally gave up my efforts and accepted reality.

However, what is incredible is that after adopting the method taught by Ms. Natalie Rogers, I recovered my reading ability. Reading aloud is where I first fell. The recovery of reading ability gave me the hope of getting up again. In my daily life, even on occasions where it was easy to stutter in the past, my condition has begun to improve. In fact, I have avoided speaking English for many years, even after I came to the United States. Because, when speaking English, my stuttering seems to be more serious than when speaking in my mother tongue. Now, with the help of Ms. Natalie Rogers, I start to try to speak English. Although I can't speak English well, I basically don't stutter. In the eyes of others, this may be a trivial step, but to me, it is a big step forward.

Ms. Natalie Rogers is undoubtedly a wise and experienced teacher. In the process of guiding me, she paid a lot of patience. If I were lucky enough to meet her earlier, especially when the stuttering first appeared, my life might be very different.

Therefore, if you are also suffering from stuttering, especially if you are still young, you must give yourself a chance to contact Ms. Natalie Rogers. This decision may change your life.

—Michael Y.

Stuttering on the Telephone

I have had the most amazing results with stutterers who experienced violent attacks of stuttering when using a telephone. Placing a weighted object in the hand and speaking on the phone, while concentrating on the weight of the object, totally erased all traces of stuttering for the people that I worked with.

Recently I have had the experience of working with several severe stutterers, and I can confirm the success of this technique. It certainly is worth a try! See the before and after video on my website stopthatstutter.com

Helpless Crying

People with a history of humiliation and public shaming live with an emotional volcano, deeply buried beneath their silence. This may manifest as a collapse into helpless tears when attention is focused upon them. In this case, a strong emotional release must happen before the Public Speaker's Bill of Rights exercise in chapter 15 can be effective.

For example, on her first day of the TalkPower workshop, Dawn broke down into tears in front of the group when she stood up to say her sentence: "Today I am going to talk about my garden." Dawn was fragile. In the initial go-around Dawn was unable to give her name. I had to interview her for the class and then, holding her hand, walk her up to the podium. Years of experience told me that Dawn's tears were tears of helpless rage, not grief or terror, as you would imagine. Terror paralyzes. Grief did not make sense in front of the group. My intuition told me it was rage.

I asked Dawn to stop crying and force herself to stomp on the floor, saying, "Today I am going to talk about my garden," as if she were very angry. She was upset by my request. At first, she refused to do this. "I am not an angry person," she cried. "I can't do this."

"Oh, yes you can," I urged her. The class watched, silent and apprehensive. What would happen? Finally, Dawn managed to begin pounding her foot on the floor.

"Today I am going to talk about my garden!"

"Once more," I said. "Do it again!"

She shouted, over and over again, as she pounded her foot.

It was a tremendous relief for all of us to see Dawn letting go, and then, radiant and smiling, actually laughing, feeling, as she said, free for the first time in front of a group. Then, "Today I am going to talk about my garden," she said calmly. She walked across the floor with poise and dignity and slowly sat down.

On the second day Dawn did an eight-minute talk without a sign of the phobic reaction she had previously displayed. "I can do this," she said. "I can do this, and I will." When Dawn did not allow her tearful childlike helplessness to take over, she was able to experience feelings of empowerment by expressing the anger she had held in check for so many years. Anger at the people who had bullied her when she was a youngster. In this case the anger strengthened her, giving her a true sense of herself. She was finally able to express her outrage at the inner voices that had bullied her, keeping her frightened and childlike, and hiding, into adulthood. Her expression of anger was totally appropriate and constructive.

If you suffer from a tearful reaction to speaking in public, chances are your hidden anger is similar to Dawn's. In your practice session, take a pillow and hit your bed with it again and again, shouting the words of your talk, or you can say, "I am so angry" or whatever comes to you yelling and screaming as loud as you can . . . "I am furious . . . You will not tell me to shut up . . . You will not shut me up. I will speak . . . I have the right to speak, and I will!" This is to be followed by a complete set of twenty or more belly breath inhalation-exhalation practices while sitting down.

By the way, as a therapist I can tell you that taking a pillow and banging it on a bed and yelling out loud is a harmless way to release frustration when there is nothing that you can do about a situation.

Imagination . . . Is Funny . . . .

The ability to imagine at will is a skill that endows the speaker with the ability to inspire or persuade his audience to follow his lead. Most people do not have this skill. They are unable to visualize with their eyes closed, and it is impossible for them to do it with open eyes. For my workshops I have created imagination exercises to beef up the picturing skills of my students.

If you would like to develop your visualization skills by taking advantage of the many benefits these skills can bring to your presentations, here is an exercise for you to practice. At first, nothing may happen, but developing this skill is just like learning to ride a bicycle. If you keep making the effort, you will see results.

Exercise: Visualization

1. Center yourself, and do ten belly breaths.
2. Close your eyes, and see what you can see (probably blank, black, light, etc.). Keep belly breathing.
3. Try to picture the letter A.
4. Stay relaxed and keep breathing.
5. Now picture the letters B, then C, then D. Continue through the alphabet for five minutes.
6. Do this once each day, for five minutes, for five days.
7. On the fifth day, picture the A plus an apple; B, a ball; C, a cat; D, a dog and so on.
8. On the sixth day, try to imagine an entire story or joke with your eyes closed.

9. On the seventh day, do number eight with eyes closed. Then imagine the story or joke with eyes open.
10. Continue picturing scenes and stories as you read from your script.

To Be Present, or Not To Be

Do people ever say to you, "Hello! Where are you?" Do you often find yourself daydreaming, thinking or worrying about the past, the future, but not the present? When your attention is not focused on what you are doing or saying at the present time, we say that you are "not present." The location of your attention determines where you are. If your distraction is intense, we call this kind of focus *obsession*. If your attention is not present, it is usually in one of three places:

1. Faraway with another person, place, or thing.
2. Thinking about something that happened last month or ten years ago.
3. Worrying about something that might happen in the next moment or ten years from now.
4. Obsessing.

Paying attention to what is happening immediately is called being present, or "being in the moment." When people are able to be in the moment we say that they have "presence." They also have good concentration skill. This subject has a great deal to do with your ability to speak in public; because if you are worried about your presentation, thinking that people will not like it, your boss will disapprove, the client will hate it, your attention will not be in the right place: focused on what you are saying and you will have poor concentration and be easily distracted.

Many of my students are not clear about what being in the moment means. Once again, "being in the moment" refers to your attention. If it is placed on exactly what you are doing or saying, with no "what if" or "last year she . . ." or "I'm afraid that . . ." or "Wouldn't it be horrible if . . . ," then you are in the moment.

If you would like to improve your ability to be in the moment, and enhance your concentration, there are various practices for growing the neural patterns in your brain that will develop these skills. The secret of training to be in the moment lies in deliberately placing your attention on whatever you are feeling, sensing, or hearing. All through the day there are hundreds of simple actions and gestures that we make that give us wonderful opportunities to practice being in the moment like the centering exercises described in chapter 6, meditation, or a martial arts practice. Feeling the weight of your hands or feeling anything that you are carrying like a backpack or a cup of tea or a can of soda are other ways of being in the moment.

Exercise: Being in the Moment Practice Opportunities That Enhance Your Concentration

1. When you are alone, pick up a cup of tea or a glass of water and concentrate on the weight of the glass or mug. Walk across the room several times with the glass or cup in your hand, maintaining your concentration.

2. As you walk down the street, focus your attention on the weight of your attaché case, pocket book, or whatever you are carrying. You will notice that you probably slow down and feel calmer and your head feels clearer.

3. In your office, have a paperweight on your desk, and when you feel that you are becoming tense, pick the paperweight up, feel the weight of it, and concentrate on the sensation for three minutes. Notice how you seem to drop down into your body and become quieter. Doing ten belly breaths with this exercise is extremely beneficial. This technique is especially effective when you are on the phone and feel tense.

4. When you sit down to dinner, if you are anxious, skip that alcoholic beverage. Try something different. Lift your waterglass about a half inch off the table, subtly so that you do not draw attention to yourself, and count to ten slowly and silently as you hold the glass, before you return it to the table. Doing ten belly breaths along with this will certainly

help. From time to time lift the glass again and hold it, silently counting to five slowly each time. Feel how you seem to drop down into your body, becoming calmer, slowing down.

Note: *These exercises always work because, as I have said before, when you direct your attention to an awareness of an inner sensation, you deactivate the part of the brain that is manufacturing the negative and fearful messages that make you tense and take you out of the moment.*

If you are worried about an upcoming presentation and are having trouble falling asleep, I suggest that you purchase a weighted blanket. In addition to your belly breathing, the sensation of the weight of the blanket upon your body is very helpful for getting you out of your left brain ruminating so that you can fall asleep.

Progress Report

Date	Time	Strong Spot	Weak Spot	Comment	Calm/Nervous (1-10)

Chapter 18

IN YOUR OWN WORDS

Toasts for Every Occasion

People think that all I have to do is stand up and tell a few jokes. Well, that's not as easy as it looks. In fact, every year it gets to be more of an effort to stand up!

—George Burns

Toasts are magical! They enrich and enliven any occasion with goodwill and can be extremely meaningful when they are personal and heartfelt. There are occasions where I can't remember who got married or who was being honored, but I can still remember amusing toasts—and the people who gave them. On the other hand, I have also been surprised to see rather sophisticated and articulate people stumble and bumble, trying to put together an off-the-cuff toast. Toasts are as much a performance situation as a formal speech, and can be accompanied by all the same phobias and faux pas.

To give you the tools you need so that you can confidently rise to the occasion when you are asked to give a toast, this chapter offers a selection of templates for every kind of toast, plus a basic rehearsal routine. Prepare them in advance. Mix and match. Include stories, jokes, poems, or any material that you think your audience will enjoy. Be sure to use the TalkPower tools to practice your toast, so that it will go smoothly without a hitch.

Basic Testimonial Toast Template

Here's to _____ *(name)*, who came into my/our life/lives as _____. No matter what the forecast—clear skies or thunderstorms, you have always stood by me/us, as dear friend/colleague/boss/other _____ .

I can remember the time that _____ _____ _____

May you see many years of health and fulfillment. May you continue to _____ _____

and _____

to _____ .

Let's see how this Toast Template looks after it's filled out.

Example: Basic Testimonial Toast

Here's to Janet, who came into our *campaign headquarters fifteen years ago as a young attorney, so eager to get involved with Mayor White's campaign.*

Through the good times and the difficult ones as well, you have always given us your best as a dear colleague.

I can remember the time that *you came into the office after your vacation and you announced that you were going to run for City Council! We were all so thrilled and surprised. When we saw your enthusiasm and commitment, we just knew that you would win!*

May you see many years of health and fulfillment. May you continue *to improve the quality of life for all your constituents* **and** *continue to reach higher and even higher* **to** *achieve all your goals.*

**As you can see, when we filled out the Basic Testimonial Template, we added more lines and more words. Please feel free to do the same in any one of the following toasts. The more personalized a toast is, the better.

Choosing a Template

Go to the Toast Template selections that follow. Pick the one that is appropriate for your occasion, look at the examples on page 308 and then fill yours out.

After you have filled out your Toast Template, the exercise on page 306 is an excellent place for you to begin rehearsing for your public debut. Make the time to do the exercises and you will be delighted with the results. In the words of a graduate of the Talk-Power Stress Seminar for Public Speaking:

> *The one joy is that I am also released from the agonies of self-doubt and recrimination that I have so often felt after an event in the past; a kind of toxic shame . . . that I still don't really understand, but know the feeling of only too well. Not only have I let go of that, but it has been replaced with a sense of inner satisfaction and joy from a job well done.*
>
> —Larry, attorney

Exercise: Basic Rehearsal/Pre-Rehearsal Routine

Set up several chairs and a designated place where you will be speaking—standing or sitting—to practice your toast. Sit in a chair, your palms face up and your hands lying relaxed in your lap.

Note: *Always begin your breathing exercise with an exhalation, never an inhalation.*

1. Concentrate, and pull your belly in slowly as you exhale through the nose.
2. Hold this for three counts: Think "1 - 2 - 3."
3. Relax your belly muscles and take a small breath. (This is one complete belly/diaphragm inhalation-exhalation set. Do not breathe so hard that your chest moves.)
4. Continue breathing and counting for ten breaths, lest your mind begins to wander.

Transitional Mantra/Pre-Talk Routine

5. Say out loud, *"I am sitting in my chair . . . I feel my body perfectly balanced."*
   (Feel your balance). Lift your hands off your lap, no more than one inch, so that no one else notices. Say, *"I feel my hands."* (Wait until you feel the weight of your hands.) Say, *"I bring my hands to my sides slowly."*
6. Say, *"I get up slowly . . . I take a small step and stop . . . I wait until I feel my hands."* Do you feel the inner click? Get up and take a tiny step (no more than three inches) in front of your chair. Stop.
7. Say, *"I walk slowly to the podium."* Say, *"I feel my hands."* Take as many steps as you need to get to the designated podium. Feel your hands at all times. Say, *"I turn around slowly . . . I face the audience . . . I stop."* Say, *"I look straight ahead . . . I stand with my feet comfortably apart."* Say, *"I feel my hands."*

This is the complete basic pre-toast routine. You can use it as a training program for practicing a toast, or any other performance event, even if you are just going to be standing in front of your chair.

Rehearsal: Toasts

Do the preceding exercises. Begin this rehearsal standing in front of your imaginary audience. You have just completed the Transitional Mantra and will now give your toast.

1. Squeeze your toes three times and read your toast to the front of the room. Do not worry about holding a glass of wine.
2. Do this for four days: twice on Day One, twice on Day Two, three times on Day Three, and three times on Day Four.
3. Day Five: Now you are ready to hold a glass of wine/juice in your hand. Prepare a glass of water next to your chair.

(Just as actors rehearse with nonalcoholic beverages, so should you.)

4. Do ten belly breaths. Say to yourself, *"I am sitting in my chair, perfectly balanced."* Pick up the glass of water. Say, *"I feel the weight of the glass."*
5. Stand up slowly, keeping your attention on the weight of the glass of water.
6. Say, *"I feel myself perfectly balanced between my right and left legs."*
7. Hold the glass to the side of your face, concentrating on the weight of the glass.
8. Say the first three words separately: *"It . . . is . . . with . . . a deep feeling of joy . . ."* etc. Say the rest of the toast normally, but slowly.
9. After the last word of the toast, slowly bring the glass to your lips, concentrating on the weight of the glass, until you begin drinking the water.
10. Sit down. Do ten belly breaths and take a moment to see how you feel. Continue to rehearse with a glass of water once a day until the day of your celebration.

Toast Templates

What follows are templates for toasting possible occasions. They are general templates that you can arrange or rearrange in any way you feel suitable. When filling them out, select descriptive stories that allow the audience to easily identify the person you are toasting.

Simple stories are the best.

Suggestions For Filling Out The Toast Templates

These ideas refer to the phrase that says, "I can remember . . ." For example: *I can remember the time we went out on a first double date with you to Coney Island and you and Jim were totally unaware of us, you were so taken with one another.*

Example: *I remember when, at that ABC conference, you said that our consulting company, which had just moved next door to us, might as well be on the moon for all the good they did us.*

Example: *I **will never forget** the first day I came to work at "Bows and Buttons." I was so confused and upset, and Jane came to my desk and gave me a little key chain that she had brought back from her holiday in Tobago, and how good it made me feel . . .*

Example: (This is a suggestion that works with the Wedding Template) *Joe and Barbara are so suited to one another. When they were planning their wedding, Barbara said, "Do you know what kind of cake I want?" And Joe said, "Of course, banana." And Joe said, "Do you know what kind of entrée I want?" And Barbara said, "Absolutely . . . prime rib!" That's the way it has always been for Barbara and Joe. They really understand one another.*

Example: *I **can remember the time** I walked into that writing group, and I heard you say, "I need someone who is completely committed." And I said to myself, "Here I am, baby!"*

Example: *I **remember the time** that you were three years old and you came back from your first day alone in the play group. You had made a dinosaur and you cried when we guessed it was a helicopter.*

Example: *I **can remember the time** that we started working here, thirty-five years ago, and we went to a retirement dinner for Al Cook. You remember Al. And you said, "That's not me. I'll never retire!" And now that your little side business is grossing six figures every year, take your gold watch and God bless you.*

Simple and Authentic

These examples are extremely simple and point to the unique experience of speaking in public. Simplicity can be compelling, if it involves people that you know. When you read them, they may sound too simple; yet when spoken in front of an audience, they take on a warmth and color that is extremely moving for everyone. This is the stuff that plays are made of—small personal stories and dialogue. The point is to be sincere, allowing your heart to lead you. Please write out every word that you intend to say and rehearse it just that way.

Birthday Toast One

Happy Birthday, _____ (name)! We raise our glasses to toast the birthday girl/boy/guy/gal! Sending you our warmest wishes for another year of health, happiness, and prosperity. I can remember when you _____

_____

_____

_____

and you _____

_____

_____

I said to myself, "What a truly wonderful person!" My admiration for you has only grown, and now that your birthday has rolled around, we would like to send you off into another glorious year of your life with a toast. Here's to _____ (name)! God bless you!

Birthday Toast Two

It is with great pride that we toast _____ (name). You have grown into a wonderful young boy/girl, whom we are all so proud of. Especially for your

   . . . leadership qualities
   . . . scholarship qualities
   . . . musical abilities
   . . . scientific abilities
   . . . athletic abilities
   . . . artistic abilities
   . . . that you have demonstrated at such a young age. We admire you and look forward to watching you develop all of your gifts and talents. I can remember the time

_____

_____

God bless you _____ (name) and your proud family.

   Let us all toast _____ (name).

Thank-You Toast

Saying thank you could never express _____

_____

_____

because _____

_____

_____. I

can remember when _____

_____

_____

And so, thank you _____. Let us toast _____ *(name)*,
with our deepest wishes for _____

_____

May you see many years of health and happiness. May you continue
to bring joy and sweetness to all those who know you.

Congratulations Toast

It's always a pleasure to talk about winning, and certainly
_____ *(name)* has given us all a feeling of great pride and satisfaction for his/her accomplishments. I can remember the time when

_____

_____

_____. We
had no doubt that _____ *(name)* would reach his/her goal
and stand so proudly with his/her prize _____.
God bless you _____ *(name)* and may you win again
and again. Let us all raise our glasses for _____

_____.

Farewell Toast

(Saying good-bye: moving, going to college, going on a long trip)
Saying good-bye to _____ *(name)* is _____
because I will never forget the way _____ *(name)*

_____

_____

_____

_____ .
So here, where I and _____ (name) have the honor of
being guests at this wonderful party, if you would all join me in
toasting _____(name) and wishing him/her _____
_____ .

Retirement Toast One
We are here today to honor _____ (name) . . . to say good-
bye to this very special person. I can remember when I first met
_____ (name). It was _____
_____
_____

All of us here at _____ (name
of firm) are so fortunate to have had the opportunity to have worked
with/for _____ (name). His/Her . . . interesting ideas
   . . . sense of humor
   . . . outstanding service
   . . . positive spirit
   . . . spiritual light
   . . . motivating force
   . . . positive example
. . . has/have made it a pleasure to be around him/her. _____
(name), before you go, there is something you really should know.
We are going to miss you very much. Tonight we raise our glasses
to _____ (name), wishing you our heartfelt very best good
fortune, health, wealth, and future happiness.

Retirement Toast Two
What an exceptional person we are honoring tonight! It is very hard
to convey the affection that we all feel for you, _____ (name).
Your outstanding years of service are a credit to our company. I can
recall the time when _____
_____
_____
_____ .
There are so many stories about _____ (name's)

    . . . helpfulness
    . . . sense of humor
    . . . creativity
    . . . imagination
    . . . dedication

that helped to make our organization the great company that it is.
For example, _____

_____

_____

_____.

Tonight we are here to say good-bye to _____ *(name)*. Let
us raise our glasses as we wish you good fortune, health, and happiness for the future.

Graduation Toast

Congratulations, _____ *(name)*! Your graduation day
has finally arrived, and we are so proud of your _____

_____. It
seems that it was only yesterday _____

_____

_____

and here we are, at *(name of establishment)* celebrating your graduation on this happy day. We raise our glasses to you and also to your
proud parents. God bless you _____ *(name)*! Our fondest
wishes for _____

_____.

Wedding Toast One

This toast for _____ *(name)* and _____ *(name)* is
such a pleasure for me because _____

_____

_____ .

I can remember when _____ *(name)* first told me that he was
going to ask _____ *(name)* to marry him. What a joyous
day that was because _____

_____

_____.
Now that all the people who care so very much for this lovely couple
are gathered together, let us raise our glasses and toast _____
(name) and _____ *(name)*, wishing them abundant health,
joy, and a sense of humor for those bumps along the way.

Wedding Toast Two
This is a toast for _____ *(name)* and _____ *(name)*.
If ever two people were meant for one another, then _____
(name) and _____ *(name)* certainly fit the description. And
I have no doubt about it because _____
_____
_____.
As a matter of fact, _____
_____
_____ .
So, let us toast _____ *(name)* and _____ *(name)*,
this very special couple, and wish for them _____
_____
_____.

Wedding Toast Three
We value the love and beauty of this relationship between
_____ *(name)* and _____ *(name)*. It makes us so
happy that _____ *(name)* and _____ *(name)*,
two soulmates who have found one another, are now pledg-
ing their eternal love and devotion. We remember the time that
_____*(name)* and _____ *(name)* first met. It was at
_____
_____
_____.
At the time, _____
_____
_____
_____.

Let us raise our glasses to this special couple to wish them health, happiness, and prosperity. God bless you.

Baby Shower Toast
Let us take a moment in all the festivities, to toast the Mom-to-be, _____ *(name)*. We open our hearts with joyous anticipation. I can remember when _____ *(name)* told me/us that she was going to have a baby. It was _____
_____
_____
_____.

What a happy moment! We wish for you all the blessings that you deserve. Here's a toast to _____ *(name)* the new Mom-to-be!

Anniversary Toast One
Here's to _____ *(name)* and _____ *(name)*. We congratulate you on this memorable day, after _____ years, sharing love and laughter. Moment by moment and day by day, life has revealed to you the beautiful gifts of your partnership. I can recall when you both _____
_____
_____
_____.

Life has certainly proven to be unpredictable, bringing laughter as well as tears, and we have shared them with you. We are so fortunate to have known you and loved you, and to be here with you celebrating _____ years of this wonderful friendship. We raise our glasses to you _____ *(name)* and _____ *(name)*. May you continue to have a healthy, happy future together for many more years.

Humorous Anniversary Toast Two
The humorous beginning of this toast can be used as a beginning for any of the other toasts.

We interrupt this regularly scheduled newscast . . . with a terribly important flash . . . Attention, Mr. and Mrs. America! Raise your glasses high: _____ *(name)* and _____ *(name)* have finally made it _____ years. Would you believe it? And not only do they still speak to each other, but they still love each other. What a remarkable accomplishment! I can remember when _____ *(name)* and _____ *(name)* took their marriage vows: _____

_____

_____.

And now, here it is _____ years later and they sit here before us, a living example of what it means to be happy together. Let us all raise our glasses to honor and celebrate our dear friends, _____ *(name)* and _____ *(name)* on their anniversary!

Toast to a Wife
Here's to _____ *(name)*, who came into my life, bringing

_____

_____

_____

_____.

You have always stood by me, a dear friend, a loving presence, a wonderful cook/mother/Den mother/artist *(or any talent you would like to name)*. I can remember the time that _____

_____

_____

_____

_____.

May we have many more years of health and happiness together. May you continue to bring joy and sweetness to all those who know you. God bless you.

Toast to a Husband
Here's to _____ *(name)*, who came into my life, bringing

_____

_____

_____

_____.

You have always been my hero, a dear friend, a loving presence, a wonderful cook/Dad/golfer/Little League coach *(or any talent you would like to name).* I can remember the time that _____

_____

_____

_____.

May we have many more years of health and happiness together. May you continue to bring joy and sweetness to all those who know you. God bless you.

Special Day Toast

We celebrate the very special occasion of _____

_____ with a toast to our _____ (host/hostess/president/founder/boss/friend/religious leader/Scout leader/teacher, etc.) _____ *(name).* Together, we have all participated . . . one way or another . . . in the wonderful work of _____ *(name)* to make

_____

possible. It seems as if it was only yesterday that _____

_____

_____

_____

_____

_____.

And here we are . . . sharing the wonderful sense of satisfaction that good work always brings, with _____ *(name)* providing an example of leadership. Let us toast _____ *(name).* We open our hearts to the inspiration that you provide on this very special day.

Chapter 19

OTHER PERFORMANCE SITUATIONS

Speech! Speech!

It is not for nothing that the word has become the most concrete expression of man's thought.

—Constantin Stanislavski

From sales presentations to testifying in court, from a job interview to a eulogy, from giving an award to receiving one—if performance anxiety is taking the joy out of occasions that could be happy and empowering, don't despair.

Peggy R. called me one day to ask for help. She was going to be honored for her life-long philanthropy at a formal dinner at the Waldorf-Astoria Hotel with eight hundred guests in attendance. In eighty years of life, she had never stood before a group to speak. To add to the terrifying aspect of it all, she had reserved several tables and fifty of her children, grandchildren, and friends were going to be present. Peggy diligently rehearsed her five-minute acceptance speech with the TalkPower program for six weeks. As she said later, her performance came off with "not a twitch or a twitter." Her family was amazed and delighted with Peggy's moving performance.

Templates for Special Occasions

The following templates will help you put together a talk for any social function. You can mix and match, substitute, or put your own transitional phrases in, to make these templates as long or as short as you like. Add funny stories, jokes (be sure to dress them up by making them personal), poems, quotations, or anything you think the audience will enjoy hearing. After you have finished all the written work and you are ready for a rehearsal, do the basic performance rehearsal routine on page 393. If you take the time to do the complete exercises, this rehearsal program will bring you to a new level of performance—and you will be delighted.

Template for Making an Introduction

Note: *Be sure to obtain the biography of the person you are introducing well in advance of the event.*

I have the pleasure, as well as the honor, to introduce . . . *(choose one)* our next guest/our keynote speaker/our dear friend/our beloved president/our honored colleague/our distinguished visitor from _____, *(choose one)* the very famous/the well-known/the world-renowned _____ (name). His/Her work carries with it a long list of accomplishments. *(list them)*

1. _____
2. _____
3. _____

(Pick three important things that this person has done, and please, NO MORE than one minute—150 words—tops.)

Let us all welcome _____
(name).

Template for Accepting an Award

It is with a deep feeling of *(choose one)* joy/happiness/accomplishment/gratitude, that I accept this award for my *(choose one)* work/contribution/winning score/years of service/ other, as/in

_____.

This is a (choose one) wonderful/fulfilling/thrilling moment in my life, to be acknowledged by _____ and I shall treasure this time in my memory. I want to thank _____, _____, and _____ *(list names here)* for their part in this achievement. *(If you wish this part can be a little longer)*
I can remember _____

_____.

Indeed, it is an honor and a privilege to be with you here tonight. Thank you for the heartfelt way that you have acknowledged me. *Remember to do the full basic performance rehearsal on page 393 when you practice this script.*

Template for Giving an Award
It is with a deep feeling of pride that I present this award to _____ *(name)*, an outstanding *(choose one)* colleague/employee/student/club member/athlete/other, here at _____ _____ *(name of organization)*.
Your exceptional contribution of _____

_____

makes this year _____

_____.

Often we find that _____

_____

but you were able to _____

_____.

Your attitude of _____,
your meeting the challenge of _____
_____;
has helped all of us to _____

_____.

_____ *(name)*, you have proven to be an outstanding

_____. All of us who have *(choose one)* worked with or for/cheered for/studied with/followed your career/benefited from your contributions to, honor and admire you. With our heartfelt congratulations, _____ *(name)*, please accept this award. *Remember to do the full basic performance rehearsal on page 393 when you practice this script.*

Template for a Eulogy for a Loved One

Following the death of a loved one, giving a eulogy can be a healing experience. Rehearsing at home will allow you to practice voicing your heartfelt feelings for when you are with friends and family. After you have filled in the template below, you will be using it as a script in your rehearsal. If you wish to add one or two stories or memories, feel free to do so. Do not exceed five minutes.

_____ *(name)* was my _____, and because his/her spirit is so very much alive with us now, I have to say that _____

_____

_____ .

I can remember *(choose one)* the first time we met/a special day we spent together and _____ *(name)* saying to me

_____

_____ . It

was _____ ago and I can recall that time as if it were yesterday. *(Tell story)* _____

_____

_____

_____ .

While it is difficult right now to accept the loss of such an *(choose one or two)* inspiring/original/wonderful/generous/creative/beloved/ other presence in our lives, it does help to realize that this life is fleeting, and the place where

_____ *(name)* has gone, eternal.

_____ *(name)* lives on in our heartfelt memories.

*Remember to do the full basic performance rehearsal on page 393
when you practice this script.*

Template for a Eulogy for a Well-Known or Famous Person

_____ *(name)* who died on _____ at
the age of _____, was known to many as
_____.

Coming from a family _____
_____.

He/she _____
_____.

_____ *(name)* always/never/chose to *(choose one)*
_____.

Although _____
_____.

_____ *(name)* was committed to _____
_____
_____.

His/Her courage/talent/creativity/vision *(choose one)* _____
_____.

showed _____
and _____.
He/She did so much in so many distinctive areas _____
_____
_____.

Over the years _____
_____.

Finally, _____
_____.

_____ *(name)* was a leader/force/inspiration/
national treasure/example/model *(choose one)* _____
_____.

*Remember to do the full basic performance rehearsal on page 393
when you practice this script.*

How Do You Get to Carnegie Hall?
Practice, Baby, Practice!

> *I never feel I have a part under control
> until I have played it in public for at least six weeks.*
> —Sir John Gielgud

The good actor or actress would never dream of performing in public without the most thorough of rehearsals and run-throughs. Similarly you, seeking a satisfying experience for yourself as well as your audience, should take advantage of the rehearsal procedures offered here. The following selections will give you instructions for rehearsing various performance situations.

Just in terms of your physical comfort, you will feel so much more comfortable if you use these rehearsal routines. Taking the time to practice, from a mind-body point of view, can transform a shaky and insecure performance into a memorable moment in your life—one that you will be proud of.

The Job Interview
There are certain situations where just a few minutes of a successful performance can change the direction of your life. A well-rehearsed job interview can mean a job offer; and a nervous, unprepared job interview can result in disappointment.

Certainly, you can see the importance of rehearsing for a job interview. Most people think that preparation means making a list of questions that you feel you will be asked, and writing down the answers. The only way to do this properly is to rehearse the answers on your lists out loud—with a friend or a tape recorder. That is the first step in the process.

You, your body, your comfort in your own skin, your ability not to talk too fast or take too much time answering the question, your sense of humor, and your ability to think on the spot, will all be evaluated in the final decision to hire you or not.

A job interview is a performance, whether you have thought about it that way or not. It certainly deserves plenty of rehearsal time and effort. Actors say, "the way you rehearse is the way you will play."

Exercise: Job Interview Rehearsal
(Five minutes plus the time for your script)

1. Make a list of all the questions you think you will be asked. Do your research and write short, clear answers to each one.
2. Do the basic performance rehearsal routine on page 393. Hold the questions in your hand. Do ten belly breaths.
   You will end up in the front of the room, facing the chair you have just left. (The reason you must work on your feet is to give you the feeling of a formal atmosphere and to shift your response from a casual conversational style—where you run the risk of speaking too quickly—to a performance style, which is what you should be doing in a job interview.)
3. Listen to the first question if you are using a recording or say the question out loud to yourself. You must say the answer out loud for this to work.
4. Squeeze your toes three times and answer the first question.

(In answering a question, it is always good to repeat the question in the answer.)

For example: **Question:** *"What is it about Goldman Sachs that makes you feel that this is the right place for you?"*

Answer: *"I feel that Goldman Sachs is the right place for me because . . ."*

By repeating the question again in your answer, you have the opportunity to frame your answer, so you do not wander—or worse still—forget the question entirely.

5. Continue reading and answering your questions until you have completed the list.

6. Return to your seat saying, *"I slowly walk back to my chair . . . I feel my hands."*

7. Do this complete sequence on your feet, for four days, once each day.

8. After you have completed four days on your feet, you can sit down and do the same routine. Always include the belly breathing and Transitional Mantra before you do the questions and answers. If you feel you are rushing, do two belly breaths as soon as you become aware of this.

The Day of the Interview

1. Have your clothes ready the night before.

2. Do not eat sugar or drink too much coffee the day before or on the day of the interview. If you smoke, cut down the number of cigarettes you smoke to one third of the usual count.

3. Do not rush to the interview. Get there ten to twenty minutes early.

4. Walk into the reception room, feeling the weight of your briefcase, or whatever you are carrying. Hang up your coat, sit down, and do your belly breaths as you wait to be called.

5. When you get up to walk to the interview room, walk slowly and feel your hands. Stay connected to your body.

6. Meet and greet. Shake hands with each of your interviewers, sit down, do some belly breathing, and wait for the first question.

7. Do two toe squeezes between each question. Do not knee-jerk your responses. Remember that taking your time is essential here

The College Interview

If you are a high school graduate or about to graduate with your heart set on a particular college and you avoid speaking in public because you become extremely anxious when people look at you, the college interview can be a daunting challenge. What if you become so nervous that you sound silly, speaking too fast and not like a serious student? What if you forget to mention that you won the city wide poetry contest for teens or some athletic triumph that is very important? What if you have a panic attack in the middle of your interview?

Now that you are about to visit the college of your dreams, these thoughts can haunt your days and nights because you are one of the millions of people around the globe who lose their bright and charming personalities and can't think clearly even when they have to answer a question at a meeting or in class. What to do? How can the situation be saved? Certainly not with a coach who is going to give you a lot of useless advice. What you need is a training program that will reduce your anxiety.

College Interview Exercise

All is not lost. Not Yet. You still have a chance to come out of this unscathed if you will just commit yourself to the following interview preparation exercise training program.

So let's get focused.

1. Make a list of all the questions you think you are going to be asked. If you feel too anxious to think clearly, ask a friend to help you out. (This part is important.)

    Write the questions and clear answers to each one.

    Now that this is out of the way, put the questions aside and let's focus on your nervousness.

    Being able to do belly breathing will really help you to control your nervousness. Belly breathing means doing the pumping with your belly instead of your chest.

    Once you begin doing this, you will soon see how much calmer you feel.

2. Go to page 53 and read the breathing instructions and begin practicing. At first, this kind of breathing will feel very strange and unnatural. That is because the way you are used to breathing now is helping to make you feel very nervous. Just try to stay with the instructions as best as you can and

in a week or two this belly breathing will feel much more
natural.

Do five rounds of twenty breaths each. Breathe slowly, gently,
and do not take any deep breaths.

Practice the round of twenty belly breaths five times, two
times a day until the day of the interview.

3. Now you must learn how to focus within so that you can
    concentrate on your answers and not on the negative thoughts
    you think the interviewer is thinking about you. You can
    learn to do this if you follow the basic performance rehearsal
    routine in the appendix on page 393 up to step number 7.
    When you have completed step number 7, walk back to your
    seat and sit down. This basic performance rehearsal routine
    should be done two times right after you have completed the
    five rounds of twenty breaths.

4. After one week of working on the first three exercises, it is
    time for a rehearsal.

    A. Sit down and do ten belly breaths.

    B. Do your inner awareness exercise. After step number 7,
    walk back to your seat and sit down.

    C. Question: Say out loud, "*Why do you think that you
    are the right fit for (name of school)?*" ... Squeeze your
    toes slowly three times. Answer the question like this,
    "*I think I am the right fit for (name of school) because*
    _____."

    D. Question: Say out loud, "*What are some of the extra-
    curricular activities that you have participated in?*" ...
    Squeeze your toes slowly three times and answer the question:
    "*The extra-curricular activities I have participated in are*
    _____."

    E. Now go through the entire list of questions that you wrote
    on the first day and say them out loud, repeating part of the
    question just as you did in the first two examples. Remember
    that after you ask the question squeeze your toes three times
    before you answer each question out loud.

F. Practice the entire routine in this order. The breathing exercise, the inner awareness exercise, and then the questions and answers out loud two times every day until the day of your interview.

It may seem like a lot of work, but the rewards, a new feeling of calm and confidence, peace of mind, and a better chance of being accepted into the college of your dreams is certainly worth the effort!

Testifying in Court

One of the most nerve-wracking experiences that the person who suffers from performance anxiety can endure is testifying in court. Even for the individual who is slightly nervous about speaking in public, the courtroom can be a shock to the system. A shock that one does not easily recover from. Hostile and belligerent attorneys and prosecutors (and judges!) can wither the coolest of cucumbers in a matter of moments. In my twenty years with the TalkPower program, I have worked with police officers, detectives, psychiatrists, and forensic experts who suffered from intense anticipatory anxiety and public speaking phobia, but nevertheless were required (because of their jobs) to testify in court.

The following TalkPower exercises were a lifesaver for them, and I am sure they will be for you if you practice these procedures with discipline and dedication. Here are a series of exercises that you can do in advance of your courtroom debut. They will allow you to function on all eight cylinders, instead of the mumbling/bumbling mess of anxiety that you anticipate in your worst nightmare.

Exercise: Testifying in Court

1. Make a list of the questions that you anticipate will be asked of you, or if your attorney has given you those questions, so much the better. Of course, you understand that questions will probably be asked that you do not expect. Turn to chapter 12 and read the Q&A instructions. Mastering the belly breathing technique is essential.

2. Write out a brief answer to each question. Make sure that you answer only the questions you are asked. DO NOT volunteer one additional word: not in your rehearsal and not, heaven forbid, in court!

3. Do the basic pre-rehearsal routine beginning with the breathing exercise on pages 53-55, and then do the pre-talk routine on pages 393-394 up to number 8.

4. You will end up in the front of the room, facing the chair you have just left. Squeeze your toes three times and ask the first question. Squeeze your toes three times and answer the question out loud. (In answering a question, don't forget to repeat the question before you answer to give yourself time to frame your reply carefully.)

I suggest that you rehearse standing up for the first four days to remind you of the formal setting in a courtroom. After this you can sit down if you wish. Run through your list of questions two times for at least three days before your court appearance.

Trial Litigation for Attorneys

"All the world's a stage." Seldom is the drama as intense as it is in the courtroom for attorneys. Cross-examinations, summations, and depositions are stressful. Constant interruptions, hostile judges, uncooperative witnesses, and formidable adversaries batter the nervous system. As a result, the tension, fatigue, and wear-and-tear upon the attorney are considerable, frequently diminishing concentration and the quality of likability that is so important to a jury.

I know that attorneys in particular are extremely busy, and it is tempting to skip the rehearsal routine; but if you examine your priorities, you will see how important it is to rehearse properly, because the final result of all your hard work will be determined by your courtroom performance.

Talking too fast, becoming confused, sidetracked or losing your concentration because of anxiety, can ruin the most skillfully prepared examination or summation. Here, likability is, at times, as vital as credibility. By likability I mean the quality of appearing warm, earnest, in control, decisive, and clear; not tense, hard, cold, or agitated. A good rehearsal routine will help you to remain in control of yourself. Therefore, it is essential if you want to deliver a strong, convincing opening or closing statement. The exercise is also beneficial for preparing for a cross-examination.

Exercise: Courtroom Rehearsal

The following rehearsal schedule is extremely effective in preparing you properly for the toughest of courtroom confrontations.

(Be sure to see *Listening Skills for Attorneys,* which follow this exercise.)

Set up several chairs, and a designated place where you will be standing, as you give your opening and closing remarks. Do the Basic Performance Rehearsal Routine.

1. Stand in front of your imaginary judge, jury, and people in the gallery. *(Squeeze . . . squeeze . . . squeeze . . . those toes.)*

    Say the first three words of your talk very slowly, with a space between each word. Continue through the rest of your talk. If you have not already made places in your talk for pauses, please note places where a pause—three toe squeezes—is appropriate for your audience as well as yourself by circling the spot on the page with a red pen. If you find that you are speaking too quickly, or you find that your talk is disorganized, I suggest you run through the TalkPower program again, starting with chapter 6. The TalkPower Action Formula is an excellent guide for developing the story logic of a summation. Also review *What if You Lose Control* in chapter 17, page 286. Say the last sentence of your presentation. *(Squeeze . . . squeeze . . . squeeze . . . those toes.)*

2. Walk back to your seat, saying, *"I slowly walk back to my seat . . . I feel my hands."* Sit down. Do ten belly breaths. See how you feel.

3. Do this two times a day for five days before your court appearance. Concentrate on the feeling of gravity pulling your hands down.

Listening Skills for Attorneys

Listening to the opposing attorney trying to totally demolish your argument (or your client) can provoke a great deal of anxiety. In addition, having the clarity and control to object, or to note some piece of testimony that you will want to explore later in your examination of the witness, demands that your thinking abilities remain as sharp and focused as possible. The key to this ideal of courtroom behavior lies in training your mind and body to remain calm, detached, and in control.

The following rehearsal procedure has been designed to reduce anxiety and strengthen concentration for the attorney who is sitting in the courtroom, listening to an adversary.

Exercise: Attorney Listening Skills

Make a ten-minute recording summarizing your opposition's argument. Do this in your own words, based on your imagination and knowledge of your opponent's case, or have someone else make the tape for you. Speak slowly and clearly. It is very important not to rush this part of your rehearsal.

Set up several chairs where you will be sitting as you listen to the tape of the opposition's argument. Do the breathing exercises found on pages 53-55 and the pre-rehearsal routine on pages 393-394. Pay particular attention to the breathing exercises, as they will prove to be essential for your courtroom effectiveness.

1. Begin by standing in front of your imaginary judge, jury, and people in the gallery. *(Squeeze . . . Squeeze . . . Squeeze . . . those toes.)*
2. Walk back to your seat, saying, *"I slowly walk back to my seat . . . I feel my hands."* Sit down. Do ten belly breaths. See how you feel.

Listening: Part I

1. You are now sitting down, listening to your tape recorder with a pad, a pen, and a paperweight in one hand.
2. As you listen, belly breathe the way you were breathing in the first part of this rehearsal. Count up to twenty breaths and then stop the recording. Relax. Make notes about what you have just heard.
3. Turn on the recording again. Count twenty breaths. Shut the recording off; make notes. Continue doing this until the entire recording is finished.

Note: *If you are concerned about not being able to concentrate on the recording while you are counting breaths, I can assure you that your concentration will be much better if you count and breathe than if you just sit there getting more and more agitated.*

Listening: Part II

Play the recording a second time. Do not hold the paperweight. This time do your belly breathing again, but stop to take notes whenever you would like to. It is important to keep counting as you breathe, listening to the recording. (In other words, you are doing three things at once: breathing, counting, and listening to the recording.)

4. Rehearse this way two times each day for five or more days before and during your court appearance. In the first rehearsal, hold a paperweight in one hand. For the second rehearsal, do not use it. Just concentrate on the feeling of gravity pulling your hands down.
5. Now you can look at your notes and formulate whatever objections or comments you wish to make in the future. After you have practiced this exercise for a week before your court appearance, you will find that your ability to listen and focus on the important points for your examination will significantly improve.

Media Appearances

If you are lucky enough to be invited to appear on TV or on the radio, then making the most of it will certainly bring a lot of positive attention to your book, your business, your career, your political message, or your project. What a great opportunity to strut your stuff! The peculiarities and hazards of the situation, however, make for a very challenging event.

The main reason a media appearance is different and unnatural lies with the very brief time that you will be given to state your message. The average TV appearance lasts from one to three minutes. Once again, the secret of success lies with a strategy for rehearsal that is customized to your specific type of guest spot. The importance of rehearsing for a media performance is even more crucial than in any of the other performance situations. Because you may be doing your spot live, even if it is being taped. There will be no chance to do it again, so get it right—invest the time and effort for a proper preparation and rehearsal.

We will cover five different types of media appearances:

1. One- to three-minute expert guest shot
2. Ten-minute to half-hour interview
3. The how-to demonstration
4. The firing line: the confrontational Q&A
5. Preparation for the one-line sound bite

On the following pages you will find examples for each one of these categories.

One- to Three-Minute Guest Shot

Often people make the mistake of thinking that if the appearance is to be brief, not much rehearsal is necessary. Actually, the opposite is true. The shorter the spot, the more time you must spend carving out a memorable moment or two for the millions of viewers who will catch your act. Make every word count.

Preparation

1. In one sentence write, "*My book/project/business is about*

_____.

For example, in her book *Open and Clothed*, Andrea Siegel said, "My book, *Open and Clothed*, tells the stories of people who have passionate emotional relationships with their wardrobes." Before she arrived at this summary, she went through a number of ideas until she determined what was the shortest and most provocative thing she could say about her book. Notice that she repeated the name of the book. Never just say "My book." Your audience won't remember the title when they head for their bookstore. This summary step is vital and must be made in advance of your appearance. Be clear and brief, and do not spread yourself all over the place. The same goes for the business owner, politician, expert, or advocate.

2. Write out in two sentences how you came to write this book/ have this business/believe in this cause. (No run-on sentences, please!)

    I got the idea to write this book _____.

    _____.

3. Make a list of the topics covered in your book/business/ project/cause. Each item should be captured in one or two words. (You may have as many as twenty items on the list.)

1. _____	2. _____
3. _____	4. _____
5. _____	6. _____
7. _____	8. _____
9. _____	10. _____

11. _____	12. _____
13. _____	14. _____
15. _____	16. _____
17. _____	18. _____
19. _____	20. _____

4. Pick out three things from the list that you wish to talk about.
    1. _____
    2. _____
    3. _____

5. Relate these three main points to three reasons people should buy your book/do business with you/support your point of view.

   I think that people should buy my book/support my cause/vote for me because:
    1. _____
    2. _____
    3. _____

6. Make a list of ten questions that you would like to be asked, and answer each question briefly. Write everything out, and in your answer, repeat the question.

Example

Q: "Why did you write your book?"

A: "I wrote my book *(name of book)* because I realized I had an important *(pick one)* message/mission/story/experience/knowledge that I knew could benefit *(define exact audience)*."

7. Once you have completed all of the previous writing, thinking, and organizing, and can clearly read what you have written, you are ready for a complete stand-up rehearsal with the questions and answers as your script.

Do the basic performance rehearsal with belly breathing and Transitional Mantra/pre-talk routine, and the job interview rehearsal, using exactly the same instructions. Rehearse your questions and answers at least five times a day, for four days before your scheduled appearance. This may seem like quite a regime, but only practice makes perfect, and on TV, you have only one chance to get it right.

Ten-Minute to Half-Hour Interview

The longer interview is the most pleasant of all the various media appearances. Here you have more time to talk and to express whatever it is you wish to talk about. Usually you are asked to submit a list of questions to your host before the program, but preparing a list is not enough of a rehearsal. Even if you could give the answers in your sleep, you must sit down and write out complete answers to each one of these questions. If you want to look good, you really must clarify and think through each one of your answers so that you sound as warm and as clever as possible. Include several humorous anecdotes or stories to enhance your appearance, and even you will love the replay.

When you have completed the writing part of this exercise, return to the basic performance rehearsal and job interview rehearsal. Use exactly the same instructions, and rehearse your questions and answers at least three times a day, for four days before your scheduled appearance. You can space out the rehearsals any way you like, but don't cut corners.

The How-To Demonstration

The how-to demonstration runs the gamut from the very active, moving-around exercise or cooking demonstration to the sitting-in-your-seat explanation of how to play a game of chess. Once again, this rehearsal model will be the one-size-fits-all general principles of the how-to demonstration that you will customize for your own particular needs.

1. Make a list of all the things that you do in your demonstration, stacking the sequence in logical order. Begin from the very beginning. Example:

    "I am standing/sitting, ready to begin my demonstration . . ."
    A...
    B...
    C . . . and so on.

2. Walk through this sequence slowly, following the order on your list. If you are handling any objects, pick up each object slowly and feel the weight of the object. Do this twice. (Think and speak the logic of what you are doing as you do it.)

3. Walk through the sequence slowly again, this time saying out loud everything that you are doing. Take your time. Do not rush.

4. Write a script for yourself based upon the steps you took and the speaking part of your demonstration.

5. List three important points that you wish to make.
    A. _____
    B. _____
    C. _____

6. Now check your time frame. How much time has been allotted to your spot? With this in mind, set a kitchen timer to ten minutes, walk through your demonstration. See how many minutes you have used on the timer. Take your script and edit it down (or fill it in) so that it fits into your time slot. If your demonstration is too long, do not count on rushing. What you must do is eliminate sections by prioritizing. Even if you show a before-and-after and explain what you did to achieve the result, this is better than dashing through the demonstration like a tornado.

7. Once you have your routine timed and edited, you are ready for your rehearsal. Turn to the basic performance rehearsal on page 393, and then walk through your written script demonstration five times each day, for five days before your scheduled appearance. Use actual objects or closely simulated objects, and do not skip any steps. Be sure to time yourself during each rehearsal.

The Firing Line: Confrontational Q&A

The firing line/confrontational Q&A is the most dangerous and unpleasant type of media appearance. Usually this type of media spot is centered on a particular issue that is controversial, inflammatory, scandalous, or in dispute. In this case it's crucial to get feedback from others you trust about how to handle the interrogation, unless you have a very strong feeling about your own strategy. With the proper preparation, the firing line can be incredibly empowering and leave you looking like a hero. The secret of success lies in preparation and training.

If you are a politician, a corporate spokesperson, or involved with public or social policy, you would be well advised to follow through on the entire TalkPower program. This will guarantee that you repattern your brain for thinking quickly on your feet, under the most aggressive conditions of media assault.

Should an emergency interview suddenly loom, and you don't have time to do the entire program, here is a shortcut. But you absolutely must turn to the basic performance rehearsal on page 393 with its belly breathing and Transitional Mantra *after* you have written your script.

1. Make a list of all of the questions that you expect your adversaries to ask you.
2. Answer every one by writing out the best brief response you can come up with.
3. I know that coaches like to bombard you quickly in a loud voice, with these questions, storming the bastions of your sanity in an attempt to toughen you up and prepare you for the media onslaught. This is wrong and can totally destroy your concentration. True learning and true training can occur only in a zone of calm, quiet, and safety. Therefore, the first step in training yourself to respond well under fire is to rehearse slowly and calmly, reading the answers to all of the questions, as you take your time, pausing and breathing. Hold a paperweight in each hand as you speak, keeping part of your attention on the weight of the paperweights. (This

will ground you, reducing your anxiety level considerably.)
Ideally, this should be done with a colleague or a coach, who
urges you to take your time, breathe, "There's no rush about
this . . ." pause, and so on. However, if you are working
alone, record the questions and allow enough time for your
response, so that you can pause and speak slowly.

4. Once you have a position, stick to it. Repeat it. Do not
    elaborate or go into detail. Here is a situation where sticking
    to your guns will really pay off. Remember, you must never
    ever testify against yourself in public. However, if you are
    caught red-handed with irrefutable evidence that you are
    guilty, then you must admit it, apologize, and hope for the
    best. Even this must be carefully rehearsed so that you give
    yourself the best possible chance for forgiveness.

5. Rehearse your complete responses five times slowly and then
    continue reviewing the list of questions, gradually speeding
    up your response, until you have a normal rate of speech (be
    careful not to talk too fast at this point). Do five belly breaths
    between each set.

Preparation for the One-Line Sound Bite

The one-line sound bite preparation follows exactly the same rules as
the firing line, except that the responses must be exactly as stated—
one short line. For example:

Q: *Don't you think that this most recent witness destroyed the credibility of the defendant?*
A: *That's not evidence. It's his word against the defendant's.*

Usually conditions for the one-line sound bite will not allow
you the luxury of a rehearsal. Therefore, you must formulate your
response wherever you are (in the courtroom, boardroom, and so on)
before you meet the media. Practicing the belly breathing in anticipation of a media attack will ensure that your sound bite is clear, crisp,
and to the point. Here are some suggestions that will always be useful in a pinch:

- We are confident that this issue will be resolved.
- We'll make an announcement to the public at the appropriate time.
- We are very close to a solution.
- Public service issues deserve solutions that address these concerns.
- We are currently taking measures to normalize the situation.
- We are taking appropriate actions.
- We are still studying the issue to determine if it has merit.

Preparing for Your Orals

Oral examinations, or "Orals," can be a time of extreme anxiety for people who are not comfortable speaking in public. They may even cause some to put off the completion of their PhD thesis. On the phone the other day, John Lakos, a computer genius, said to me, "Orals are no challenge at all. Just teach a course in your subject for seven years, like I did, and that will straighten you out." I can just hear my students saying, "Seven years? I don't think so."

The basic performance rehearsal routine is the perfect solution to the problem of Orals trepidation. If you take the time to learn how to do correct belly breathing and practice the inner awareness walking exercises, not only will you perform brilliantly on the day of your Orals, but those sleepless nights with bouts of anticipatory anxiety will be completely eliminated.

Although I cannot present a strategy for every kind of Orals procedure, I can give you a general, one-size-fits-most model that you can customize to your own specifications.

Exercise

Now do the basic performance rehearsal routine on page 393 up to the point where you are standing in front of your imaginary committee.

Oral Examinations

Prepare a summary of your thesis to last about ten minutes. Use the TalkPower templates for a writing model, if you wish. If you intend to use PowerPoint or any other audiovisuals, have them ready. Prepare a list of questions that you expect to be asked by your committee.

After you have run through the belly breathing and Transitional Mantra, read your summary out loud. Remember to put pause points (squeeze two times with your toes) in your script with a red pen about every 200 words. Write this into your script and deliver your PowerPoint presentation on your computer.

Complete all the answers and walk back to your seat, saying, *"I slowly walk back to my seat . . . I feel my hands."*

Do this routine while standing once per day, for four days. Then you can do this one time standing up and one time sitting down each day until the day of the examination. The entire rehearsal period should include at least ten rehearsals beginning two weeks before the scheduled date of your Orals.

Walking Down the Aisle

Many people do not realize how traumatic walking down the aisle can be for a person who is uncomfortable when he or she is the center of attention. The bride or groom (or wedding party member) who suffers from intense self-consciousness, can go through weeks of painful anticipatory anxiety, worrying about that moment when he or she hears the organ playing "Here Comes the Bride." They think, "Oh God, will I faint?" "Will I be able to breathe?" "I am going to spoil the wedding!" "I wish I could call this off . . ." and so on.

Only the person who suffers from performance anxiety can possibly understand the grief that comes with this unfortunate condition. However, if you rehearse walking down the aisle using the TalkPower belly breathing exercise, plus the Transitional Mantra, or the basic desensitization exercises at home, well in advance of the wedding date, you will find that your comfort level on the day of the wedding has increased by 100 percent. As a matter of fact, you may even enjoy your own wedding, much to your surprise and delight. In this book, I previously quoted a student who said, "I actually enjoyed my own wedding." That was something he could not possibly imagine before he signed up for the TalkPower Workshop.

Exercise: Wedding March

Rehearsals should start one month before the wedding. You will need a recording of the "Wedding March" or whatever music the bride plans to use for the processional, and two small paperweights or two cans of soda for the Transitional Mantra.

1. Do the entire breathing exercise on pages 53-55, and the standing up and walking exercise on page 84. When you do this basic performance rehearsal routine, hold a paperweight or a can of soda in each hand. Do not shake or jiggle the paperweights; just feel the weight. Do this routine two times. Now you are ready to rehearse walking down the aisle.
2. Play the processional music tape. Slowly stand up with the weights in your hands, concentrate on the weights, and slowly begin to walk around the room, taking medium steps to the rhythm of the music. You will find that just the act of concentrating on the heaviness of the paperweights makes you feel a bit calmer immediately. You will become calmer and calmer as you continue to practice.

This entire exercise should be done once a day for five days each week, for four weeks before the wedding. On the day of the wedding, run through it again if possible. By now you should be significantly desensitized to the feelings of embarrassment that come when you are the center of attention.

Walking into a Restaurant Alone

Some people suffer from a form of social phobia that leaves them unable to walk into a restaurant alone. This event, which most people never even think twice about, can produce anything from a mild feeling of anxiety to a major panic attack for those who cannot bear standing apart from a crowd and being looked at. There are many people who fall into this category; their pain is invisible, their isolation terrible. If you are not comfortable about walking into a restaurant or a hotel lobby and being seated when you are alone, the following exercise will help you overcome this problem.

Exercise: Walking into a Restaurant

Set up several chairs and a designated place in the imaginary restaurant where you will eventually sit.

Part One: Breathing

Note: *Always begin your breathing exercise with an exhalation, never an inhalation.*

1. Sit in a chair far away from the designated place in the imaginary restaurant where you will eventually sit. Hold one paperweight in each hand; your palms face up and let your hands lie relaxed in your lap. Concentrate, and pull your belly in slowly as you exhale through the nose.
2. Hold this for three counts: Think "1 - 2 - 3."
3. Relax your belly muscles and take a small breath. (This is one complete inhalation-exhalation set. Do not breathe so hard that your chest moves.)
4. Repeat this breathing routine ten times. At the end of each exhalation, count the breath you have just completed. Counting each breath is important, lest your mind begin to wander and you are no longer fully present.
5. Now that you have completed ten breaths, take a moment to see how you feel. Go immediately to Part Two.

Part Two: Transitional Mantra/Pre-Talk Routine

1. Say out loud, *"I am sitting in my chair . . . I feel my body perfectly balanced."* (Feel your balance.)
2. Lift your hands off your lap no more than one inch, so that no one else notices.
   Say to yourself, *"I feel my hands."* (Wait until you feel your hands.)
3. Say, *"I bring my hands to my sides slowly."*
4. Say, *"I get up slowly . . . I take a small step and stop . . . I feel my hands."* Do you feel the inner click? Get up and take a tiny step (no more than three inches) in front of your chair. Stop.

5. Say, "*I walk slowly across the floor . . . I feel my hands.*" Take as many steps as you need to get to the imaginary front of the restaurant. Feel your hands at all times. Say, "*I turn around slowly . . . I face people seated in the restaurant . . . I stop.*" Say, "*I look straight ahead . . . I stand with my feet comfortably apart . . . I feel my hands.*"

6. At this point, begin walking toward the imaginary table where you will sit.

7. Sit down, do ten belly breaths, and see how you feel.

8. You can reinforce this exercise by concentrating on your hands or anything you are carrying when you walk past a restaurant or a diner or any kind of dining establishment.

9. Do this twice a day for four weeks. In the fourth week, do this exercise without the paperweights, concentrating on feeling how gravity pulls your hands down. Then do a test run by walking into a restaurant alone during the slow part of the day. As your confidence increases, you can try to do this during the lunch or dinner hour.

Introducing Yourself to the Group

People who are extremely uncomfortable whenever any attention is directed toward them dread waiting their turn to give their name and whatever information the leader of the group requests. Once again, a structured procedure will work wonders for reducing the stress of this situation.

Your Script

Fill in the following script on a card.

"*My name is* _____," or "*I am* _____.

"*I work for* _____" and/or "*I am a* _____" (choose one or both)

Say, "*I am here because I would like to . . .* (state one, two or three things)

1. (fill in) _____
2. (fill in) _____
3. (fill in) _____

Or else you can say, "*What I would like to get from this experience is* _____."

Rehearsal Format

1. Place several chairs together to simulate a part of a circle. Sit in the middle chair. Hold your script in one hand and a paperweight in the other.
2. Imagine that you are in a group and the leader has asked each person to introduce himself to the group.
3. Do ten belly breaths, beginning with an exhale. (Now it is your turn to speak . . .)
4. Slightly raise your hands imperceptibly above your lap and concentrate on the weight of your hands while you say, "*I am . . .*" or "*My name is . . .*" and the rest of your prepared words. Return your hands to your lap.
5. When you stop talking, immediately exhale, and do ten more belly breaths.
6. Do this rehearsal three times each day for seven days, before you attend a conference, begin school, or go the initial meeting, etc. Do not use the paperweight on the third try. Work with the weight of your hands. Use exactly the same words each time. Do not change anything.

Meetings and Classrooms

I am at a professional conference, in a meeting, and I have a great idea. My face gets warm and I feel my heart starting to beat quickly. I know just what I want to say . . . I don't know what happens, but the moment passes . . . I hear my colleagues saying exactly what I wanted to say . . . everyone is smiling and saying, yes, that is a great idea . . . I feel cheated, dumb, disappointed.

—Doug, dentist

Does this story sound familiar? I ask the question in my workshops, and most of the participants sadly agree that this is a frequent experience. Fear of public speaking creates inhibitions that prevent you from expressing yourself in a variety of situations. As a result, you are unable to ask questions or make comments in a class. Meetings and conferences are also a problem.

Neurologically, what is happening? You are sitting in a meeting; something is said that triggers an idea. In your brain a network of neural transmitters becomes excited, vibrating in preparation for you to state your idea. An inhibitory impulse appears, blocking the transmission of chemicals and electrical signals that facilitate the final expression of the idea. You shut down; you do not speak. This happens in a flash, faster than a heartbeat. You are betrayed by your own neural network, and you have no idea what happened to you.

How can you get rid of this mental shutdown or, as we say in behavioral terms, extinguish this inhibitory impulse? When the TalkPower training program is carefully followed, there is a big reversal in avoidant behavior, and students find that they are able to participate in meetings when previously they never could. If you wish to improve rapidly, practice the rehearsal exercise described below. You will have more success with this exercise after you work with the basic performance skills in the beginning of the book.

Exercise: Participation Practice

Bring your phone to a meeting or a class. Or ask a colleague to discuss some relevant issues about your work situation and record the conversation. Or read notes about the class onto your phone's recording app. Try to keep the entire session to about fifteen minutes.

STEP ONE

At home, place your phone on speaker-phone. Sit in a chair with a paperweight in each hand, your hands resting on your lap. Center yourself by being aware that the right side of your body is balanced with the left side . . . do ten belly breaths. Inhale with your nose, and exhale with your nose . . . Keep your eyes open or closed as you wish. Listen to the questions on your phone. You will probably feel your heart jump when you hear the discussion. This is perfectly natural. The discussion stimulates higher levels of excitement.

As you listen, breathe, when you feel your breath flowing in a comfortable rhythm, pick your hands up off your lap no more than one inch . . . concentrate on the weight of your hands. (If your hands become tired, bring them back to your lap, let them rest, and then pick them up again.) Listen to the entire message. Prepare to write a script for participating in meetings.

THE STRUCTURED SENTENCE FOR PARTICIPATION IN MEETINGS

Just as the TalkPower Action Formula helps to organize your ideas for a speech, a simple structure for your comment will help you to formulate your ideas into sentences so that you are able to participate at meetings.

1. *(A comment)* In reference to _____
I think that _____
because _____
_____ and _____ because
_____.

Example

In reference to *speaking up at meetings, I should promise myself to make at least one statement at each meeting that I attend,* because *this systematic plan will reduce the inhibitions I have about speaking up at meetings,* and *if I make up my mind to do it, I will not have to make a decision about it at the meeting. I will speak at every meeting because I promised myself I would.*

In addition to the structured comment, asking a question, or agreeing or disagreeing with what someone else has said, is another way to participate in a meeting.

2. *(Asking a question):* I need some clarification. Could you explain _____

_____?

Note: *Even if you know the answer to a question, ask the question anyway to practice participating.*

3. *Picking up on what someone else says, by agreeing or disagreeing with a previous statement.*

Example

"I agree with Brad. I think his idea about half days on Fridays in the summertime would boost employee morale and will be more productive in the long run."

Any one of these three responses gives you an A for participating in meetings.

STEP TWO
Write three different comments and three different questions that you might have made had the phone recording been a real meeting.

STEP THREE
You have written three comments and three questions that are relevant to the discussion. Sit in your chair. Hold one paperweight in one hand and your cards with the comments in the other hand. Center yourself . . . be aware that the right side of your body is balanced with the left side . . . do ten belly breaths, inhale with your nose and exhale with your nose . . . keep your eyes open or closed as you wish . . . let go of your tensions . . . When you feel that you are listening and breathing in a comfortable rhythm, concentrate on the paperweight in your hand. When you have a comment to make, pause the recording and make your comment. Speak slowly and clearly. Listen to your phone until there is a point where you can ask one of your questions. Ask your question. Continue in this manner

until you come to the end. If you think of a new comment or question, shut the tape off and state your comment.

Practice this entire exercise once each day for one week. Then put yourself on a real-life practice schedule. Ask one question or make one comment at every single class, conference session, or meeting that you attend. Do not wait until you have something brilliant to say, as you previously did. Even if you know the answer, ask a question. The point is to speak up once at every single meeting so that your presence is established.

If, after one week of practice, you feel that you are not able to ask any questions, continue rehearsing at home with your phone for one or two more weeks. After the third week, try a real-life experience. If you have practiced the TalkPower program described in the beginning of this book, plus three weeks of rehearsal, you will probably be able to handle asking one question or making one comment. When you have asked one question at each meeting or classroom session often enough, you will be ready to make a comment. Decide to ask one question and make one comment at every single meeting or classroom session that you attend.

Behavioral Schedule

In behavioral psychology, putting yourself on a regular schedule of asking one question and making one comment at every meeting would be called putting yourself on a "behavioral schedule," a systematic method for changing behavior. In this way you can plan a routine of new actions that will eventually become integrated into your own repertoire of behavior. Use any one of the three strategies: make a comment, ask a question, or agree with someone else's comment.

If you do plan to make one comment at every meeting, it is important not to skip a week or to wait until you feel like saying something. You cannot pick and choose your time to speak. This is avoidant behavior.

All serious athletic training, such as training to run a marathon, observes the same principle. If you want to run a marathon, you must commit yourself to a regular training schedule of running at least three or four times a week, progressively increasing the distance over time. Even people who are initially in terrible shape can hope to eventually complete the marathon with this kind of dedication. If you adhere to a behavioral schedule for speaking at meetings, gradually, in three to six months you will find yourself becoming a player in your organization, feeling empowered by participating in all the meetings. Your self-esteem will be over the moon.

PRESENTING AN IMPROVISED PROFESSIONAL TALK AT A MEETING

Presenting an improvised talk at a meeting, though not as formal as a stand-up presentation, can be just as intimidating. However, now that you have experienced the TalkPower Action Formula, it will be easy for you to use parts of the TalkPower Action plan as a model for an improvised talk. Here is an outline you can follow for an improvised professional presentation at a meeting. When speaking at a meeting, the Introduction and the Background templates are not included.

TOPIC SENTENCE

(CHOOSE ONE): Today, *(pause)* I am going to talk about *(or)* in reference to *(pause)(or)* other

_____

MESSAGE SENTENCE

(Choose one): I think *(or)* I feel *(or)* I believe *(or)* it has come to my/our attention *(or)* our findings suggest that *(or)* studies suggest that

_____

MENU

In my talk about *(topic)*

The issues that I will discuss include:
List items like in a table of contents (Limit your list from two to
seven items).

_____

_____

_____

"and finally" (*the last item*) _____

Go back and discuss each item on your list.

Try to remember to include the message sentence or a similar
idea, in as many of the items that were on your Menu as possible.

Q&A

"Before I conclude, are there any questions?"

Remember to repeat the question in your answer.

"Thank you for your questions."

CONCLUSION

"In conclusion, I have tried to familiarize you with (*repeat the
Menu list*) _____

_____

_____

_____

_____ "

"and finally" _____
(*the last item*)

   (Closing Statement: Use either A or B)

   (A) I would like to remind (*or*) suggest (*or*) recommend (*or*) appeal (*or*) confirm (*or*) other

_____

_____

_____

Because _____

_____

   (B) Moving forward (*Make a statement*)

_____

_____

Auditions for Actors

Professional actors are no more spared the effects of stage fright than the most inexperienced novice. Even though it doesn't make sense that an actor would ever have stage fright, the fact remains that many actors are not able to maintain their concentration and self-control in new environments such as auditions or interviews because although the actor may have a brilliant acting technique, he does not have a developed performance technique and probably has anxiety when he is acting in a play.

The following rehearsal schedule will give you the technique for overcoming your pre-audition stage fright.

Preparation

1. Thoroughly read chapter 4, *Breath is Life*, and practice the belly breathing exercises carefully and completely.
2. Before and after each rehearsal for your audition, do a thirty-cycle slow belly breath exhalation/inhalation practice.
3. Sit in front of your imaginary audience or casting director.
4. Focus your attention on your body balance for thirty seconds.
5. Use the technique you are trained in to go into the emotional mood or color of your character.
6. If you have to, stand up, feel the weight of your hands as you leave your chair and walk to the place where you will be standing. (See the complete Transitional Mantra on page 393.)
7. Say the first three words of your script slowly with a space between each word to ease into the spoken word.
8. If you are doing a monologue, make rest points in the script where you will stop talking and try to sense your body balance. If you are in a scene with one or more actors, make rest points in your script where you will try to sense your body balance. These pauses will stop you from becoming tense.

Do this rehearsal two times.

Rehearsal Practice

Detailed below is an excellent rehearsal aid to overcome the feeling of disassociation some actors feel when working on monologues:

1. When you are rehearsing your script, at the end of each line, stop talking.
2. Make contact with whatever you are feeling such as tension, stiffness, stress, pressure, tightness, racing heart, etc.

3. Take the awareness of that feeling into your next line.
4. Stop at the end of that line and, again, make contact with whatever you're feeling.
5. Continue reading and stopping in this way until you are finished.
6. Go through the entire piece a second time without the stops.

TalkPower for Kids
Part One

Here is an overview of the entire TalkPower for Kids Program.

First read the entire section by yourself and then begin with the breathing exercises.

(This program is for eight- to twelve-year-olds. For children over thirteen, the regular TalkPower program is suggested. The instructions here are designed for classroom participation. However, they may be used for one on one home use by a parent.)

If you would like to introduce children to leadership skills such as public speaking, here is a model that you can practice together. This model is also recommended for use with children in any performance situation: chorus, plays, playing a musical instrument, or talent shows when they are afraid to stand in front of an audience. The following exercise (modified to your needs) can work wonders and is especially recommended for the shy child.

For some children this is a very sensitive and possibly a difficult exercise. Before you begin the first lesson you might even read a children's book about space to them. Take the actual TalkPower exercise as far as the child is willing to go. You may not get beyond the breathing part. That is fine for the first few times. As the lessons progress, you will go further and further into the exercises. But above all, do not push or pressure the child. With patience and your self-control, amazing things can happen.

Use the following script. Please feel free to add your own words and ideas.

Say, *"We are going to the moon in outer space, and we have to learn how to do belly breathing so that we do not lose our oxygen as we take off in our great space capsule."*

Sit in a chair and give the instructions for the following belly breathing exercise out loud. First, get it right yourself, then show the children how you are doing it. It is very important to be relaxed about this. Do not criticize or command even if someone is doing it wrong. It has to be fun! If it gets too difficult, pleasantly discontinue the exercise and try again the next day. Say, *"That was a great beginning! That's enough for today. We'll do more tomorrow."*

Belly Breathing Technique for Kids

I suggest you practice by yourself until you feel confident that you know how to do this. If you need more information please review chapter 4, *Breath is Life*. During this exercise, you can also quietly play non-rhythmical, somewhat ethereal music to set the scene.

1. Sit in a chair. Give each child two small wooden blocks to hold in their hands. We will call the blocks *moonstones*.
2. Say, *"Pick up one hand and hold it under your nose. Now blow out on the block that is in your hand. Can feel the air?*
3. Say, *"Now pull your belly in slowly as you blow out through the nose."*
4. Say, *"Now relax your belly muscles and take a small breath in."*
5. Demonstrate to the child what this looks like.
6. Say, *"Put your hand down."* Repeat these steps five times to the child.
7. Say, *"Take a moment to see how you feel."* Pause silently for approximately 20 seconds. Say, *"By now you should have landed on the moon."*
8. Say, *"Lift up your hands and feel how heavy these moonstones are."* (Let the child experience the weight of the blocks for half a minute or so.)
9. Stand up and say, *"Now, get off the chair and begin walking around the room very slowly with the moonstones, feeling*

their weight in your hands all the time." Say, *"This is how you would be walking if you were on the moon, where there is very little gravity."* Ask the children to follow you as you walk around the room. (This walk will feel robotic. That is correct.)

10. After the children have walked around the room twice, let them walk back to their seats to return to earth.

Part Two

11. Say these sentences out loud
    "I am sitting in my chair . . . I feel my body perfectly balanced . . .
    I feel the moonstone in my hands."
    Now have the children say it.
    Tell the children to wait until they feel the weight in their hands.
    Say *"I bring my hands to my sides . . . I stand up slowly and take a small step and stop . . . I wait until I feel my hands."*
    Now have the children say it.
    Ask the children if they feel their hands.
    Say *"I walk to the front of the class feeling the moonstones in my hands . . . I turn around . . . I face the class . . . I stop . . . I stand with my feet comfortably apart . . . I feel my hands."*
    Now have the children say and do this.
    Tell the children that now you are standing in front of your imaginary classroom on the moon.
    Tell the children to squeeze their toes slowly three times.
    Squeeze, release, squeeze, release, squeeze, release.
    Say, *"This is how we walk up to the front of the class on the moon."*
    Now have the children squeeze their toes three times.

12. Say, *"I walk back to my seat . . . I feel the moonstones in my hands."* Now the children say, *"I walk back to my seat,"* and the children walk back to their seats.

13. Now you can ask the children if they have any questions or comments about walking on the moon.

14. This is the end of the first lesson.

For lesson number two, repeat the breathing and walking exercise and ask each child to select a topic from the following list.

Here is a selection of topics for a talk. Have each child select one.

• An outer space trip	• Sports
• A jungle safari	• A pet
• A trip to Disney World	• A hobby
• A favorite vacation	• Summer camp
• Science experiment	• A special interest

You might ask each child why he/she chose the topic. And have a discussion.

At this point the lesson is over.

Lesson Number Three

Repeat the breathing and walking "moon walk" exercise.

Now ask each child to fill out the template on the next page, using the topic they have chosen. If they can do it alone, fine. If you have to help a particular child, read the template with her/him and gently coax out the answers. Be very patient and allow each child time to think. Do not under any circumstances rush or pressure the child. Read a magazine if you have to, while they are thinking. Do not in any way reject or criticize any choices, even if they sound wrong or awful. The point is to get the children to participate comfortably. Eventually, things will be corrected. If any child is so shy that they cannot think at all, then say cheerfully, "That's OK. Why don't I show you what it looks like, so you can have a better idea of what to do?" Fill out the template yourself with a topic from the list. Start by reading it out loud and ask if there are any questions or comments.

Have each child read from his/her template two times.

The lesson is over.

Lesson Number Four

Do the same as the previous lessons, only this time the children will read in front of the class.

The point is to familiarize the children with the concept of standing up in front of a class alone and speaking. This can be done by first demonstrating how you look when you do it, and then having the children do it themselves when they are ready to do it. Remember ... no pressure.

TalkPower for Kids Template

Topic Sentence: Today I am going to talk about _____.

Message Sentence: I think _____
_____.

Background: When I was in/with/making *(choose one)* _____,

(Menu/Points) I saw (or did, or learned) three things:

    1. _____

    2. _____

    3. _____

What I liked best was _____
_____

because _____
_____.

Conclusion: Next time I would like _____
_____

because _____
_____
_____.

(Squeeze your toes three times.) Thank you!

Standing in Front of the Class

1. Script for teacher: We are now going to practice standing in front of the class and reading from our scripts. First, we will review all of the steps that we have done on the other days.

2. Complete the entire exercise with the children, including the belly breathing segment, up to step 11. However, this time do not give the children the blocks. Encourage them to feel the weight of their empty hands at their sides.

3. Now you are ready to work individually with each child. Give each child a number or a letter from the alphabet and gently call each child in order.

4. One at a time, have each child walk up to the front of the class, saying all of the steps out loud. He can read from a paper, you can call out the instructions, or he may already know them by heart. Do not rush or criticize the child in any way. He says, *"I am sitting in my chair . . . I feel my body perfectly balanced . . . I feel my hands . . . I bring my hands to my sides . . . I stand up slowly and take a small step and stop . . . I wait until I feel my hands . . . I walk slowly to the front of the classroom . . . I feel my hands . . . I turn around slowly . . . I face the class . . . I stop . . . I stand with my feet comfortably apart . . . I feel my hands . . . I am now standing in front of my class . . . I squeeze my toes slowly three times. Squeeze, release, squeeze, release, squeeze, release."*

5. As the child stands in front of the room, holding his script, ask him to read it out loud. Do not criticize, correct, or change anything that the child has done, no matter how poor you think his performance has been. (This part is absolutely essential. If you are unable to control yourself and must comment, it is better not to do this exercise at all.)

Ask the child to walk slowly back to his seat, saying out loud, *"I slowly walk back to my chair . . . I feel my hands."*

Say, *"That was great! What a good try! That sounded so interesting!"* or some other appropriate, yet always positive and complimentary remark. Depending on how cooperative the children are, try to do this rehearsal three times a week for one month. If you wish to continue working with it, pick a different topic and go through the same routine.

If you wish to reward each child with a gold star, or a sticker, or some other small reward, by all means do so. However, every child should get an equal reward. There is absolutely no place for competition or ranking in the TalkPower system.

Note: *Please refrain from suggesting how the child could have improved his performance.*

With gentle encouragement, each child will improve with the doing, at his own pace.

Chapter 20

IN CONCLUSION . . .

True Confessions

Physician, heal thyself.

—St. Luke 23

Years ago, when I was an actress on the road in a play, I had my first panic attack in a plane that was landing in Cincinnati. Just as the pilot was dipping his wings, my heart began to race uncontrollably. I could barely breathe. I thought that I was going to die.

Somehow the plane landed and eventually I got back to New York, but I never, ever again would get into an airplane. If I couldn't go somewhere in a car, taxi, train, boat, or sled, I didn't go! It was a small price to pay for safety and peace of mind. The irony was that previously, in one of my incarnations, I had briefly worked as an airline stewardess. Now I couldn't fly.

From the sidelines I saw my friends going to wonderful and exotic places. Not me: I was grounded, shot down in my prime. Time passed. I became a therapist. And one day the publisher of my first TalkPower book called to tell me that my book was one of their lead books for the season. I was to be sent on a national tour, flying from New York all the way across the country and back, with the tour lasting four weeks.

I was thrilled. Of course, in my heart, I knew I would never go. How could I? Now I was a mother. I had a little girl: my darling Colette. How could I put her in jeopardy of becoming an orphan? Which, of course, I was sure would happen once I set foot in a plane.

The tour would not begin for six months, and living in the moment, I decided to bask in the glory of my alleged national tour, just for a few weeks, just long enough to tell all my friends and to feel like a celebrity. How I enjoyed the attention and the status of being an author with a first book, about to go on a national tour!

Time went by, and I began to hear voices of conscience urging me to pick up the telephone and call the publisher. It wasn't fair. They were making so many plans. They had even hired an outside public relations person and arranged glamorous breakfasts at the Brasserie just for me.

I had to tell them: I simply couldn't go. How could I do that? Would you?

I delayed. Another month went by. . . . You understand. I just couldn't let go of it. Sleepless nights obsessing about catastrophes in the sky collided with dreams of book signings and TV interviews. I was going mad. And there I was, a therapist. It was so embarrassing. But I didn't tell anyone.

I too said, "I can't believe this is happening to me!" Finally, it was too late to refuse. A voice deep within me said, "Natalie Rogers, if you are going to die in an airplane you might as well, because life is no longer worth living this way." And this is how it was settled. The tides of embarrassment and desperate ambition had sealed my fate: I was going. No turning back. I had eliminated my conflict, but instead I was hit with waves of anxiety, anticipating the panic attacks, the terror, the fear, the possible end that lay in store for me in the air, day after day, on a national tour. I kissed my daughter good-bye, seriously wondering if I would ever see the dear child again.

The first flight was a nightmare: flying to Chicago in November with the wind chill factor (whatever that is) as low as only Chicago can get. I curled up in a fetal position with a blanket over me, belly breathing my little heart out, watching the scrambled eggs on my neighbor's tray bounce twelve inches into the air again and again.

What did I get myself into? Help!

And so on . . . as we traveled from Chicago to Minneapolis, to Texas, Indiana, and California, from city to city, landing and taking off every day for four weeks. How I survived, I will never know.

Obviously, I did. I took note of the fact that the minute we landed and the wheels touched the tarmac, the interior of the plane seemed to brighten. Other times, when we were about to take off, the plane seemed dark and foreboding.

Finally it dawned on me that the danger was in my head. That my terror was based upon some madness that had nothing to do with the plane I was flying in. It was an intellectual observation, but interesting nonetheless.

On the way home, as I entered the Houston airport to pick up a plane for Dallas, I noticed immediately something peculiar: I was calm. I felt . . . well, the best way to put it is . . . "normal."

I stopped examining the faces of the other passengers in search of a terrorist profile or trying to identify some angry man about to put a bomb on a plane to dispose of his mother-in-law. This sensation of tranquility lasted for about twenty-five minutes, and I took note of it because it was so strange, so different from the usual state of hysteria I had suffered during the previous trip. Of course, my stress and tension returned as soon as I was buckled in my seat.

Thank God! The tour was over. Heaving a sigh of relief, I was home, bringing with me a major change. Still terrified of flying, I was actually willing to consider going on a vacation in an airplane. "Major" is an understatement.

And so, as a family, we began flying to Snowmass in Colorado, to Europe in the summer . . . here, there, and everywhere. I also accepted invitations to speak and to teach.

Of course my hypervigilance was on active duty at all times, smelling the interior of the plane to detect smoke or any untoward and dangerous aroma; examining the faces of the flight attendants to see if they knew anything terrible that I didn't know; checking the weather (on land and in the air). An empty seat with a briefcase sitting on it was enough to bring on an arsenal of relaxation techniques and listening to the voice of the captain. (Oh, that was a good one.

I was a therapist, and I could tell from his voice in just one or two sentences, if he was intoxicated, a dope addict, possibly psychotic, or had not had enough sleep the night before. Oh yes, I was working all the time.)

And then one day I was sitting in a plane, waiting to take off for Great Britain. I was scheduled to do a TalkPower seminar at the Barbican in London. Reading a book, I was blithely unaware of the comings and goings of other passengers, which in itself was no small miracle because I had never been able to read a book while waiting for a plane to take off. Oh no, not me! I had always been much too busy, checking the vibrations, the faces, the crew, the captain, belly breathing, listening to my relaxation tapes, praying. I looked out the window, and I was amazed: I saw beautiful white clouds all around me.

The plane had actually taken off without the assistance of my consciousness.

What a pleasant surprise! Letting down on the job? Was I becoming casual about this?

Perhaps not. Perhaps something else was happening.

As time went on, my feelings of terror gradually disappeared, decreasing with each new flying experience. Today I must admit that I love to fly. I love it! I sit in my seat and play with my toys: my phone, my books, my notes, my letters . . . no appointments, no responsibilities. It seems the only place I am truly free is in an airplane, and I love it. I even look forward to my tray of airplane food, sitting in my seat watching a movie, pressing a button to summon the flight attendant. "More ginger ale, please."

And I ask myself: What happened to my terror? Where did it go? I grab my arms, I squeeze myself, looking for that feeling of dread that was so much a part of me as soon as I walked into an airport and the night before. Looking for terror and fear, that black cloud of anxiety, I pinch myself. Perhaps I am not alert. Where is it—that sensation of angst and tension as I sit, buckled in my seat, flying high over the oceans, plains or mountain ranges?

It's gone! It's totally gone. I do not have one drop of fear of flying in my entire body. I fly in the winter. Lightning cracks above the wings; hail pelts the plane; we drop and climb. No problem. I am dozing in my spa in the sky.

Last year, returning from the Bahamas, my plane was the object of a bomb scare. Not a peep out of me. I was sure everything would be all right. I am a naturally optimistic person. How did I do it? And this is like a Zen parable. I did it by doing it.

Why am I telling you all of this? I am telling you this story because, first of all, I think it's very funny, and I enjoy sharing funny stories about myself. But more to the point, many of my students tell me that they have heard that once you have a fear you can never get rid of it, that there is always some tiny vestige (or some big vestige) of that original terror that remains forever and ever.

It's not true. Look at me. As I said before, there is not one speck of fear about flying in my body or brain, and I would fly anywhere in a heartbeat. Just give me the chance.

So I say to you, Dear Reader, just as I say to the students in my seminars: There is hope. I learned to love to fly, and you can learn to speak in public and love it. You can feel great and powerful doing a talk; give yourself that chance. For each moment that you invest working with the TalkPower program, you will be repaid a thousand times over. The skills you will learn when you do the assignments and rehearsals are permanent, lifelong acquisitions.

Just as drivers never forget how to drive cars, actors never forget or lose their performance skills, even if they have not performed for many years. Once you have gained these performance skills, you will have them for the rest of your life. You will not believe the compliments that will come your way. At first, you may be nervous, but then you will have the feeling of satisfaction that comes with being able to stand up and express yourself fully and well. If for some reason you stop practicing in the middle of your training period, you can always pick up where you left off at a later time, because a skill is derived from a network of neural patterns that become a permanent part of your muscle memory, who you are, and what you can do.

Chapter 21

HOW TO WRITE A MONOLOGUE

Monologues are a unique form of theatre where one person stands or sits on the stage and talks to the audience or to him or herself.

Monologues are different in structure from the usual business or educational presentation, previously the subject of this TalkPower book. For example, when preparing a business or an educational presentation, the intention of the speaker plus the agenda, informed by facts, drives the speech forward, in a linear progression. The goal is to motivate the audience to buy something, take some kind of action, or learn something. On the other hand, the monologue is a creative form of dramatic expression. It follows a complex and subtle narrative line, intuitively informed by meaning, emotion, and psychological nuance. These emotional and psychological components, expressed within the twists and turns of the story, drive the monologue forward as the audience (hopefully) becomes emotionally involved.

Note: *If you are not an experienced writer and you would like some practice writing with a structured outline plus templates to guide you, I strongly suggest that first you try to complete at least two or three formal presentations using the TalkPower Action Formula. This Action Formula will help you to understand what structure, thematic element, and beginning, middle, and end are all about. These three elements are crucial to the creation of a successful monologue. In addition, since the Monologue is an intuitively creative art form, an internal sense of narrative flow (logical story continuity) is very important. The TalkPower Action Formula is an excellent tool for giving you these necessary skills.*

Different Kinds of Monologues

Monologues fall into various categories. Here are a few suggestions:
comedic, romantic, personal/family life, horror, mystery, and sports.

Different Prototypes

Looking at the various monologues, we see that there are three main
prototypes: (1) The story monologue, (2) the poem that tells a story
and is acted out, and (3) the soliloquy—a monologue that might be
an examination of one's inner conflicts and concerns, for example,
Hamlet's soliloquy "To be or not to be." In this segment, we will be
developing the story monologue with step-by-step instructions.

Step 1: Picking a Topic for Your Story

Note: *If you already have a story that you would like to develop into
a monologue, skip the first three steps.*
Brainstorm your own list of five to ten topics that interest you.

Possible topics

+ a great experience
+ your pet
+ your family
+ a love story
+ your hobby
+ a sports story
+ a wonderful or horrible teacher
+ an important life principle
+ a famous historical figure
+ elaborating upon a quote
+ a historical event like a famous battle
+ your mother, father, or siblings
+ a life lesson learned
+ a humorous story
+ a spiritual experience
+ a transformation
+ other

Step 2

Narrow your list down to three topics.

Step 3

Now narrow your list down to one topic.

Step 4

Put that topic on the top of your page.

The Message Sentence

In one sentence: what is the one most important piece of information that you would like to convey about your topic? (Make this short please. No more than twenty words.)

For example, if I were writing a monologue about my passion for the Tango, the piece of information that I would like to convey to my audience would be that my passion for the Tango has revitalized my life.

This message sentence is a thematic element. It will pull your entire monologue together because that one message sentence will appear each time a new major idea is introduced. It is very much like the message sentence in the TalkPower Action Formula. This message sentence should be placed anywhere within each one of the major ideas that you have fleshed out and included in your mono- logue. (An example of my idea list will follow. See below.) You can vary the words in your message sentence, but the original meaning of your message must be retained.

Idea List

Make a list of all the ideas that relate to your topic. One sentence please for each idea on your list, like a table of contents. Do not reject any ideas.

Example:

I am going to do a monologue about my passion for the Tango. Here are a variety of ideas, some of which will help me to enrich my story.

How the Tango came into my life

Taking lessons
My Teachers
Learning to Follow
Tango music
Dancing in heels
The Tango cruise I took to Italy
The international Tango community
What the Tango means to me
My partners' different styles of Tango
The history of the Tango
Giving up Salsa for the Tango
Buenos Aires

How to Start
There are many different ways to begin a monologue:
+ A short funny story about yourself or another person that relates to your topic
+ A short moving story that relates to your topic
+ A quote that relates to your topic
+ A short poem that relates to your topic
+ A headline from a newspaper
+ Other...

Templates for Monologues
(If you do not wish to use the templates, by all means follow your intuitive sense.)

The following group of templates is composed of transitional phrases that will support your thinking and help you to get your monologue off and running. (Transitional phrases are phrases that frame your ideas, introducing them or bringing closure in an elegant manner. See the templates for examples.) Use these templates so that they help you to develop your story.

Do not limit your writing to the exact spaces provided on the template page. Write as much as you like.

Please feel free to change or rearrange the order of the transitional phrases as well as the wording so that your monologue flows naturally and makes sense.

Combine templates or transitional phrases in any way that will help you to flesh out your monologue in a clear and interesting manner.

In addition to the templates, you can use the "Personal Background" we covered earlier in this book as a template after your opening section if you wish. Please do not use the menu section of the TalkPower Action Formula. It is not appropriate for a monologue.

Before you begin, look at all of the templates, become familiar with them, and choose one that will give you a good start.

Each time you finish a piece of writing, see if you want to include your message sentence. Then go back to your idea list and select another idea and add it to your story with a different template.

As you are writing, don't stop and try to edit or censor yourself. Write whatever comes to your mind. When you are no longer writing, then you can edit and change.

As you develop your monologue, include the actual words that the characters say in different parts of your story, one to two sentences, not more than three sentences for each inclusion. This gives color and texture to your story.

It may take several drafts before you get it really right.

Mix and match. Do not hesitate to use parts of one template with a part of another template.

Empty References

Constantin Stanislavski said: "A word can arouse all five senses. One needs to do no more than recall the title of a piece of music, the name of a painter, a dish, a favorite perfume and so on and one immediately resurrects the auditory and visual images, tastes, smells, or tactile sensations suggested by the word."

In other words, whenever you refer to anything in your monologue—a dog, a child, a wife, a husband, a company, a school, a car, a movie, a food, a restaurant, a country, and so on—GIVE IT

A NAME (my dog PLATO). Otherwise it will be an empty reference and will go in one ear and out the other of your audience.

Templates to help you write your monologue
(Look them all over before you choose one.)

Monologue Template #1

When I was growing up I thought

_____

I can remember

_____

I even tried to

_____

_____

My family

_____

Eventually

_____

Do not limit yourself to the spaces on this page. Continue writing as much as you like. When you have completed your first template and you do not know where to go from there, go back to your idea list for something else that you wish to develop and add to your story. Continue writing, trying to flesh out whatever comes to your mind about that idea, adding it to your monologue. Again, do not censor or critique yourself while you are writing. To be sure that your monologue stays on track, check to see if you are including your message sentence into some of these idea items. When you finish a section, read what you have written out loud to yourself to see if it is working and that it makes sense or if it needs to be revised or the ideas put into a different order.

A monologue needs "slow cooking." It's like how a baby grows. Don't expect to create your monologue in one sitting.

Because of the intuitive artistry involved, many drafts may be necessary before you feel that the story holds together.

Monologue Template #2
Whenever I think about

_____

_____

So many memories come to mind, like the time I

_____

_____

(Don't limit yourself to the space on this page. Write as much as you wish.)

As a matter of fact, it seemed so

_____

_____

I even knew someone who

_____

_____

Go back and pick another idea from your idea list, fleshing it out and adding it to your story/monologue wherever it is appropriate and

makes sense. Keep reading your monologue out loud to yourself to
see if it is working or how it has to be revised or the sequences put
into a different order.

Monologue Template #3

I guess you could say that I was looking for love in all the wrong
places because

_____

_____

It's not that I

_____

_____

I always thought that I

_____

_____

There was a time when

_____

_____

_____

It's really so

_____

_____

Continue writing by looking at your list of items and fleshing them out and adding them to your story/monologue where they are appropriate. Keep reading your monologue out loud to yourself. Clarity is very important. If something is not clear, look at it, simplify it, or take it out and put it aside. Do not assume that the audience will figure it out (perhaps you can use it at a later time).

Monologue Template #4

Being a chubby/shy/aggressive/musical/artistic/fearful/stubborn/outspoken/other child was

_____

_____

My mother

_____

_____

Once, when I was

_____

_____

So all through my

_____

_____

It was really

For example

_____

_____

Even my

_____

_____

As you continue writing, fleshing out your ideas one by one, add them to your story/monologue. From time to time, look at your message sentence and see if it belongs anywhere. Keep reading your monologue out loud to yourself to be sure that it is working or if it has to be revised.

Monologue Template #5
I had the opportunity to

_____

_____

_____

(state when)

_____

_____

at that time

_____

_____

So

_____

_____

Also,

_____

_____

one time

_____

_____

it was obvious that

_____

_____

because previously

_____

_____

and so I tried to

_____

_____

I said to myself

_____

_____

Well, at least I made the effort

_____

_____

Monologue Template #6
It is difficult to imagine

_____

_____

but

_____

_____

An example is

_____

_____

In fact,

Once I even

My friends all

It seemed so

What could I think, when

Building Your Ending

In the last part of your monologue, you will begin building up to your ending. If any of the templates work for the ending, by all means use it. I think that it is very important not to have several little false endings that level off to a continuation of more dialogue. So just bite the bullet. Cut out your mini endings and concentrate on "the big bang" that is the real ending. Grow it, enhance it, and develop it so that when the last moments of your monologue arrive the audience is just wowed out of their seats with admiration.

The Final Editing Process

Begin your final editing process by reading your entire monologue out loud and changing, moving, erasing, adding, rearranging, cutting, and pasting to clarify and smooth out your story monologue. Again, if something is not clear, look at it, think about it, simplify it, or take it out. Then put your monologue away and take it out the next day or at a later time. Look at it again and continue editing. Do this as many times as you feel it is necessary for a final draft. When you are satisfied that you have a finished piece of work, you can think about performing it for an audience.

The Importance of Pausing

> If speech without the logical pause is unintelligible, without the psychological pause it is lifeless.
> —Constantin Stanislavski

Read your finished monologue out loud again and wherever you find a place where you feel that you must pause for dramatic effect, write "(pause at this exact spot; squeeze your toes one time)." In this way you will be sure to include that second of silence for dramatic tension. You must write this pause note right onto the spot in your script where it belongs because when you are performing for a live audience you may have a tendency to rush. As a result you will disregard the pause places, your monologue will speed up, and you will lose control.

If you are a person who speaks too quickly when you stand in front of an audience, you must stop at the end of each sentence and give a quick squeeze of your toes. Then go to the next sentence and give a squeeze at the end of that sentence and so on. This little squeeze can mean the difference between an enjoyable experience for your audience or a bummer where people cannot understand what you are saying.

Example

Suddenly, I heard footsteps, (*pause & squeeze your toes*) I froze. (*pause & squeeze your toes one time*) Who could that be?

Do this little example out loud and see how effective the pause is.

The Acting Part

I never feel that I have a part under control until I have played it in public for at least six weeks.

—Sir John Gielgud

Rehearsals

1. Always begin your rehearsals with a brief breathing routine and a complete Transitional Mantra.

2. Now close your eyes and try to see in your mind's eye where your monologue is taking place. Try to see as many details as possible. Which room are you in? Where is the door? Is there a window? Can you see the furniture? What are you wearing? Remember, the creation of a monologue is a process. Spend several minutes imagining the place, and then read your monologue slowly. (This is very important.) If you feel that you are rushing, squeeze your toes one time at the end of each sentence. If you can't remember to do this, write "(squeeze)" at the end of every sentence.

3. Do not try to act your script until you have read it out loud about four or five times in the following days so that you are familiar with it. Do not try to memorize it yet.

4. Now you can begin to explore the acting, movement, and gestures that fit with you and your monologue.

5. The first rehearsal is exploratory. Do not hold back. Don't try to be logical or even to make sense. Just do anything that you have the urge to do: yell, whisper, scream, sing, jump up and down, spin around, sit on the floor as you speak the words of your monologue—the bigger, the louder, the better! Do this kind of a kinesthetic rehearsal for three days, once or twice each day. This will really loosen you up and help to dissolve your self-consciousness.

6. When you feel ready to perform it somewhere, you can begin memorizing at this point since you have been reading it over and over again. It will be fairly easy to learn it by heart.

Be sure that you do your breathing exercise and your Transitional Mantra before each rehearsal.

Last Minute Changes

Do not make any major changes the night before a scheduled performance even if you had the most brilliant idea since the discovery of the iPhone. It's too late for this. You will only upset yourself and end up feeling so insecure with the new material that your performance will suffer and your confidence will be damaged. Save the changes for the next performance.

The Try Out for Your Friends and Family

Be sure that you do not invite a friend, colleague, or relative who is judgmental, negative, nitpicky, or competitive with you to be your audience.

I would suggest a Toastmasters club. They are the very best place to receive support and encouragement.

Good Luck!

Feedback

Feedback after your first performance can be extremely constructive or it can seriously damage your confidence. If you want to make this a positive experience, say to your audience, "I want you to answer only three questions. Did you follow my story? Was there any part where you lost interest? Was it clear?" Ask them please not to critique your acting. Your acting abilities will develop over time with more experience.

Sample Monologue

This is a sample monologue about me and my daughter. As you can see, there is no identifiable structure at work here, but you can sense the beginning, middle, and end.

Colette's Husband to Be

by Natalie H. Rogers

Humorous Story Monologue

(Notice the (pauses) at the end of each sentence.)

I was totally unprepared for my daughter Colette to have a husband. (pause) Yes, I said a husband and I might add totally unprepared for the displacement such a person would bring into my life. (pause)

Oh please don't misunderstand. (pause) I certainly expected her to marry. (pause) Of course to marry! (pause) Some day! (pause) Recently, I began to seriously wonder when that someday would take place, given that on her last birthday she turned thirty-three. (pause) There I was, walking down 19th Street when I came upon the Kleinfeld store. (pause) Kleinfeld? (pause) On 19th Street, the Elysian Fields for brides who dream about fairy tale weddings and princess wedding gowns and there it was ... the primordial bridal scene. (pause) Encased in a huge glass box of a terribly elegant window display was a tall, smashing, larger than life Bridal Mannequin swathed in a white tulle wedding gown with the sheerest of lace panels billowing out in every direction. (pause) Complete with matching lace trimmed bridal veil and arms outstretched, she seemed to say, "Catch this! I'm just about to throw my bouquet of blood red roses over my head and into the air." (pause) The vision took my breath away. (pause) Oh, I can just see my adorable Colette in such a gown. (pause) I continued walking up the street, trying to convince myself that of course, eventually she would fall madly in love with some fabulous man, the right man for a change, and he would sweep her off her feet to become her husband. (pause) Her husband? (pause) Well actually, I prefer not to dwell too much on that part of the scenario. (pause) I prefer rather to picture her ensconced in a cloudy dream-like vision of romance-doves, heavenly bells, celestial chimes, flowers flown in from Andalucía and of course a Kleinfeld Wedding Gown. (pause) To be perfectly honest this particular fantasy took me completely by surprise. (pause) Me the flower child before her time, previously a free spirit. (pause) So rebellious and unconventional in my youth. (pause) On the other hand, I certainly had every reason to believe that she would wed because what does that say about me if my lovely, smart, talented, independent daughter were not to find a partner, a permanent companion, a soul mate? (pause) Somehow soul mate comes easier to my lips than husband to nudge her into womanhood, wife, mother, all the right things. (pause)

And so, think of my chagrin when Colette, my daughter who fought so vigorously to maintain her identity as the gifted playwright, the enchanting actress, having recently become "engaged," actually insisted upon taking this designation of "husband" seriously. (pause) It happened right after I complained that she ratted me out to "him" when I brought her near to tears by suggesting, rather persuasively, that she bring a favorite denim skirt to the thrift shop because it was not becoming. (pause) "Of course I tell him everything Mom. (pause) He is going to be my husband." (pause) You see what I mean. (pause) It's over She and Me. (pause) And we were so great together. (pause) Sort of a poster couple for how a mother and daughter should be. (pause) Don't laugh. (pause) That time we went away to that week long writers' conference. (pause) Didn't people say that they were amazed to discover that she was my daughter because we got along so well, eating lunch together each day and talking and laughing just like old friends? (pause) But now with this husband. (pause) This husband to be, this "other" who suddenly pressed himself into our scene to relocate me out of the picture. (pause) Well, not totally. (pause) I mean, we still have lunch together once each week. (pause) But I just can't get over the idea that she actually tells him in great detail how I upset her by giving her too much advice and he agrees with her and has a momentary bad opinion of me. (pause) And he and she alone decide upon the color of their living room and that my cousin Stuart who I adore will not be allowed to speak more than five minutes at their wedding because he is verbose and on and on. (pause)

Betrayed, abandoned, dejected, after all I have done for her. (pause) The trips each summer to Europe. (pause) The private school, the special programs for young writers, the riding lessons, the Safaris to Bloomingdales, even the gorgeous Vera Wang wedding gown that I made sure she had. (pause) And who found the perfect venue for her wedding? (pause) I'll give you one guess. (pause) Well, I will admit this very charming fiancé of hers who I happen to be quite fond of, on his own has his appealing qualities. (pause) A very smart, very kind young man with a wonderful sense of humor who always takes my phone calls and was actually instrumental in getting my publisher to pay me the royalty check she owed me instead of the books she wanted me to accept in lieu of payment. (pause) He really is quite a catch. (pause) But still that thought does not in any way compensate me for my loss since "husband to be" has stepped up to the plate and without even trying has erased my significance so far as my daughter is concerned. (pause)

Well, you see it's complex because there she is with this tall, take charge guy who is as committed to her safety and comfort even more than his three times a week ice hockey game. (pause) So where does that leave me? (pause) Who am I now? (pause) What am I now? (pause) The intruder? (pause) The third wheel? (pause) The infamous "mother-in-law"? (pause) To my very own darling daughter? (pause)

Come to think of it, the foreshadowing for this shake-up had been brewing for some time. (pause) And had I been clever enough and paid attention I would have realized that something terribly amiss was developing because appearing regularly in several of my daughter's most recent plays was her creation of a spacey, half-cocked therapist mother character, living in an apartment not unlike my own, overflowing with books and photos and memorabilia and would you believe it—a pink depression glass collection! (pause) Yes! (pause) Just like mine! (pause) Her last play called "Breaking Up With My Mother" was indeed the overture to our present situation. (pause) Her total renunciation of me as the all-knowing best friend Mom. (pause) Shamefully demoted to pain in the butt annoying phone caller who she shuts her phone off to avoid when she is with him. (pause)

People tell me that this is all very healthy and "normal." (pause) People who seem to know about such things because they have married daughters and have traveled the very same road. (pause) Like my neighbor Debby at my summer house in the Catskills, who had a

magnificent rapprochement with her daughter Rachel upon the birth
of Rachel's daughter. (pause) "Mom," Rachel said to Debby one day,
"You are a genius because you know all these things about babies
and that this rubber pad you put under the baby's tush when you
diaper her will keep the sheet from getting wet. (pause) "You'll see,"
Debby assures me. (pause) "Just you wait. (pause) Husbands bring
babies and then Colette will need you to babysit and to give her
advice when the baby is coughing or choking and she is hysterical.
(pause) You'll see. (pause) She will call you all the time and you can
go flying over there as often as you like and you won't even mind
that Colette has a husband. (pause) As a matter of fact, and you
can quote me on this. (pause) You will absolutely say a prayer of
gratitude every day that Colette has a husband. Just wait, you'll see."
(pause)

Obituary Collage
by Natalie H. Rogers

This is a sample monologue using a poem about a funeral. Notice
how effective it becomes when the spaces are added in between the
sections. These spaces create the pauses that give the monologue dramatic tension. Once again the beginning, middle, and end have been
arrived at intuitively through many drafts and readings.

She liked to make a splash
To make an entrance
With a big Ta Da!
And so
In the midst of the Christmas festivities
She died
They found her on the kitchen floor
I went to the funeral

I didn't know her very well
She was a friend of a friend
From long ago
Her daughter called, asked me to attend
I was surprised
Because as I recall
Her mother never liked me very much I was too demanding of
attention
And she needed her attention for herself

So preoccupied was she
With this endeavor,
Paying attention to herself,
That at parties she
Would cut me off
By interrupting my responses

Cut me off!

In her prime, she was Practically stunning
She was tall and wore beautiful clothes
The color of jewels Ruby red and emerald green
Purple Quartz and Safire blue

The funeral was in a church
I wore a great fur hat
It made a statement
"At your funeral
I will be noticed
Whether you like it or not ...
Dear"

Rumor had it
That her daughter had some mental issues
Ran away
Became a homeless person
Finally was rescued by a halfway house

Years ago when she was twelve
I came to visit
I still remember the lace canopy
Above her bed
And she had long blond hair
A tall young goddess
In a long white nightgown

The sounds of organ music wafted through the church
Like heavy vapor on a misty day
The coffin was an ornate copper box
Hours away from its rain drenched resting place

I was amazed she found my number
I suppose they needed bodies in the pews

Perhaps less than a dozen friends and
Relatives attended
Scattered about the Church
Consumed by that gigantic space

I see someone I know
That woman in the pew
Across from me
The mutual friend
We no longer speak
She had gotten very very fat

It all came back to me
From some smelly Internal repository
Bubbling up into my thoughts
Whispers, that the mother
The deceased
Chased her daughter through the house
With sharp knives
Screaming, calling out with nasty names
Saying she was worthless, a mistake

Sitting there alone
In my pew
The gray light
The morning chill
The organ like a giant sponge
Squeezing soft groans into the
Cavernous space
I drift into a semi slumber

She was a therapist
The deceased,
The deceased all laid out
In that beautiful copper box
A therapist,

And when her name came up
At social gatherings
There was a pause
So much was left unsaid
One had to wonder

Me, alone with my fabulous hat
I fade in and I fade out
The priest performs his final genuflection
The organ gasps it's last and labored breath
We are done

And I approach to render my condolences
The daughter's gaze is puzzled and confused
Her tattered face has
Deep grooves and a pallid pasty skin
She wears white tights and sneakers
And an old plaid coat
She still is sweet
I remind her
She remembers,
She ask's about my daughter,
Is she married?
Has she any children?

I don't accompany the party to the gravesite ...
I am done
It's enough
I am done
I leave for
My next appointment
Only half an hour later
Scheduled weeks before
My yearly medical
Just around the corner from the church
I found that odd coincidence ironic

She cutting me off the way she did
Me not going to the gravesite
Apparently her scorn still smolders
When I rake the coals of memory
When I contemplate
 the past

Why did I attend?
It's obvious isn't it?
To have the last word . . .
Dear

APPENDIX

Basic Performance Rehearsal Routine: Belly Breathing and Transitional Mantra

Set up several chairs and a designated podium. Place a sheet of paper on the floor where you will be standing. If you wish to use a podium and don't have one, use a music stand (if you have one), or invert an empty wastepaper basket on a table or a desk and use that as a podium.

1. Sit in a chair, palms up and relaxed in your lap. Be aware that the right side of your body is perfectly balanced with the left side.
2. Do five belly breaths. (Pull your belly in. Exhale through your nose. Hold it to the count of three. Relax your stomach muscles. Take in a small bit of air. Do not move your chest.) Repeat five times. Count each exhalation and inhalation set as one count.
3. Say out loud, *"I am sitting in my chair . . . I feel my body perfectly balanced."* (Feel your balance.)
4. Say, *"I feel my hands."* (Work with the feeling of the weight of your hands. Lift your hands up subtly, so as not to be obvious to others.)
5. Say, *"I drop my hands to my sides slowly."*

6. Say, *"I get up slowly . . . I take a small step and stop . . . I wait until I feel my hands."* (Get up and take a tiny step—no more than three inches in front of your chair.)

7. Say each of the following aloud: *"I walk slowly to the podium . . . I feel my hands."* Take as many steps as you need to get to the designated podium. Feel your hands at all times. Say, *"I turn around slowly . . . I face the audience . . . I stop . . . I look straight ahead . . . I do not scan the room . . . I feel my hands."*

8. You are now standing at the podium. Be sure that your feet are comfortably apart. Squeeze . . . squeeze . . . squeeze . . . those toes, and begin your talk. Remember to squeeze between each section.

9. After you have said the last word of your conclusion, say, *"Thank you."* Squeeze three times with your toes and say, *"I walk slowly back to my chair . . . I feel my hands."*

10. Sit down. Do five belly breaths. Be aware of how you feel.

11. Repeat this entire sequence. To help you prepare for your debut in the real world, do not say the instructions out loud this time. However, you must say them to yourself as you go through each step.

FINALLY

I was born to be a teacher. As far back as I can remember, my job has been to clarify and to inspire. The rewards are enormous. Nothing can compare to the satisfaction that I feel when a student tells of a moment of personal or professional triumph. Sharing many such moments with thousands of students over the years has given me an enormous feeling of validation. Not only have I shared their triumph, I have seen the impossible become possible.

Several years ago, I had a student who fainted on the platform during his valedictory address. Afterward, he went through the TalkPower program and ultimately became one of the spokespersons for his professional organization. Another young man in one of my classes suffered so severely from fear of public speaking that he lost his vision whenever he stood in front of an audience. His courage and commitment to his practice of the TalkPower program helped him to work his way out of his terrible fear. Today he is a technical consultant for his company and gives lecture demonstrations all over the world.

Not as dramatic, but just as satisfying, have been the achievements of students who came to the seminars with a minimum of nervousness but whose presentations were quite ordinary and rather repetitive and dull. After they had followed through on the rehearsals and assignments, these students became polished speakers, glowing with a warmth and charm they never dreamed they possessed.

These real-life accounts are not unusual. You are no different from any of the people who have come to the program over the years with a strong desire to overcome the terror that prevented them from speaking in public successfully. Give yourself a chance! You, too, can feel good about yourself when you get up to speak.

Keep up with the work. Put aside the small but realistic amount of time that you will need to keep working on the rehearsals and assignments. With only twenty minutes of practice a day for the next three weeks, you can make a major breakthrough in your life.

> *Don't exclude yourself from giant dreams.*
> —Aaron Yazzie, *Mechanical engineer*
> *at NASA's Jet Propulsion Laboratory*

> *Isn't it time you came out?*
> *Isn't it time we heard your voice?*
> *Isn't it time your shimmering soul was revealed?*
> *We are waiting . . .*
> *We believe in you . . .*

INDEX